Corrections:
A Humanistic Approach

Corrections:
A Humanistic Approach

Hans Toch

University at Albany
State University of New York

CRIMINAL JUSTICE PRESS

Monsey, New York, U.S.A.

© Copyright 1997 by
Criminal Justice Press.
All rights reserved.

Printed in the United States of America. No part of this book may be reproduced in any manner whatsoever without written permission, except for brief quotations embodied in critical articles and reviews. For information, contact Criminal Justice Press, division of Willow Tree Press, Inc., P.O. Box 249, Monsey, NY 10952 U.S.A.

ISBN10: 0-911577-40-8.

ISBN 13: 978-0-911577-40-2.

Library of Congress CIP:

Toch, Hans.
    Corrections: a humanistic approach / Hans Toch
      p. cm.
    Includes bibliographical references and index.
    ISBN 0-911577-41-6 (hard : alk. paper) —
    ISBN 0-911577-40-8 (paper : alk. paper).

  1. Corrections—United States. 2. Corrections—Philosophy. I. Title
HV9471.T64 1997
365' .973—dc21

                              97-16295
                                   CIP

To the Memory of

Joan Grant

A consummate humanist.

Table of Contents

Foreword ix
Preface xiii

One   **Where are prisons today?**
       Introductory note 1
   1. Prison policy in the nineties 4
   2. Warehouses for people? 16
   3. "Just deserts" prisons? 27
   4. Functional unit management 30

Two   **Reforming the prisons**
       Introductory note 35
   5. A revisionist view of prison reform 37
   6. If DeTocqueville were with us today 44
   7. Rewarding convicted offenders 49
   8. Enhancing the quality of survival in prisons 60
   9. Democratizing prisons 66
   10. Inmate involvement in prison governance 74

Three   **Reforming Prisoners**
       Introductory note 84
   11. Correctional rehabilitation 86
   12. Psychological treatment of convicted offenders 90
   13. Regenerating prisoners through education 99
   14. Inmate classification as a transaction 107
   15. Dealing with long-termers and old-timers 113

Four   **Working with disturbed prisoners**
       Introductory note 119
   16. Ruminations about prison mental health work 120
   17. Mainlining disturbed offenders 126
   18. Coping with noncoping inmates 135
   19. The disturbed disruptive inmate 147
   20. Managing the disturbed disruptive inmate 159

Continued...

Table of Contents (Cont.)

Five		**Addressing prison violence**	
		Introductory note	165
	21.	Prison violence in perspective	167
	22.	Hypermasculinity and prison violence	176
	23.	Social climate and prison violence	184
	24.	The violent prisoner	190
	25.	Creating a niche	201
Six		**Research and reform in corrections**	
		Introductory note	208
	26.	Prison research and prison reform	209
	27.	The convict as researcher	215
	28.	The impermanence of planned change in corrections	221
		References	234
		Index	244

Foreword

by John Pearce

Regional Director, Scottish Prison Service

When I began my formal training to become an Assistant Governor in the Scottish Prison Service I was particularly struck by the writings of Donald Clemmer about American prisons, and his observations and descriptions of the inmate society therein: "The Code" as he specified it, seemed to be virtually a universal point of commonality across prisons in a variety of jurisdictions.

Over the years I have been fortunate to have visited, and to have been visited by, colleagues in other countries and have noted the similarities in our day to day experiences and the pressures we are subject to. Certainly there is a very obvious movement, in a political sense, of ideas and influences from North America to Europe, with perhaps a general time lag of some three to five years.

Now, nearing the end of my third decade of senior management of prisons I can look back and recall my first decade, the 70s, as largely stable, following as it did other decades of the stability of an established prison system. Our main statutory instrument was still almost wholly intact from 1952.

In 1975 I was working in an institution for males up to age 21 when a United Kingdom Government White Paper was published concerning a review of the treatment and training of Young Offenders, that is, offenders 16-21 years of age (Advisory Council, 1974). The document was weighty, with a major radical recommendation that prison staff should continue to supervise and support offenders at release. The White Paper recognized the distinct and special relationships frequently found to have been formed between inmates and members of the staff of institutions. Indeed, great emphasis was placed on the positive potential in such developed relationships. This in itself was very noteworthy, but I remember the document for a specific quote by one of the review body who within a personal note of comment wrote:

> Prisons are rare amongst institutions in that the reasons for sending people to them differ largely from the objectives of the institutions once people have arrived. We send someone to school or hospital so that he may be educated or treated and that is what schools and hospitals set out to do. We send an offender to prison largely to deter him from further offenses or to register Society's disapproval of his action. Once he is there we try to treat him. Only keeping the offender out of circulation is common to both sets of objectives.

Herein lies the very essence of the task facing all prison managers and staff, and that is to balance the dual responsibility of enforcing the sentence of incarceration and that of maximizing the period as a useful and relevant piece of activity in order to minimize recidivism.

The first half of my second decade I recall as a morass of riotous incidents, assaults on staff and hostile litigation in the prison where I was Deputy Governor. This was followed in the second half of the 80s with violent incidents and hostage taking across the Service, together with the concomitant heightened media and political focus. There were times when individual establishments were almost down on their knees as problem succeeded problem, and indeed the whole Service teetered toward breakdown. Matters were not helped by the despair of the "Nothing Works" doctrine and it could have been all too attractive to resort to a strategy of mere containment.

Thankfully, professional experience and managerial skills prevailed and through a very robust and searching strategic planning approach we both regained necessary control and initiated a new and meaningful direction for our Service with a theme document entitled Opportunity and Responsibility.

One thing is starkly apparent in the 90s — change is here to stay and the management of that change is a key task, particularly for operational managers in prisons. The pace and the flavor may vary across different jurisdictions but there is one constant shared by us all and that is the context of the prison community itself.

The interaction between prisoner and prisoner, staff and prisoner and indeed staff and staff creates a powerful and crucial resource. Therein lies both the opportunity *and* the responsibility for all of us who work in and around prisons. The quality and style of these relationships and the management frameworks they exist in can either enhance or confound the use of expensive and finite resources. The goal is to change from a mere human warehouse to a productive unit with a clear view of the product and the process, and thereby the potential to influence and have real impact upon the quality of the end product — the release back to the community at large of a valuable and valued human being.

The modern prison manager and staff member needs a framework to make sense of what are, at times, the conflicting pressures and objectives laid upon them. I frequently note copies of a management cartoon on the walls of some of our prison offices, and there surely can be no more appropriate place for the words "It is difficult to remember when you are up to your backside in alligators that the actual objective was to drain the swamp!" It can be all too easy to retreat into treating the symptoms rather than the disease.

But where to find recourse to the necessary objectivity and the repertoire of techniques under extreme pressure? I have been most privileged to engage with Hans

Toch for several years following a fortuitous encounter in Scotland at a Fulbright Colloquium on punishment. Face to face he can be a disconcerting individual, having a seemingly bottomless capacity to absorb information but with also the ability to digest and distill to the essential issues and questions which cut to the heart of the matter. He has made significant, learned contributions to important debates in our prison service and he has frequently helped a number of Governors to bottom out their own strategic approaches.

His writings have the same impressive quality in distilling a huge range and amount of information into sharply focused discussion. The particular thread he "pulls" for me is the potential lying within enabling relationships and of appropriate supporting structures which recognize and utilize the powerful potential of a dynamic prison community. Key amongst all this is a participatory approach and dare I say, democratization of the prison process.

My own career journey has been at times a painful and stretching process tinted with some hard lessons. It really is remarkable that Toch is so at home with operational people like myself. His feel for the task and his frameworks of response are perceptive and spring, I believe, from a barely concealed love of prisons and the people therein: He has a marvelous affinity for a very complex business!

The pace of change in corrections will not slow, rather it may quicken. No longer will those in charge of prisons have the luxury of a couple of decades to experience the problems in order to sort out a successful response. This book will be an important reference manual for those who work in prisons. It will stimulate many questions and pose great challenges, but above all it will be relevant because it is about the real world of prisons.

I can think of no better writer than Hans Toch to assemble such a menu of challenges to the prison practitioner nor to guide towards a practical and coherent response.

At the start of my career Donald Clemmer captured my interest by *describing* the prison community. Towards the end of my career Hans Toch has done much to set out for me the opportunities and responsibilities which lie therein.

Preface

Where there is life there must be reliability, even for those—like myself—who are given to short-term involvements. Where we hop and skip with abandon, pattern and consistency may emerge when we are observed by others, or by ourselves in retrospect.

One reason this is so is because we enact what we inherit. I, for one, am a psychologist reared in the humanistic tradition, though I have spent much of my life researching prisons and prisoners. Such facts are intertwined. A humanistic perspective affects the questions one asks when one does research, and how one asks them. It affects the inferences one draws, and what one does with these inferences once one has drawn them. Applying knowledge in the case of prisons leads to concerns about inmate management and prison reform; such are the subjects of this book.

What follows was not written starting at the beginning and working toward an end. Rather, the chapters are essays produced at various times for different audiences, to make points that it seemed important to make at the time. Somehow, the points have converged, and the suspicion has grown that I had been groping toward something that is defensibly coherent.

This book is a book about corrections. The term derives from a period in history during which the application of knowledge about prisons meant individual treatment and rehabilitative programming. The dictionary definition of correction(s) says that it means "the treatment and rehabilitation of offenders through a program involving penal custody, parole and probation; also: the administration of such treatment as a matter of public policy." The first sentence refers to prisoners; the second, to prisons.

The link between "penal custody" and "the treatment and rehabilitation of offenders" has become attenuated since the dictionary definition was coined. Most corrections practitioners see treatment or rehabilitation as a goal for a minority of their charges, such as sex offenders and nonviolent youths; there is no goal on which they have agreed for most other imprisoned offenders. By default, penal custody has become an end-in-itself.

So why do we not talk of "penology?" The dictionary defines this word (from the Greek *poine*, for penalty) as "a branch of criminology dealing with prison management and the treatment of offenders." Treatment, in this definition, does not mean therapeutic ministrations. Instead, (as per the dictionary), it refers to "techniques or actions customarily applied in a specified situation."

Penology need not denote callousness. The field of penology accommodates concerns with fairness, humaneness and decency. *Penology: A Humanitarian Approach* would be a viable title for a book. But humanitarianism and humanism are somewhat dissimilar (though compatible) perspectives. For a humanist, the concern is with action based on understanding. The humanistic psychologist is person-centered and prizes empathy; for him or her, the experiences and perceptions of others are the focus of attention. The humanist is also attuned to suffering and interested in reform and improvement of the human condition. A tenet of humanism is that, given opportunities, most people can learn and make constructive contributions.

Penology deals with policy and administration, process and procedures. Corrections has a broader purview, which encompasses the impact of policy and procedures. When we study interventions, correctionists assume that we must assist those who do the intervening and those who are their targets, even where the prison no longer defines rehabilitation as its central objective.

In focusing on corrections, we shall first deal with policy, and ask questions of impact. Next—in Section II—we shall consider how impact can be improved and ameliorated. In the third and fourth sections we sample questions that a humanistic psychologist would address in working with offenders in the prison. Section V centers on one specific area of behavior—prison violence—which is of interest to criminologists. Our final section deals with issues of prison research and prison reform from a humanistic perspective.

This book enables me to review and to relive observations about prisons essayed over a period of decades. I obviously hope that some of these observations may be of interest to others. My publisher Graeme Newman has acted as midwife to the book, and I owe him a sizable debt of gratitude. Sally Spring—a virtuoso at deciphering scribbles—has helped me with the process of cumulative revisions.

Many mentors have taught me what I know: My prison induction began with the late Ross Pascoe and with Robert Scott, after whom a Michigan prison was named, and culminated with Ed Wozniak and John Pearce of the Scottish Prison Service. A heavy indebtedness (as always) is to Doug Grant, former Director of Research, California Department of Corrections. Among younger colleagues—who learned along with me—are Kenneth Adams, Mary Finn, Michael Fischer, Gail Flint, James Fox, John Gibbs, Alice Greene, Robert Johnson, John Klofas, Steve Light, Daniel Lockwood, Lucien Lombardo, Dorothy McClelland, Leonard Morgenbesser, Joycelyn Pollock-Byrne, Marc Renzema, Belinda Rodgers, Bob Rogers, Richard Shaw and John Seymour; also (hopefully) their future students, and my own.

Hans Toch
Albany, May, 1997

Part One

Where are Prisons Today?

PRISONS HAVE been called garbage bins of society, but the phrase is less than apt. Few offenders who are in prison today have been permanently "discarded;" most will at some juncture be released from prison to rejoin the outside world. "Garbage bins" is also not an apt appellation for settings in which men and women labor mightily to preserve meaning or self-respect. Moreover, staff are presumed to support their charges. Corrections, after all, is a profession, and has its own desire for self-respect. Corrections has also had help and constructive advice from benevolent outsiders, first from devout, self-invited "prison visitors," and recently, from the courts.

Today, many people *want* prisons to be the garbage bins of society, and the decibel-volume of their voices is increasing. Some of the demands are peremptory, in that they shrink resources, fuel intake populations, and lengthen the time prisoners must serve. More and more offenders thus find themselves presumptively "discarded;" there are more death-row prisoners-turned-lifers, lifers-without-parole, and felons whom no sensible parole board can release.

Such facts pose a challenge for prisoners and for those who run prisons within current force fields and constraints. In the chapters that follow we address the second dilemma: Can one (and how can one) run a prison acceptable to the public, that provides safety, sanity, activity, purpose and hope to incarcerated offenders?

Where political considerations are paramount, the question may not be posed. The public, or what one may think of as the public (Chapter 1), can be titillated with chain gangs, and appeased with correctional austerity, sterility and congestion. But one cannot sustain stultifying regimes over time. Chronic stress leads to tension (collectively and individually), tension leads to conflict and violence, and violence invites repression, resentment and further violence. Such escalation stems from a familiar dialectic of keeper and kept—one that has been solidly and redundantly documented: Captives who are dealt with insensitively build a wall of sullen secretiveness that protects their thoughts and actions; those who are treated cavalierly construct an abrasive world of their own, and those treated repressively react with thinly disguised rage. The game of cops and robbers is reciprocal and symbiotic; the more policelike the keepers become, the more their charges engage in subterfuge, delinquency and subversion. Punitive subcultures give rise to defensive subcultures. Control leads to surface acquiescence and subsurface evasion, or rebelliousness.

How one proceeds in appeasing a fearful and angry public is often as important as the content of what is done. Prisoners know the climate as well as do their keepers, and can make required allowances for actions reluctantly taken. They can accept externally imposed cutbacks of perquisites, for example (such as retrenched education), if steps are taken, within constraints, to fill voids with substitutes. They can be mobilized to assist by providing some services or engaging in self-help. Given adversity, prisoners respond to approaches in which they are treated as intelligent consumers and fellow-problem solvers. But this is easier said than done.

A prison system abroad provided a dilemma that illustrates some of the options and consequences. The issue was random mandatory drug testing of prisoners, which the public demands and expects. The demand, on the face of it, is reasonable. We are waging a war on drugs; prisons are full of men and women who have committed drug-related offenses. Since these persons are sent to prison for using drugs and engaging in drug-inspired offending, drug use in the prison is arguably farcical, and makes prisons look silly. There is sound justification for administering tests, assuming safeguards for misdiagnoses and procedural snafus.

Prisoners, however, did not see it that way. Some saw themselves not getting help for crushing addictions. Others classed the ingestion of marijuana as an innocuous pastime that eases pains of imprisonment. They resented the ease with which traces of marijuana can be picked up after weeks, while hard-drug residues dissipate. Most mistrusted the testing process, and anticipated being targeted for harassment. All viewed the instituting of tests as politically tainted punitiveness.

Given such resentments and anxieties, how is a program to be introduced? How are lead-in steps to be taken in the initial introduction? Who is to be charged with details of implementation? How are the prisoners' fears and misapprehensions addressed? How well can one allay their concerns about equity and fairness? How does one promote some openness of discourse (including disclosure), protecting confidentiality of those who need help? How does one deal with issues such as the relative seriousness of marijuana smoking and hard drug use — a distinction of no concern to members of the public, but important to the prisoners?

If one starts a program of this kind with a trumpet blast, makes it a centerpiece of policy, defines implementation details unilaterally and proceeds self-righteously and peremptorily to the administration of tests, one has no right to pained surprise when chaos ensues, resentment simmers and subcultural attitudes harden. To coin a saying, the devil lies in details of implementation.

There is no point in expressing helpless rage at the punitive ethos that engulfs corrections today. In the short run, the walls of Jericho are obdurate, but they are bound to crumble in time. In the interim, the challenge I shall delineate (in Chapters 2 through 4) is to exercise ingenuity in the face of political adversity. Responding to this challenge involves proactivity and contingency planning, as opposed to prevailing reactivity and crisis management. An important goal of such planning must be to preserve attributes of the prison environment which make it possible for prisoners to preserve sanity and psychological integrity. These are subjects we shall address later in this book.

1

Prison Policy in the Nineties*

THOSE WHO look for philosophical consistency in prison policies are apt not to find it. There are several reasons for this fact. The first is that sentencing provisions can be enacted as political statements. The second is that the public to whom such statements are addressed can be ambivalent about the way prisons are deployed.

Politics as it affects policy is the art of compromise, presaged by Solomon when he resolved a custody dispute by offering half a child to each parent. Compromise can occur between corollaries of diametrically opposed values or goals, by allocating a portion of the pie to each. A prison system that evolves in this way can embody responses by legislative factions to divergent constituency pressures. Lawmakers may sense pressure from crime control-oriented constituencies that demand escalating efforts to "lock 'em up and throw away the key;" they may also know of welfare-oriented constituencies who want different approaches, such as prevention and

---

*A modified version of this chapter was presented at a 1992 Fulbright Colloquium at the University of Stirling, and published by the University of Manchester Press in Volume 14 of Fulbright Papers, under the title *Penal Theory and Practice: Tradition and Innovation in Criminal Justice*, edited by A. Duff, S. Marshall, R E Dobash and R P Dobash. It is here reprinted by permission of the Manchester University Press.

treatment of offenders. Some groups of citizens are envisioned as opposed to spending money; other are seen to have competing uses for the money they want to spend.

The combinatory political formula for arriving at prison policy today requires legislators to be tough on crime and kinder and gentler to people with problems. But offenders are often people with problems which our toughness exacerbates. Our actions spawn problems which we then try to solve through crisis management. Instead of tempering justice with mercy, we temper retributive overkill with safety nets of hasty remedial services that ameliorate the consequences of retributive policy. To take an example, it is an inconsistent policy to incarcerate women on a large scale and make gargantuan efforts to find placements for children, to open cooperative nurseries in prisons and to worry about reunion and visiting programs. Clients of dissonant policies sense the dissonance, and we cannot keep a young mother from asking whether our welfare concerns could be better reconciled with our punitive dispositions if we punished her in the community.

Seed and sweep

I do not here suggest that combinatory formulas intrinsically preclude coherent approaches. A tough-and-kind blend can have a purpose. For example, a "sweep and seed" approach advocated for drug-infested communities several years ago (US Department of Justice, 1992), was a "left hook-right hook" sequence that made conceptual sense. The communities were presumed to be intimidated, paralyzed and emasculated by endemic drug dealing. The prescribed first step was a massive enforcement drive — a sweep — to close drug bazaars and clear away drug merchants who insisted on conducting intrusive business at the expense of law-abiding citizens. But it was recognized that drug merchants are replenishable, and that sweeps provide evanescent respite from community disorganization and decay.

The answer was the "seed" phase, which denoted follow-up interventions that empower community residents to recapture their neighborhoods. Seeding provided for organizing residents so they could address conditions in their communities that underlie drug addiction and crime. Seeding was symbiotically related to sweeping. Sweeps offer short-term solutions that are preconditions to long-term solutions. Community responses could not be easily initiated until citizens were free from intimidation; arrests in turn would make no sense unless prevention efforts followed. Other links could be appended to taste. One such link was that of prisons that would do seeding follow-up work by subjecting swept addicts to rehabilitative interventions before reintegrating them into the community.

Prisons and dustbins

But seeding did not take place as envisaged. Prisons became the congested repositories of sweeps, and the beneficiaries of draconian measures that were aimed at the recidivistically swept. As a combined result, prison populations came to overrepresent young, addicted property offenders—mostly under two-to three-year sentences, and nonviolent recidivists sentenced for inordinate periods of time. Prisons face this influx while operating under politically-inspired mandates that vary in detail from jurisdiction to jurisdiction.

Many mandates are originated by conservative legislators, and conceded by liberals as a trade-off. This includes building as many prison cells as it takes to accommodate intake populations. The counterpart liberal thrusts—conceded by conservatives in exchange for tough sentencing provisions and runaway construction funds—provide for treatment aimed at addiction, and due process in administrative proceedings.

Legislators, of course, may see logic where it does not exist for nonlegislators. In this sense, consistency may be the hobgoblin of persons caught in cross-pressures from their constituents. Consider the following sentiments that were expressed by legislators in New York State in response to a survey (Flanagan, Brennan and Cohen, 1991): Eight out of ten who answered this poll (82 per cent) opined that "unless we do something about the root causes of crime such as poverty and unemployment, the crime rate will remain high"; three out of four (73 per cent) said "it would be better to treat drug abuse as a disease rather than punish it as a crime," and a comparable proportion (72 per cent) argued that "the best way to reduce crime in America is to expand social programs that will give disadvantaged people better education, job training and equal employment opportunities" (pp. 24-25).

Two-thirds of the same group (67 per cent), however, responded that "stiffer jail sentences are needed to show criminals that crime does not pay"; nine out of ten (85 per cent) said that "even if prisons can't deter or rehabilitate criminals, long prison sentences are needed so that we can keep habitual and dangerous offenders off of (sic) our streets," and two-thirds (64 per cent) felt that "punishing criminals more harshly would reduce crime by setting an example and showing others that crime does not pay" (p. 26). Yet four out of five legislators (79 per cent) indicated in the survey that "rehabilitation programs in our prisons should be expanded," and three of four (74 per cent) argued that "rehabilitating a criminal is as important as making a criminal pay for his or her crime" (p. 27). It is off-hand difficult to see how beliefs such as these can cohere philosophically, and how they could inspire legislation that one could call a "policy" relating to imprisonment.

This picture is discouraging enough, but incomplete. Ultimately, more discordant developments can occur as nonpolicies are enacted or implemented and expenses and population pressures mount. Chaos can begin to threaten as components of the system fight each other to fend off the onrush of bodies with intersecting lawsuits and other forms of internecine warfare. The response requires economy-inspired legislative retreat that can only be effected at the expense of residual consistency, blunting thrusts painfully arrived at through compromise.

The Great American Prison Crisis — or "The Crunch," as it is known in the profession — climaxed in the early eighties, when it had become obvious that we could not stuff more offenders into oversubscribed prisons that were bulging at the seams, and that construction could not keep pace with the demand for additional cell space. The realization that Something Had to be Done sparked a search for politically acceptable solutions to the problem. I shall center on one clear-cut example of such solutions, because it highlights the difference between politically-inspired acts and genuine responses to public opinion.

The swagger was gone

In a report issued by the Georgia Department of Corrections (Flowers, Carr and Ruback, 1991) it was noted that "by the early 1980s, jail/prison overcrowding was universally recognized as the single most serious problem facing Georgia's criminal justice system" (p. 3). In one twelve-month period (1983), for example, the state's prison population increased from 14,057 to 15,504. Not coincidentally, in November of that year, Georgia began use of what it called "Special Alternative Incarceration," or SAI (much effort in correctional reform is expended on innovative acronyms).

An early description of the Georgia program in a *New York Times* article (Clendinen, 1985) opens with the following vignette: "Five young men—three burglars, an arsonist and a car thief—arrived at the Dodge Correctional Institute two hours southeast of here by car last month with long hair, designer jeans, tattoos and an attitude of independent swagger. In short order, the swagger was gone."

The New York Times accentuated the harshness of the offenders' reception in the camp, and described it as an integral program ingredient. The Georgia Corrections Department acknowledged that "the appeal to the media of a military-style prison program in terms of its 'filmability' ... cannot be underestimated. The media vividly captured the image of young men who have broken the law being verbally disciplined and marched through their daily activities of hard work and calisthenics" (Flowers, Carr and Ruback, 1991, p. 1). The routine in the Georgia camp called for head-shaving, delousing, and barked stentorian commands. "That," writes the *New York Times* reporter, "was their welcome to a Georgia program meant to give young criminals a tough 90-day experience of prison life that they will never wish to repeat. The program, which the state describes as 'shock incarceration,' is one of a number of new measures being taken across the South to keep criminals out of overcrowded and increasingly expensive prisons."

The New York Times reporter quoted an official who described the *sine qua non* of prison reform as follows: "It's got to be safe, it's got to be tough—or punitive—and it's got to be inexpensive." The dominant message to be conveyed to young inmates as they entered the Georgia program was that of "toughness." A second reporter, who covered the opening of an SAI-derivative institution in another state (Michigan), highlights the same emphasis:

> The booming commands of a drill sergeant echo through the halls of Camp Sauble, where beginning this week convicts will trade a year or more in prison for 90 days of hard labor, intense physical training and intimidation....
>
> Pool tables, television sets and other means of recreation have been moved out of Camp Sauble....
>
> The 156 inmates will have little time for recreation. The inmates will rise at 5 a.m. and prepare for an inspection of bunks and uniforms. After breakfast they will fall in for a workout before heading out in eight-man crews for about seven hours of unpaid work in and around Mason County.
>
> Military protocol will be strictly enforced. Inmates will be required to stand at

attention when in the presence of an instructor. They will receive demerits for violations (Associated Press, 1988).

One corollary of the theme in this second state was that some constituents concluded that their prisons should emulate the boot camp regime. The Prosecuting Attorneys Association of Michigan, a lobbying group, released a policy paper in which they proclaimed,

> We are deeply concerned that many young offenders view the prison experience as "easy." ... Earlier this year the Department of Corrections reported that 40 per cent of convicts eligible to repay their debt to society with only 90 days in SAI chose instead to spend 2 1/2 years in a state penitentiary. Doubtless, this disturbing trend is partly due to an attitude reflected in the report, which says, "SAI is tough, as well it ought to be, as it is an alternative to prison."
>
> Why should "tough" only be found in "alternatives to prison?"... Legislative action should be taken now to remove the layers of prison freedoms and amenities... Only under an in-prison routine of demanding exertion and actively earned privileges can the prison system move toward more limited periods of rehabilitative punishment instead of long, facility-glutting periods of room, board and idleness at taxpayer expense (Prosecuting Attorneys, 1989).

In my own vicinity shock incarceration began on a somewhat inauspicious note. The first group of young volunteer prisoners changed their minds after arriving at their camp. According to one published account,

> Nine inmates at the state's first military-style prison camp have been sent to Attica and Elmira state prisons after they injured two guards while protesting against the harsh and regimental treatment.
>
> The six-month programs of militaristic treatment, modeled after some prisons in the South, started 10 Sept. ... two inmates became upset Monday morning about the rigorous training method imposed at the camp. One of the inmates struck a guard and a fight ensued between two guards and the two inmates ... After the fight broke up, six more inmates started to complain about the harsh treatment.

"They didn't like the shock training" (*New York Times*, 20 September, 1987).

New York offered shock incarceration to 225 youthful offenders on an "experimental basis." But only a year later, with no research returns available, that population was doubled. A 1989 legislative package provided for an increase to 1,200 shock incarceration beds. It also raised eligibility age standards and made the program available to women. Similar expansions occurred on the national scene. Starting with Georgia in 1983, the number of states using shock incarceration totaled 11 in 1989, 14 in 1990, and 17 in 1991. By mid-1992, there were 59 boot camps in 29 states, with a capacity of 10,065 beds (Cronin, 1994). A federal omnibus crime bill called for federal camps. Urban detention centers showed parallel interest. In covering the mayoral election campaign in New York in 1989, the *New York Times* reported that "the program of choice for most candidates appears to be establishing work camps, which combine boot-camp discipline with drug treatment and education. The idea allows candidates to talk tough, but convey a hint of sensitivity as well" (Barbanel,

1989). The winning candidate, Mayor David Dinkins, proclaimed that "this is one marine who believes in the value of discipline and respect... and I'm going to make sure that some young guys get a whole lot of it early on." An opponent wanted it understood that the offenders under his administration would lead even more Spartan lives: "They would do calisthenics at 5:30 in the morning," he said, "mow the grass in 95-degree heat or shovel snow at 15 degrees below zero." New York's retired mayor, Edward Koch, joined by claiming intellectual primacy. He observed that "the Governor and I have been way out in front on this a long time ago. The others are wrapping themselves in the boot camp [flag]. I would like to give them the boot" (Barbanel, 1989).

Ingredients of a winning recipe

Shock incarceration is an instructive concept because it is an example of a politically acceptable alternative selected out of a range of truly intermediate punishments (Morris and Tonry, 1990). Georgia, which had opened the first shock camp with its prison population at 15,500 in 1983, expected to imprison 39,257 people by 1993. An emergency Early Release Program had to be instituted, but a Governor had been elected after promising to rescind it. The Georgia Corrections Department pointed out that "it soon became apparent that early releases could only be discontinued if another program was initiated that would keep the backlog from becoming prohibitively high and would provide a publicly acceptable degree of punishment for offenders" (Flowers, Carr and Ruback, 1991).

The result of this discovery was a more intense interest in shock incarceration. This interest sparked a number of variations on the theme, which had varying political advantages.

One part of the Georgia package was the original garden-variety SAI model, in which young, non-previously-imprisoned offenders undergo a thirty-day military-type experience as a condition of probation. The candidates are selected by judges from a pool of convicted offenders who are eligible for up-to-five-year imprisonment. This eligibility requirement was dropped along the way, making boot camps a potential corrective for more draconian sentences. An obscure amendment that gives judges the power to de-escalate punishments made it possible for the legislature to advertise its punitiveness with impunity. On the other hand, the provision also made it possible for judges to become punitive (and risk-aversive) by placing would-be probationers in boot camps. There is evidence, however, that this is not what judges decided to do in Georgia. They used their discretion — as judges use any discretion — to "tailor-make" dispositions, gratefully escaping from silly, politically-motivated determinacy. Flowers, Carr and Ruback (1991) touchingly report that "the judges like SAI because it gives them 'a sense of being respected' in their sentencing practices" (p. 47).

The second part of the Georgia package were honest-to-God Boot Camps, introduced in July, 1991 for prison inmates. In this program, the selection of campers is made by the Parole Board, which could also exercise a great deal of discretion. Boot camp graduates were placed on intensive parole, with provision for mandatory treatment participation.

The concept of mandating involvement had become an important theme in the nineties, and it is politically critical. Making treatment available to offenders sounded mushy and uninviting, but mandating treatment sounded hard-nosed and responsive to the problem (drug-related crime) that is of concern. Moreover, the no-nonsense premise is appealing: irresponsible people are not entitled to be bums—or drug-addicted bums—at public expense; society is entitled to create incentives that make chronic irresponsibility unattractive. The ethos is nonlibertarian, but constraints are designed to produce volitional behavior in the long run, when the no-longer-irresponsible person is ready for it. Discipline produces self-discipline, and the freedom to exercise it. Freedom for irresponsible people produces irresponsibility.

The Parole Board's selection of Boot Camp candidates provided early release without early release. The Parole Board did not "release" inmates, but changed the modality of their confinement. The system remained *de jure* as it is, but *de facto* diluted determinacy and defused advertised punitiveness through selective de-escalated punishment.

The third part of the Georgia package were SAI/Probation Boot Camps to which offenders are sentenced as a condition of probation. These Camps provided an intermediate punishment for nonrecidivistic drug offenders and for probation violators.

Functional equivalents of Siberia

The fourth component of the Georgia package was called Intensive Discipline Units. The IDU program was Georgia's version of the "maxi-maxi" prison concept that had started to sweep the country. A "maxi-maxi" prison is a segregation facility. Viewed in administrative terms, it is a consolidated, centralized way of dealing with prison infractors. IDU is also a specialized setting in which staffing is less rich—therefore less expensive—because inmates stay in cells. The defenders of the concept also contended that an IDU makes conventional prisons more relaxed because these prisons need no longer take turns accommodating recalcitrant offenders.

It is obvious that in IDU-equivalents a less-than-attractive aspect of imprisonment — punitive isolation or segregation — acquires visibility it does not normally enjoy. Citizens who have no preconception of prison read about men who are "kept isolated, shackled at the waist and wrists when allowed out of their 6-by-10-foot cells and made to spend their daily recreation hour in newly built cages" (*New York Times*, February 20, 1991). They also read about prisoners being fed tepid food in cells, and about the solidity of doors needed to protect the guards from the excrement thrown by the helplessly angry inmates. Public relations officials do not enjoy such accounts, nor do they like the civil libertarian critics they invite.

There is, however, no cause for public relations concerns. A typical editorial notes *in passim*, "critics have argued that locking an inmate in solitary for 23 hours a day is no way to encourage social skills," and rejoins, "That is not a self-evident proposition. It might just be that a period of quiet and lonely reflection on crime as a way of life is just what many of these men need. Moreover, it shouldn't be forgotten that those

Prison Policy in the Nineties

inmates . . . had already demonstrated quite clearly that their personalities were more than a little disordered. Many of them are simply sociopaths" (Albany *Times Union*, 7 June, 1991).

One feature of this argument is that, though the dichotomy that it proposes between sociopaths and decent people is sharp, the conclusion it draws is not retributive. "Discomfort," the argument goes, "can be a regenerative experience. It can be particularly regenerative for irresponsible hedonists who have done what they like at other people's expense, and who must learn to control themselves." The "pain-is-good-for-them" formula converts a setting self-consciously designed to lack rehabilitative programs into a rehabilitative enterprise. The view seems to be, "we can rehabilitate you the hard way or the easy way." Hard cases are not hopeless, but invite more austere regenerative approaches. The tough-but-optimistic stance is typified by a provision of the Georgia and New York maxi-maxi settings which lets inmates earn their way out of segregation before their sentences expire, by behaving in exemplary ways.

Elsewhere, as I noted above, there is stress on compulsory participation in regenerative experiences. Prisoners across the US and in Canada are told that they must work or partake of educational offerings, and that the length of their stay hinges on their compliance. Drug-related offenders are assigned to drug programs under similar injunctions. Boot camp residents return from forced marches to nonoptional-but-benevolent group therapy sessions. A similar incoherence characterizes the Mutt-and-Jeff interplay of determinacy and diversion in Georgia. Draconian sentences—embodying retributionist policy—feed offenders into a system that must shorten sentences because it cannot afford to retain the offenders for the full length of their assigned terms.

In other words, logically inconsistent perspectives prop one another up through their cohabitation. We wage a retributive war featuring wholesale arrests and hefty determinate sentences. This congests prisons and strains budgets to an impossible degree. It also punishes many nonviolent addicts, who return to prison to be punished again. We discover that this is expensive and senseless, so we opt for a hard-nosed version of rehabilitation tied to reductions of time. We reintroduce discretion in a system in which we have forced judges to dispose of offenders in harshly punitive ways. The machine becomes a strange assortment of pulleys and rubber bands, serendipitously arrived at.

The public and prison policy

In 1958, S. I. Hayakawa wrote an article called, "Why the Edsel Laid an Egg." The Edsel was a large, ungainly, chromium-plated car which consumers refused to buy. The auto maker (Ford) said that it had based the car's design on consumer survey responses. Ford blamed the recession for the debacle, but Hayakawa (1962) wrote, "one wonders . . . whether the recession itself is not partly to be blamed on carmakers who, in defiance of all rational consumer interests—economy, convenience, safety, maneuverability and beauty—have been trying to foist on the *majority* of the public fabulously overpriced jukeboxes such as only people of deprived origins or the neurotic would want to buy and only the prosperous can afford to maintain" (p. 171). Hayakawa pointed to a "doctrine" which "implies that if you hold the key to people's irrationality, you can exploit and diddle them to your heart's content and be loved for it" (p. 172).

While Hayakawa talked of irrationality because he suspected Ford of succumbing to the "phallic symbolism school" of design, others reported that Ford's consultants had used more pedestrian approaches. They had surveyed female consumers and male consumers, and pooled the desiderata of the groups into a hermaphrodite composite.

Whichever version one accepts, the lesson applies to the way in which prison policy has been formulated in recent times. The problem lies with the process whereby consumers are stereotyped in efforts to assess what consumers want (Wilkins, 1986). Legislators segmentalize publics into predefined interest groups (as did Ford with Edsel customers), to which they seek to appeal. They are also attuned to the voices of constituents who approach legislatures with strongly worded predilections and sentiments. Such constituents are often self-selected, but are hard to ignore.

The fear of crime issue illustrates the problem of assessing citizen input. The issue is volatile (disappears in wartime or becomes displaced by economic concerns), but politicians know that it is risky to discriminate between long-term and short-term apprehensions. Fear, in particular, can never be adjudged illegitimate. If the threat is crime, something must be done about the perception of crime. Prison construction responds to fear of crime, even if prisons remain after fear has dissipated.

Fear can be admittedly less-than-rational. Constituents who demand more prisons tend to live in small towns or suburbs. They fear—but rarely experience—crime. Many urban citizens live with crime. But they are less apt to demand wars on crime, because they know better from experience. The drug dealers arrested in last night's raid have been instantly replaced; gang wars (in which innocents are shot) are fought to name successors. Urban citizens may know a great deal, but can be superseded by sentiments of suburbanites.

Citizens in general are also better at detailing needs than at spelling out solid, long-term solutions to needs. This does not mean that politicians are better at this. Nor does it mean that one needs experts to do the job. But one has to find some way to translate raw sentiments into policies responsive to problems the public perceives. One must find a way to explore public opinion in depth, and consider consequences and ramifications of solutions that are proposed. This includes hypotheses to be tested through evaluations of outcomes.

The process needs nurturing and patience. People with strong feelings (such as fears) start by ranting and raving, or doing magical, top-of-the-head thinking: "We need lots of executions." Why? "It would teach criminals a lesson." After they are dead? "We must think of the victims." How do victims benefit from executions? "They feel vindicated."

All right, a first try. Are there other things we could do? "We could make the offender help the victim." (Great. The Anglo-Saxons did it centuries ago. They called it *bot*). "You have the offender indentured to the victim, who'd get everything he earns." Until they are even? "That's not enough. You could add punitive compensation, like they do in civil trials."

That sort of thinking (or something like it) is called planning. Legislators and administrators do it, but worry needlessly about what the public might accept—the public being presumptively vindictive and bloodthirsty. (The public in turn feels inhibited by red tape they expect from officials.)

Stereotypes of the public can provide officials the wrong premises for things that they do. In New York, for example, they appropriately stressed work for inmates. Why should a prison system do this? An official was quoted as follows by the press:

> "I've been troubled for years by the public perception that inmates sit around all day watching TV or pumping iron while the average guy is trying hard to make ends meet," said Thomas A. Coughlin III, Commissioner of the State Department of Correctional Services. "We fully intend to change the perception of inmates getting a free ride" (Sullivan, 1992).

As it happens, the public perception existed, but it does not follow therefrom that work should be provided to ease suspicions about the Good Life prisoners lead, nor that boot camps are appropriately set up for their "filmability." Such rationales keep the public and officials from centering on sounder justifications for policy development.

Exploring public opinion

In a recent analysis of opinion poll data, the Edna McConnell Clark Foundation (1992) concluded that "when asked, citizens reveal that they are afraid of crime. But perhaps unexpectedly, they show that they are not nearly as punitive as some of their leaders think" (p. 23). Citizens (unlike most academic criminologists) favored rehabilitation as the "primary purpose of criminal sanctions"; citizens also liked a system that gives judges "the flexibility to make the punishment fit the crime." Given a forced choice between prison and probation, respondents often opted for imprisoning the offender. They did this because they (correctly) equated probation with *de facto* freedom. But if provided with a choice of *intermediate* options, most survey respondents favored their use with nonviolent offenders, assuming rules are enforced and backup options exist.

These conceptions are better highlighted when citizen opinions are explored in more detail. Two studies sponsored by the Clark Foundation (Doble and Klein, 1989; Doble, Immerwahr and Richardson, 1991) transcended explorations which relied on spontaneous focus groups. In these studies, a philosopher was used to feed information to citizens and supervise discussions of issues. Groups were filmed to assure their dispassionateness and fairness. Pre/post-instrumented surveys asked the groups to suggest sanctions for contrasting types of offenders.

The most salient finding was that the citizens studied held coherent positions which become articulated as information is assimilated. The citizens favor imprisonment because it is closer than nothing (i.e. probation) to what they want. They basically want offenders to be changed. They are unhappy with prisons in this regard (even as they opt for sending people to prison) because prisons may not do the job. For the public, rehabilitation means that you move from undisciplined hedonism to self-control and disciplined work. One sends people to a setting that provides the ingredients of such change which are (1) work (2) supervision (3) discipline and (4) a modality of self-improvement, such as education, vocational training, and therapy for offenders with problems (e.g. addicts or sex offenders).

The public did not feel the need to see an offender imprisoned unless the offender is violent and poses a threat. It wanted to see offenders engage in serious toil under strict supervision, repaying victims if possible. It wanted to see effective rehabilitative experiences imposed on offenders in a businesslike setting. It wanted serious sanctions to back up less serious sanctions for recalcitrant offenders.

How does this view differ from stereotypes of public opinion on which legislation is based? For one, the public is not retributionist and desirous of "throwing the book" at offenders. Prisons are not envisioned as places of storage and idleness. For the public, prisons belong on a continuum of stern rehabilitative efforts that range from enforced labor in the community through institutional programs that require disciplined activity. The public likes work-as-restitution sentences. The public also favors shock incarceration, but does not see boot camps as safety valves for congested prisons.

The public is not in the pain-amelioration or time-shortening business; it does not care that prisons may be crowded. The public, however, is not in the discomfort-inflicting business either, as the "filmability" school implies; it does not want boot camps simply because they are "rough." The public's view of corrections is a secular version of the puritan ethic that envisages redeemability through works, and reassimilation into the community. It is an optimistic, anyone-can-make-it, never-give-up stance which observers (including De Tocqueville, 1956) have dubbed the American ethic.

The public thinks that offenders can progress in the same way others should progress—through hard work, discipline and unflagging dedication. It thinks of criminal sentences as incentives to change, and punishment as indentured change experiences. Deprivation is seen as the means to an end. Moreover, citizens see intermediate punishments as appropriately targeted change modalities for offenders who do not need to be sequestered to protect the community.

Lawmakers who respond to this view of dispositions need not ask themselves, "How much deprivation does the offender deserve?" but can instead ask, "How substantial is the compulsory rehabilitative experience we are entitled to exact, given the nature of the offender's transgression?"

Fortuitously, the shock incarceration setting encapsulates desiderata that citizens want highlighted in correctional experiences. Other intermediate punishments would have popular appeal to the extent that they feature similar combinations of work, discipline and self-improvement options. Within the prison, trends such as compulsory drug treatment, work and educational involvement are congruent with consumer sentiment.

The public opposes draconian sentences for nonviolent recidivists, but sees prison as a backup for offenders who do not comply with intermediate punishment regimes. And the public does not like the use of unadulterated probation. Citizens endorse determinate sentencing as a concept (equivalent dispositions for comparable offenders for the sake of fairness) but like flexibility that permits judges to individualize dispositions.

If citizens had their way, the pendulum of correctional policy would swing to rehabilitation and individual deterrence as a goal. Dispositional options would proliferate, drug offenders would be treated, and prison population and probation would shrink. Communities would see offenders in substantial numbers in public service projects, and short-term confinement settings — including half-way houses, work-release institutions and prison camps — would be opened in large numbers.[1]

If we ended up doing what the public wants, we would free legislators from having to prove how tough they are. We could permit offenders to be more constructively engaged and let them contribute to their communities. We could experiment with new modalities of treatment. And we could ease prison crowding and rethink the use of prisons.

By conveying to people that we are listening to them, we might also persuade them to take more of an interest in improving the system. And if we then provided opportunities for more than top-of-the-head (or gut) reactions, we might contribute to democracy-in-action — which is responsive-but-rational government — as opposed to a government of elite planners or one of politics as usual.

Note

1. A recent article on crowding-reduction strategies that have been successfully implemented (Greene, 1997) quotes the Corrections Secretary of North Carolina as asserting that a public opinion survey in his state "has been an essential element in the state's effort to strengthen the community sanction system ... We learned that there was strong support for certain intermediate sanctions," he says. "The poll results helped us to get them 'framed right' so we could continue to build even stronger support for our strategy" (p. 65). Similarly, in Oregon, two polls conducted in 1994 pointed to "a solid base of public support for using community corrections and intermediate sanctions to help nonviolent offenders" (p. 53).

2

Warehouses for People?*

IN RECENT prison history two disasters converged to cancel each other. The advent of unprecedented overcrowding coincided with the loss of faith in correctional rehabilitation. The latter made the former more viable, because to have rehabilitative goals for overcrowded prisons would be a particular travesty.

But can prisons be viable warehouses? In such warehouses prison wardens could record successes as fewer than expected riots, and the uncluttered mandate of inmates could be to serve time. But simplicity disguises complexity. Congested prisons could be embarrassing for staff and intolerable for inmates. Men and women may not be the sort of commodities than can be stored, shelved, and retrieved.

Some hints from research studies

The question at issue in this chapter is; Are crowded prisons marginal or inadequate human environments? If so, for whom? In what way? With what effect? Unfortunately, defensible prison studies often tend to ask more circumscribed ques-

---

*This chapter originally appeared in *The Annals of the American and Political and Social Science*, 1985, 478, 58-72. It is adapted and reprinted with permission from Sage Publications.

tions.[1] Recent research questions — "Do inmates in dormitories violate more rules than those in cells?" "Do crowded inmates experience more frequent illnesses?" — skirt the edges of the coping-with-warehousing issue. But there are hints as to the shape of the problem, which include some well-established findings.

First, we know that prison crowding, which is usually defined as social density — the number of inmates who sleep in a room — is an arrangement that obliges some people to intrude in the lives of other people who live with them, so that they impinge on each others' privacy. Among susceptible inmates, this experience can engender psychological problems that find expression in behavior that is obviously related to stress, such as somatic complaints and symptoms (D'Atri, 1975; McCain, Cox and Panlus, 1980). For others, the same problems increase behavior that is disruptive to the institution and may appear to the prison's staff to be purely discipline-related (Megargee, 1977, Nacci, Teitelbaum and Prather, 1977).[2] In a few inmates, the stress of crowding may contribute to behavior that is extremely violent (Ellis, Grasmick and Gilman, 1974).

Second, it matters who is being crowded, because persons of differing vulnerabilities tend to react differently. Young inmates are most likely to react disruptively. Older inmates may be more likely to develop health problems, and there is a suggestion that some may even die prematurely.

A related fact is that different inmates feel more or less crowded, in the sense of more quickly or more slowly concluding that their privacy has been violated. Personal past experiences with uncongested accommodations in the community can prove a liability in prison. The reverse also holds, in that early adversity can prepare one to cope with crowding (Baxter, 1970; McCain, Cox and Paulus, 1980). The fact that one feels crowded, depressed, or helpless also does not mean that one will react in the way that researchers or administrators measure. Blood pressure readings, disciplinary incidents, and other rosters of inmate reactions are not uniformly correlated with the degree of crowding that is measured in studies of crowding. Some inmates quietly or not so quietly suffer, while others become repeat clients of infirmaries or of disciplinary tribunals, but researchers cannot infer who does which, in part because their studies deal with prisoners in the aggregate.

We also have discovered, by comparing prison studies to studies of crowding in other institutions, that reactions of crowded persons vary with available options; social density may increase the disruptiveness of some young inmates, but it leads students in dormitories to social and psychological withdrawal (Baum and Valins, 1977). Of course, it is hard to find retreats even in ordinary prisons except in segregation settings, which are burgeoning, but young prisoners do not appear eager to retreat. Finally, disrupted routines combined with physical crowding seem to be especially stressful, and it is the composite — crowding and disruption, rather than crowding alone — that is measured in prisons, because the two conditions go hand in hand (Megargee, 1977, Porporino and Dudley, 1984).

There may be more room for concern about crowding than the formal research findings suggest when we start to consider a plethora of informal observations that are prevalent among prison experts. Among these are the following contentions:

1. Congested prison systems must play musical chairs — or rather, musical beds — to accommodate inflow. This means that the inmates in a congested prison system are much more frequently transferred between and within prisons. Such transfers not only disrupt the lives of those who are transferred, but destabilize the environments — including work environments, classrooms, and living spaces — of those who remain.
2. Congested prisons increase the chances of incompatible inmates being thrown together. Despite frequent transfers, congested prisons become fruit salads, with the mixes of people largely left to chance. This is a corollary of congestion because arrivals must rapidly be placed in vacated space.
3. As accommodation becomes noxiously congested, inmates find themselves at large or sequestered in their cells for longer periods of time. This occurs because programs fill up and program-related space becomes less available.
4. Noxious behavior that is inspired by crowding produces more of such behavior. Violence spawns violence and increases the experience of being crowded. Settings that have higher levels of aggression are experienced as more crowded because their tension levels and the chance of involvement in conflicts increase for all inmates (Ellis, 1982, Freedman, 1975).

Crowding and the prison guard

Staff are mostly neglected in research studies, though "social density influences the behavior and attributions of both prisoners and guards" (Ellis, 1982, p. 2). Among ways in which guards tend to become affected by density is the fact that guards feel crowded in the same fashion in which inmates do. In addition, crowded prisons make custody much more difficult and onerous. A company of prisoners that is marched into a prison yard which is already flooded with teeming humanity becomes a potential mob. It is harder to supervise crowds than it is to monitor isolated groups, and much harder to control them. The same point holds for public settings such as dining halls, in which every incident carries the potential for explosive contagion.

A congested prison also reduces the opportunity for positive contacts between individual keepers and their charges. One reason for this is the stretched span of supervision or control; another problem is transience of staff as well as inmates, which makes it harder to establish relationships. A third reason for the increase in social distance is tension, because tension translates into apprehensiveness and withdrawal at work: Officers in some crowded systems are more likely to operate in pairs and to converse only with each other.

It is also obvious that the officer's job can change its shape as the custody component — as contrasted with the human service component — of the job becomes more salient (Lombardo, 1981; Ross, 1981). For some officers, job satisfaction levels decrease, and job stresses increase as the officers are reduced to turnkeys. As tension levels in prison rise, staff turnover rates increase, and inexperienced new guards are disproportionately brought into contact with inmates. This trend is exacerbated by the accelerated tendency of experienced officers to bid themselves into non-inmate contact assignments. The increased custody concern of officers can also leave the more vulnerable inmates, who are marginal survivors at best, deprived of a key resource for them — the more counseling-oriented officer — and this increases the chances of such inmates experiencing psychological breakdowns, self-injury, and similar stress-related symptoms (Chapter 8).

Finally, as the custody concern increases, the success of the custody enterprise diminishes. Desmond Ellis points out that "less effective social control measures tend, to an increasing degree, to replace reliance on 'the program' (dynamic security measures) as crowding increases," and that "under crowded conditions the ability of staff to move inmates to a 'worse' prison condition (e.g., a punitive segregation cell) decreases because these tend to be already occupied by prisoners" (Ellis, 1982, p. 18).

Crowding and idleness

Crowded prisons must spread their resources — with the possible exception of custodial resources — over an expanding pool of clients. As a result — even if prison administrators still felt that rehabilitation matters (Chapter 1) — fewer inmates would be engaged in program-related activities and more inmates would lie idle for larger portions of time.

By far the most universal concern expressed by inmates anywhere revolves around the issue of using prison time profitably through program involvement of some kind. Less prevalent, but more urgent, is the need felt by some inmates to engage in continued activity as their chief means of adjusting to prison life (Toch, 1977; Glaser, 1964). Idleness increases the chance that such inmates will break down and become mental health clients. This further destabilizes the social world of other inmates, who feel surrounded by persons who are unpredictable and therefore dangerous.

There are also more subtle effects of idleness, which have to do with traditional benefits of work settings (Chapter 12). Prison programs, as Daniel Glaser points out, forge "respectable" links between prisoners and staff figures, such as civilian supervisors (Glaser, 1964, p. 142). Work situations can also be places of refuge in which vulnerable inmates can temporarily escape from the hustle of the yard and the tier (Hagel-Seymour, 1982). Staff-inmate and inmate-inmate social links, which form around constructive activity or in special settings, are diminished as programs become scarce.

Even more subtle is the effect of having to do time without a way to give time meaning — probably the oldest of correctional concerns, as the phrase "doing time" suggests. Moreover, program involvement must include a modicum of variety and the distraction that is afforded by keeping busy. Little is known about such effects, but it seems plausible that activities accelerate the subjective passage of time and enhance one's ability to keep past and present stressors from becoming salient in one's mind. If "doing time" means anything, it means expediting the passage of time and easing the day-to-day experience of deprivation. These are minimal requisites, which reduce prison time to an interregnum in which life is suspended. Beyond such minimal requisites is that of compensatory meaning, in which — as inmates put it — "you do time instead of time doing you." When one does time in this sense one can experience long-term profit, and the program in which one does time runs the risk of rehabilitating the participants in defiance of prevailing fashion.

Regenerative impact in this sense is one of three — and only three — logical ways in which an inmate may be affected by prison. Another is the change in inmates who are somehow damaged by their prison experience. A third path is that of prisoners who emerge from prison unchanged, which presupposes that they have spent a quiescent period eating, sleeping, playing dominoes in the yard, not caring about the months that slip away, being oblivious to the tension around them, and being otherwise resilient. Noncongested prisons usually made these relatively low-key methods of adjustment possible, providing various time-doing options for vacationing isolates who kept their noses clean. Some prisons — especially those for old timers and long termers — even specialized in quiescent routines.

Today these same prisons are as noisy, intrusive, confused, and confusing as the rest. Stay-as-you-are time-doing, with — in the words of old timers — "no one's nose in your pocket," becomes less possible with closer proximity of noses to pockets; program retrenchment breeds forced human contacts. Antisocial options — including drugs, gambling, and gang formation — become competitive program substitutes. The abandonment of a serious rehabilitative philosophy increases the potency of such anti-rehabilitative thrusts, and as a result more inmates are induced to become more antisocial in their orientations.

Breakdown of classification

A critical topic we must attend to has to do with the enterprise of allocating different inmates to varying living spaces, programs, and other assignments, because how well this is done vitally affects life in the prison (Chapter 14). There are two ways of viewing this process. One is as a method for separating people who must on inspection be separated, such as potential aggressors and victims. This is sometimes called "internal classification." A second function of sorting is to match inmates with available programs, staff, and fellow inmates (Levinson, 1994). These aims are intertwined, in that programs are useless unless staff ministrations are appropriate to their clientele and unless peers reinforce — or at least refrain from disrupting — the beneficent impact of the programs. Disaggregation — the separation of different types of inmates — is a requisite to matching — the creation of compatible inmate groups in settings that are relevant to their needs — because minimal compatibility can be assured by keeping the wrong people out of the wrong groups.

Most experts agree that a prison is crowded when more than 85 per cent of its cells are occupied. The extra beds provide room in which to juggle inmates; one can place the vulnerable and the dangerous on hold in spare space until the least destructive permanent assignments can be worked out. The absence of such provisions at best yields chaotic interludes and unmanageable places. At worst, the effectiveness of programming and the viability of living and working can be systematically undermined as rotten apples end up in every barrel.

The inevitable consequence of extreme crowding is that security risk becomes the only classification criterion that is used. Other criteria, such as matching work and education needs with program opportunities, can no longer be invoked. The system must react in this way because officials would suffer if a hardened offender who had committed notorious crimes were discovered in a low-custody setting. There is little risk, however, in leaving such an offender illiterate, should the only available walled prison contain no classrooms.

The solution of putting programs where the action is — in the largest of prison fortresses — makes logistical sense, but nonhardened offenders must now join hardened ones to get schooling, training, or mental health assistance. Research and common sense tell us that such a prospect is uninviting. Unless low-pressure settings are provided in high-pressure prisons, victim-prone inmates will be victimized, and inmates whose mental illness is borderline will become disproportionately certifiable. The environment of the large prison is a jungle, which invites nonsurvival of the unfittest. The struggle for survival leads less advantaged prisoners to flight (self-segregation) and sometimes to fight; in either case, their lives are, at the very least, apt to be program-impoverished. Compromise resolutions include second-choice or third-choice program assignments, classrooms filled with rowdies, and overstaffed and underemployed vocational plants.

Compromise programs damage staff and clients. Job satisfaction decreases and staff cynicism increases as goals of education and production are subverted, and as inmate-staff contacts are diluted through wait-and-rush routines and the nonappearance of scheduled clients. Motivated inmates lose motivation, semitrusting inmates lose vestiges of trust, and those who are bitter become even more bitter at the way they are treated in prison. The fact that no one is responsible for structural unresponsiveness to inmate needs is obvious neither to the inmate nor to the staff who experience the inmate's reaction in the shape of disciplinary violations. This sort of game escalates: inmates who are disciplined have their anti-staff perceptions reinforced; they then cement their reputations by escalating their disruptivness.

The sick get sicker and the bad get badder

It is axiomatic in prison circles that institutions are increasingly populated by hard-core, unmanageable inmates and that larger segments of inmate populations are emotionally disturbed. Sociological trends are invoked to explain such impressions. They have to do with the proportions of violent offenders who are sentenced to long terms — to explain disruptiviness — and with the dumping of mental patients by hospitals — to explain mental illness. The trends are real and may contribute to the variance. But correlations between free-world crime and prison disruptiveness have been notoriously unimpressive.

Some habits and attitudes are imported into prison. Young street toughs disproportionately are prison rule violators; chronic mental health patients disproportionately are prison mental health clients. But risk is a far cry from predestination, and the majority of inmates in high-risk groups make adequate adjustment to prison under normal circumstances. Congestion, however, produces abnormal circumstances, and these often push predisposed persons over their respective brinks and keep them there.

Defiant disrespect for prison rules ordinarily brings reprimands and admonitions, but it invites formal sanctions where congestion makes disrespect a public spectacle. Sanctions reinforce bad reputations and invite efforts to live up to them. Incipient careers snowball and provide models for predisposed peers.

Contagion varies with mixtures of subpopulations. In noncongested settings, security personnel can seek to control explosive admixtures of people; but when options become preempted by crowding, mixes that facilitate both contagion and conflict are more likely to brew and to produce confrontations to which staff must reflexively react.

In sum, the most tragic brinkmanship entailed by congestion centers on the problems of men and women whose adaptive repertoires are limited. Coping ability is challenged by every consequence of crowding. Some inmates react to overstimulatuion, including not only social density but also confusion and noise. Pre-psychotics have problems managing their own drives and fears; the struggle requires relative quiescence in the environment. When too much stimulation impinges, the more precariously equilibrated inmates become disequilibrated.

The difference is not between inmates who can cope and inmates who cannot, nor between environments that permit survival and those that preclude it. All environments to some measure tax coping competence; the point is that some conditions pose more serious challenges for an increasing number of people. Environments contain pressures that are difficult to escape; conditions no longer present mere problems, but instead promote crises, which are seemingly insoluble problems that overwhelm people (Toch, 1975).

For the majority of us, stressful pressures stem mostly from other humans. This does not mean — as crowding research at times implies — the excess presence of humans; it means the behavior or actions of humans. In crowded settings some people are in a position to annoy other people, reliably interfering with their lives. Some interfered with persons break down when they encounter interferences they cannot tolerate or escape.

A chaplain, Father Shaw, makes the point about a congested jail. He writes that "overcrowding at the [jail] has become so explosively acute that only one inmate classification remains unbroken; men and women are still kept on separate tiers." Shaw observes that predatory inmates get increased opportunity to exert pressures on fellow inmates who eventually reach breaking points:

> An old alcoholic who is perpetually in jail for disorderly conduct doing, as they say, "life on the installment plan," has been caged on the kiddie tier where the inmates are 16 and 17 years old. It is the most brutal tier in the jail. As in an unruly schoolyard bullying macho fights are constant. During the past couple of weeks it had become a growing game to bait an ever more maddened old man. When I approached his cell today youngsters in both adjoining cells were pounding on the metal walls making his cell a giant drum of noise. Though he has always been a gentleman in the years I have known him in jail he turned angrily and snarled at me: "Get the . . . .away from here. What good are you?" (Shaw, 1983).

Warehouses for people?

Coping failures lower self-esteem, which further reduces coping competence. Incompetence often consists of efforts that reliably boomerang or backfire. Fear becomes panic, and panic brings panic reactions. These include self-mutilations, and cornered explosions of rage.

Crowding and collective reactions

One argument against crowding is that crowding leads to prison riots. Administrators claim that they make increasingly hopeless efforts to keep the lid on, and the claim is correct if one means that custodial emphasis is dominant and centers around preventing and controlling riots.

It is not ascertainable whether a control emphasis contributes to riot prevention, because riots are sparked by grievances rather than lax security. This point was brought home nicely through a crowding-related disturbance that erupted at Sing Sing prison in January 1983. The incident was later analyzed in a report by former New York Criminal Justice Director, Lawrence Kurlander.

Sing Sing, or Ossining Correctional Facility (OCF), is a study in irony. At one time the prison represented the nemesis "up the river," where felons did hard time at hard labor. At the time of the 1983 riot there was no labor to be done, nor were there places to do it. The prison had become a depot of decrepit cells, a place of transit for prisoners and staff wanting to go elsewhere. Twice slated to be closed, OCF was reactivated to accommodate inmate overflow, and particularly the incoming overflow of the prison system.

The result was pure warehousing. Kurlander's report notes that "the reality of Ossining is that there is practically no educational program provided to anyone. According to a recent estimate (by the New York Commission of Correction), only 60 of 1,500 prisoners attend school" (Kurlander, 1983, p. 242). Kurlander records that "when interviewed for this report, the president of the local officers' union cited the prison's 90 per cent idleness rate as its biggest problem" (p. 88). On the other side of the fence, rioting inmates "were virtually unanimous in their complaints about the lack of programs to fill their time and improve the quality of their lives" (p. 78).

Riot participants and 1,200 others at OCF were officially "transient," meaning that the inmates were classified as falling in a category "awaiting transfer to other general confinement facilities." The TI or Transient Inmate status carried serious penalties. These penalties included restrictions on visits and program participation, incoming packages, and personal possessions. The reasons officially given for such restrictions were practical, and had to do with the logistics of transience. In response to one inmate grievance, for example, the warden wrote:

> The Executive Team has determined that the status of "transfer inmates" precludes the acquisition of more than three (3) softcovered books due to their short stay at this facility. The package list for transfer inmates was designed to curtail the accumulation of personal property that requires repackaging (p. 79).

Another inmate was told on appeal that:

> A substantial portion of the package mail for such inmates would thus have to be

forwarded or returned as inmates were transferred. CORC [Central Office Reviews Committee] believes that the facility should not be required to shoulder the heavy administrative burden that such a change would bring about (p. 81).

One problem with the officials' rationale was that the image of convicts zooming through the prison with no time to fill out mail-forwarding forms was badly outdated. Kurlander's report points out that:

> Although facility or DOCS [Department of Correctional Services] officials often stated that the inmates would remain in transient status for only a few weeks, at the time of the disturbance some "transients" had been at OCF for more than a year, and many had been there for several months (p. 82).

Prisoners were told that they had to pay the price for the prison system's congestion, but this explanation did not satisfy them. The problem of perceived injustice was compounded because some late arrivals left the prison early while many early arrivals lingered.

The point is that the preconditions of the Ossining riot included clumsy and insensitive responses to the crowding problem. Kurlander's report points out that:

> By withholding privileges from inmates based on their status rather than their behavior, DOCS eliminated incentives and other tools of control from the apparatus usually available to enforce discipline in a prison, and many inmates came to feel that they were being treated unjustly . . . . It's [the "transient" label's] inhibiting effect on inmate social structure, for example, stunted the growth of constructive inmate leadership which could have been useful in preventing or helping to more quickly resolve the uprising. A lack of clarity marked the facility's status, function and procedures (p. 75).

The issue of "lack of clarity" of "status, function and procedures" often proves crucial to the genesis of a riot. The Ossining riot's precipitating sequence began when several capricious alterations of the routine of a cell block were instituted by a corrections sergeant against the advice of his experienced officers. As a result, many of the inmates were locked in and/or unfairly penalized. Rumors circulated, spawning more restrictions of movement, and tension on the tier continued to build. Frustrated inmates expressed their resentments, voiced long-term and short-term grievances, and demanded that the culpable sergeant be moved. Efforts to restore order took place, but they occurred too late in the inevitable transformation from an unhappy crowd to an uncontrolled mob.

Do we need riots to institute reforms?

Prison riots spark reforms because they alter our mind sets, placing the problems of prisons among those problems that must be given precedence in planning agendas. Riots are peremptory bids. They get attention because they raise the threat of more riots if we do not attend to them. They also imply that any riots that may occur will be blamed on those persons — penurious legislators, corrections commissioners, and others — who did not profit from their experience.

It could be a constructive exercise to review every riot with the premise that unforeseeable human errors must have been made during pre-riot conditions. Such a premise provides the chance for us to do constructive self-examining and remedial thinking. But bureaucracies invariably operate in public, and they operate competitively. To admit fallibility invites scapegoating, and it can be political suicide for an administrator to be self-critical.

The problem is compounded by the crisis management style that is prevalent in overcrowded systems.[3] This style rests on premises which managers attribute to experiences such as

- there is no real point in doing long-term planning because data on which planning must be based — such as population projections — are notoriously untrustworthy;
- any provisions made to accommodate Monday's problems are bound to become superseded by Tuesday; some of Monday's problems will dissipate if one does not act, but others will become more serious, and one cannot tell in advance which will do which;
- the real legitimacy of a need cannot be ascertained until things break down;
- to improve a system requires time and energy that is not available when the name of the game is to keep afloat; and
- any administrator's personal survival — not being fired, demoted, or embarrassed — hinges on not being successfully sued, getting no adverse media attention, experiencing no felonious conduct by employees, and so forth. System survival therefore has to get top priority attention.

Crisis management may be less than effective, but management that is oriented to expect crises and forestall them may be even worse. Such management feverishly attends to behavioral incidents or trends in incidents, and seeks to reduce them. It does so by watching, moving, and isolating people.

Unfortunately, behavior incidents mean little if we do not understand the concerns and goals of incident participants. If we address people's behavior instead of their perspectives and motives, our responses are apt to be unresponsive. For example, a self-conscious riot-prevention strategy invites custodial concentration in predetermined riot-prone hot spots. This approach can make hot spots hotter by increasing tension. Another example is the enterprise of suicide prevention, the activity through which unhappy inmates who need human contact are physically isolated. Unsurprisingly, preventive segregation promotes suicides that otherwise would not occur (Toch, 1975, p. 304).

Overcrowding invites the ignoring of inmate needs other than the need for a place to sleep. In a system that is relatively uncrowded, it would not be conceivable for inmates to be assigned to cells without simultaneous inquiry about the availability of programming. When we place inmates we would ask as a matter of course: How will these inmates spend their time? Will they occupy enough of their time? Will they profit from the way they occupy their time? Will their fellow inmates be the right peers? Can fellow inmates harm or corrupt the new inmates, or be harmed or corrupted by them? Can loved ones stay in touch with them? Are the staff they will need available? Are the inmates' interests accommodated and their fear allayed? Are they fully informed and oriented? Are they ready for their prison experience?

To not ask or be able to ask such questions not only certifies, by default, the death of rehabilitation, but announces the advent of anti-rehabilitation. In such a system some inmates will become less stable and less competent, and less able to deal with life. Some who survive prison will have done so at unknown costs, laboring under uncharted but resilience-taxing pain.

Notes

1. Most research studies fall in the positivistic tradition that was adopted by the social sciences from the physical sciences. This tradition places a premium on correlations between neatly specified independent and dependent variables. Unfortunately, simple designs do not permit fleshing out the effects of complex sets of conditions such as those of overcrowded prisons — on persons subjected to them.
2. The fact that prison conditions can produce stress than can lead to violent behavior among some inmates is discussed in DeWolfe and DeWolfe (1979). Though DeWolfe and DeWolfe are among the few experts who recognize that extreme prison conditions can produce stress-induced violent behavior and that more punitiveness is no solution, they also conclude that "inmates who are violent or exploitive, or both, must be excluded from rehabilitation programs," so as to protect the other program participants (p 529).
3. Kurlander (1983) describes typical management reactions as "schizophrenic, haphazard, and wrecked by an endless train of 'unforeseen contingencies,' many of which might have been anticipated if there had not been such confusion." Kurlander adds that "the Ossining disturbance was simply the most immediate and most dramatic consequence of a crisis management response to complex problems" (p. 235).

3

"Just Deserts" Prisons?*

ENVISAGE the following scenario:

The young man from corrections headquarters, clad as usual in dark slacks and a loud sports jacket, takes a seat in the warden's office.

"It's happened," he says. "They went and passed another determinate sentencing law. You ought to get ready."

"You mean, rehabilitation is definitely dead?" the warden asks.

"You better believe it. We're now in the just deserts business."

"Rats! Last week, after ten years of looking, I find a psychiatrist who speaks English. I hate to see the fella go."

"You can call him a psychosis prevention agent. We can justify that. But why don't you be a good warden and prepare a list of services you can dispense with now that rehabilitation is dead. We sure can use the money to add more cells."

The warden shakes his head. "You forget, chum, that what you call 'services' keeps the residents busy. You want them to spend their time planning the next riot?"

---

*This chapter is a revised version of an editorial contribution to *Corrections Magazine*, 1980. 4, 22-23.

"OK, forget about saving money. But what are you going to do to retool from rehabilitation to just deserts?"

"You tell me. What is a just deserts prison?"

It is fairly obvious that this dialogue is unconvincing. In practice, a prison is the sum of what it does. If a prison has a rich panoply of services — no matter what administrators call them — it becomes more "rehabilitative," because more services can make an impact on more inmates. Rehabilitation is not built into the title on someone's door: While a concerned officer may be rehabilitation agent, a counselor who shuffles papers is a fixture. Mental hospitals can be custodial settings when they tranquilize residents into half-heartedly playing cards; psychotropic medication (unless followed immediately by therapy) is a custodial tool. Elementary schools can be custodial; so can graduate schools.

Most of the fuss about the "goals" of prisons derives from a desire to make the criminal justice "system" look like a system. People who talk of prison goals think of prisons as instruments of judges. They think of sentencing philosophy — or philosophy about sentencing — as a set of marching orders. It is as if inmates arrived at reception centers in stately buses marked with signs such as, "Shape them up," or, "Make them pay commensurately."

Inmates enter prisons because judges send them there. Analogously, food arrives in my stomach because my hands feed me. But no one has suggested that my hands shape the process of digestion. My stomach, like the prison, is an autonomous professional agency whose job is digestion. How much transformation my food undergoes depends on its obduracy and on the availability of digestive juices; however, my stomach does the best it can with the mess I feed it. If a prison, like my stomach, is to exercise its expertise, we must accord prison managers the privilege of shaping their domains. We may assume that services in a professionally run prison would go beyond inmate storage and the prevention of institutional hyperacidity. The point being that once the punishing switch has been pulled it becomes the job of prison staff to enhance the profitability of the experience for the inmate.

That is not to say that one statement in the dialogue is not absolutely valid: Indeterminate sentencing had been thought of as an adjunct to rehabilitation. The prisoner would be released when "ready," which implied prison input into parole deliberations. Such input addressed inmate behavior and misbehavior, perceived "progress" or lack of it. No such impressions are transmitted by prison officials under the determinate (just deserts) model. But what does that really mean? One could argue that it reduces the need for game playing and pretense, phoniness, manipulation and acting by inmates, and that it thereby reduces the roadblocks to helping. This permits the serious rehabilitator to get on with his or her business, which is not that of sitting in judgment over offenders or pretending to foretell their future.

The danger of having unfinished business interrupted by discharge is inconsequential, except for inmates who are seriously mentally ill. A prison rehabilitator operating under a determinate sentencing system could be better off than his free-world counterpart because he would know how much time he has, which would help him plan his work. Change, after all, is intrinsically a process, not a product. It is improvement that counts, and this makes an advance of three grade levels for an illiterate burglar no less a success than a graduate degree for a lifer who has all the time in the world.

The confusion of indeterminacy with rehabilitation is the anachronistic residue of the overly optimistic dreams of a simpler age. It was an age in which parole proponents had a naive faith in the science of assessment and prediction, in the myth of an "optimum point" for release. That is not to say that parole boards were a mistake, nor that links between prison and parole could not be forged. However, the honeymoon between treatment "goals" and parole decisions never was what it was cracked up to be and the marriage between less-than-potent rehabilitation and less- than-fair parole made a vulnerable target. Support for the misalliance made it possible to impugn prison services by yelling, "Blackmail!"

Prison and parole were also separable enterprises. For Inmate A, prison could be rehabilitative and parole reintegrative. A's cell mate could elect to vegetate in prison, although he might seek counseling after release. Parole boards could deal in commodities such as "community conscience," scientific prophecy or the dispensation of amelioration and mitigation as well as in rehabilitation and integration.

Obituary notices for rehabilitation and parole were placed by the same alliance of nihilists and conservatives whose sentencing proposals resulted in stacking inmates like sardines, paralyzing prison programs, increasing stress and generally creating mayhem. In this fashion, by a self-fulfilling prophecy, their death wish did — in the short run — come true. Prison crowding killed rehabilitation and converted prisons into warehouses (Chapter 2). It did not create "just deserts" prisons. What it created is suffering, tension, defensive inmate groupings, fearful staff, crisis-studded management and organizational conflict. This was a cure worse than any alleged or imaginable disease.

4

Functional Unit Management*

A RECENT article about the US prison system contained a list of "Firsts and Mosts." It is an impressive list, but there is one entry that I missed. There was no mention in the list of the introduction of functional unit management in 1970, and of its dissemination in the mid seventies. This development was unquestionably a "First." And it is an ongoing development: We have just begun to explore what units can achieve, and what we can do with them.

The idea of functional units was simple: Take a prison and divide it into enclaves of prisoners and staff members. Each group of inmates (50 to 100 in 1970) would have its own staff team. The inmates would stay with their units and would be individually programmed. Each unit would become a specialized "mini-prison" within a larger prison and share facilities of the institution with other units.

An analogue of the arrangement is that of neighborhoods in a city, in which each neighborhood can be neighborly and intimate, but is part of and has access to the amenities of the city. Each neighborhood receives municipal services, but has its own

---

*This chapter is reprinted from the *Federal Prison Journal*, 1992, 2, 15-19, by permission of the Federal Bureau of Prisons.

Functional Unit Management

cultural flavor which is different from those of other neighborhoods.

A second analogy — which emphasizes programming — is between a prison and an automotive plant, which has disparate assembly areas for different cars, and "can continue production of Cadillacs even when the Chevy assembly line has run into some snags."(Levinson, 1980, p.51)

Bob Levinson, the author of this analogy, created a fictitious automotive empire (Flivvers Limited) as example. He writes:

> So FL establishes several subsidiaries, one for each model — Bearers, Seattles, and Tallyhoes. In this way some of the expensive effectuation equipment can be shared while workers specialize and develop expertise in producing exemplary automobiles of each type. Moreover, if there is trouble with the brakes on the Bearers, FL can still go on producing acceptable Seattles and Tallyhoes (Levinson, 1982, p. 244).

The flexibility of Levinson's assembly lines does not spell anarchy: Flivvers Limited decides whether market trends favor small cars (Tallyhoes) or limousines (Bearers). It sets policies that affect what its assembly lines do. Levinson and Paul Gerard write that "one of the dangers in a decentralized facility is that the Functional Units may become totally 'out of step' with one another, so that the institution appears to be headed in all directions at the same time" (Levinson and Gerard, 1973, p. 15). It follows that there must be ways of coordinating what units do. As example, "the Unit Program Plans can become part of a total Master Program Plan for the entire facility." (*Ibid.*)

One reason units need some freedom is so they can run programs that meet the unique needs of their residents and use the special skills of their staff to design and run these programs. Autonomy also lets units develop their own cultures and identities.

What can units do best?

Levinson and Gerard distinguished among three functions of units. One is that of *correction*, the design of tailor-made inmate experiences that are shaped by staff who are closest to the inmate. The second is *care*, which means efficient use of relevant resources to run programs that do the correcting. The third use is *control*, which means monitoring the inmate as he remains in the unit, so that one can work with him.

One fact which is critical for all three functions is the fostering of staff-inmate relationships that benefit from a shared environment and closer acquaintanceship. The foundation for this notion had been laid fifteen years before the advent of unit management in a study of the Bureau of Prisons conducted under Ford sponsorship. The director of the study, Dan Glaser, had complained about the fact that:

> The caseworker in a large prison inadvertently reduces his chances of knowing the social environment in which his clients live. By scattering his caseload throughout the prison population, the caseworker minimizes the probability of his also knowing the cell mates or dormitory colleagues, coworkers, recreational partners, or other close inmate friends or associates of any specific client.... Also, when the caseload is scattered, it clearly becomes more difficult for the caseworker to see his client's customary behavior in the institution (Glaser, 1964, p. 193).

In Glaser's reports to the prison system, he had suggested attaching caseworkers to tiers or work assignments, where each worker could get to know residents in their natural environment, observing the pressures to which they were subjected and their capacity to cope with them. Glaser also talked of staff teaming, and of "facilitating communication across traditional intra-staff lines" (p. 197). Among innovations Glaser reviewed, for example, were "treatment teams" which included custody officers assigned to dormitories who observed inmate behavior. With respect to the teams, Glaser reported that "before long the line custodial staff seemed unanimous in considering the new system 'the best thing that ever happened' in the prison. They feel it gives them a chance to be heard, and it raises their prestige with the inmates" (p. 209).

Another long-standing question was how to deal with anti-staff norms of "inmate subcultures" in custodial prisons (Chapter 22). Glaser speculated that "inmate pressure on other inmates to avoid communication with officers varies directly with the extent to which there is an impersonal and authoritarian orientation of staff to inmates" (p. 128). The corollary is that a setting in which inmates and staff could relate to each other would be inhospitable to the advent of an anti-staff prisoner culture. Such a setting might do more. Gerard and Levinson observed that:

> Both staff and residents come to feel a sense of pride in "their" unit and its accomplishments. Rather than offenders finding a common cause to organize against staff, competition develops along more desirable lines; e.g., which Unit has the best record in achieving some positive goal (Levinson and Gerard, 1973, p. 9).

Functional units call for participation and involvement. And just as officers, teachers and clerical staff could be involved as teams, residents could play a more active role than they customarily do in prisons. The inmate would thus "be viewed as a member of the Unit team and have a voice in program decisions affecting him" (p. 14).

Staff and residents would have more control over their environment, and new means to enhance their own development. The vehicle for accomplishing this would be small, self-governing groups working behind walls of prisons.

Early experiments

The invention of units can be compared to that of wheels. Wheels and unit management are tools: Wheels make sense as we use them in watches or on tricycles and roulette tables. Units have had to show that they can earn their keep as they are put to use.

In 1970 the Bureau of Prisons had two salient needs. One was the need to reduce disruption and violence in prisons, and to protect weaker inmates from exploitation. It was assumed that units could help to solve this problem because one could use them to separate predatory prisoners from those susceptible to predation. Such sorting had occurred in the past, but the separating could now be done on a larger scale, based on observations at intake. And incident rates could be measured before and after sorting the inmates, to verify the efficacy of the sorting.

The second use for some units would be to house drug offenders who were being committed to the system. The units made it possible to keep these offenders in regular prisons. They also made it possible to experiment with different treatment approaches to addiction. Most of the approaches capitalized on the fact that the offenders lived together as a residential community. This made it easy to use experiences of living and working as grist for treatment (Chapter 12). It also enabled teams to mobilize constructive peer pressure in resident groups. This type of treatment modality, called the therapeutic community (Toch, 1980), could be combined with other modalities — such as token economies — or used by itself. The Bureau of Prisons in the seventies had thirteen "official" therapeutic communities. Some had siblings outside, to which they sent graduates. Others thrived in model prisons, but one TC (Asklepieion) ran for six years in the Federal Penitentiary at Marion.

Types of units

TCs — which are now being reconstituted — are examples of units that provide *treatment*. Inmates are selected for such units because they have problems such as alcohol or drug addiction that can be ameliorated or remedied.

Other units provide *education, training or work* experiences, and "an appropriately designed counseling program" (Levinson and Gerard, 1973, p. 10). The inmates in such units have deficits (marginal literacy, lack of employable skills and so forth) that can be addressed by the unit. A third type of unit, which covers most current units in the federal system, is management-related.

"Management-related" does not mean that the prisoners' interests are not served. For example, when inmates are sorted by personality type to separate "aggression-prone" from "victim-prone" inmates, this reduces rates of predation. Prison management benefits through fewer incidents but the most direct beneficiaries are prisoners who are no longer victimized. The same point applies to other sortings in which prisoners are isolated to avoid trouble or conflict.

One can form groups to facilitate service delivery. A unit composed of elderly inmates, for example, can adjoin medical or pharmaceutical services. Young inmates can be assigned to staff teams with expertise in adolescence. (A side benefit is that older inmates get peace and quiet.) Other teams can have expertise in problems of long-termers, immigrants, persons diagnosed as HIV positive or other homogeneous groupings.

But sorting of prisoners and specialization of program and staff requires time and attention, and uncrowded conditions (Chapter 2). Where prisons compromise, a bifurcated situation arises in which this process is reserved for high-priority programs, and remaining units receive prisoners on a first-come, first-served basis. A few units thus get to be specialized, and serve treatment, training/vocational or management functions for special populations. Most units receive representative intake subpopulations, and these are programmed in more or less standard fashion. Teams can still introduce program variations (if they have autonomy). But they cannot apply Levinson's model and produce Bearers, Seattles and Tallyhoes under the auspices of specialized experts.

Patterns of unit management

The import of the status quo is that unit management survives crises such as the extreme overcrowding we are seeing today by changing the ratio of special to general units in the system. The challenge for management is to create special units that serve the needs of the system and the inmates, given available resources. Today, resources are scarce, but drug-related offenders need specialized drug-treatment units (Early, 1996). Other programs could be inspired by intake disproportions involving long-term offenders, violent offenders, emotionally disturbed persons, or other groups that may need tailor-made programs in special settings. With respect to this issue managers have to ask questions such as:

- How seriously would the inmates be handicapped if they were integrated into the general population?
- What problems would be created for others if these offenders became part of the population?
- Do these offenders require a specialized program, and are staff available that can administer the program?
- Can the program still be effective without segregating the offenders or dealing with them as a group?
- Does an institution exist in which the program (say, residential drug treatment) can be set up without playing musical chairs?

Should answers to such questions favor the creation of a unit, new questions arise having to do with the patterning of units in a system. One option involves the creation of institutions which are conglomerates of special units, that can be different or of the same kind. Another option places one or two special units in prisons that are otherwise unspecialized. The former model permits the concentration of resources, and the latter allows partial mixing of special and general populations and commonality of custody grading.

Beyond immediate questions there are long-term questions, involving a future in which special programs can be routinely created, and we can afford to decide whether to move an illiterate drug addict from a therapeutic community to a remedial education unit, or vice versa. When that time comes — unless impending senility intervenes — I shall plan to write a sequel to this chapter.

Part Two

Reforming Prisons

PRISON REFORM, according to Johnson (1996), "means improving existing prisons, however many prisons there may be in existence, so that they reach or approximate our notions of decency and produce a reasonably effective prison enterprise. As a practical matter, this means that the pains experienced in any given prison must be kept to a minimum....The ultimate goal of prison reform is to produce mature adults who can live in society and cope with daily problems of life without harming others" (pp.253-255).

One can think of reforming prisons as emergency repair work or unfettered creativity. The minimalist position (Chapter 8) calls for ensuring survival for prisoners — especially for those who are least resilient and least able to care for themselves. One step removed (Chapters 6 and 7), we can reorganize resources to make the prisoner's experience more meaningful and profitable, or we can disaggregate resources to link prisoners to the staff who are best qualified to deal with them.

The fact that prisons are in crisis does not prevent one from taking the long term view, which says, "Eventually, the sort of progress that had been achieved over time is bound to continue." This perspective involves a study of history, which tells us about improvements in prisons that may not yet have reached full fruition (Chapter 9). Such clues about what is possible are especially convincing where some prisons are experimenting with innovations that could be replicated elsewhere, once the climate improves (Chapter 10).

A humanistic approach to reform carries two implications. The first has to do with the issue of impact. Instead of contemplating change across the board, we think of *where* we need to do *what* to improve the lives of *individual* inmates or staff (Chapters 5 and 8). The second implication has to do with what improvement consists of. Three premises enter into this view. First, we assume that when individuals are provided with opportunities for personal development, they will demonstrate a capacity for self-actualization. A related assumption is that change in people is best accomplished when those to be changed are engaged as partners in the change process. The third assumption has to do with the type of human organization (participatory democracy) which lends itself to active involvement and personal development.

No one objects to such statements until we apply them to the prison. We then run into widely prevailing assumptions about differences between offenders and nonoffenders. We are very likely to be informed that while the rest of us have the capacity and potential for improvement, offenders have demonstrated that they lack this capacity and potential. If we furnish offenders with opportunities to make contributions, they will respond by making negative contributions, if they make any contributions at all.

A second response we can expect is that prisons by their very nature must be authoritarian, because this is an attribute that is built into the prison as an institution. From this perspective — which is shared by observers on the left and the right — it is naive to conceive of a prison that is run democratically, or that can acquire features that make it more of a community.

Other sources of resistance one can expect lurk among long term habits and attitudes of those within the system. The beneficiaries of our reform are apt to be skeptical of our intentions. They may react with defensive hostility, confirming the expectations of those who see change as impossible. Opportunities will be co-opted to antisocial ends, or may mobilize passivity and apathy. Such results will inevitably derive from experiences with the traditional prison, and the feelings prisoners and staff have about each other.

The prison breeds paranoid perspectives and a stance of reciprocal suspicion among prisoners and staff. Disconfirmation of such premises is not a one-step process, but a turbulent struggle that calls for steadfastness, persistence, and an abiding faith. This faith must not only sustain the reformer, but must be shared by the high-echelon correctional manager who has to risk his or her job by sponsoring reforms in the face of a less-than-sympathetic public.

5

A Revisionist View of Prison Reform*

MANY PRISON experts hate prisons, and this stance, on the face of it, has merit. Traditional prison architecture — which is inspired by a consuming obsession for security — is, to say the least, depressing. The spectacle of human beings living in cages or crowded into a prison yard strikes decent observers as dehumanizing. The prison, with its obvious regimentation and custodial emphasis, violates assumptions about appropriate social organization. Deprivations of prison, such as separation from loved ones and forced association with dangerous peers, seem unnecessarily harsh. Prisons also do not appear to dramatically reform people. The expert therefore asks, with the best of reasons, "Why don't we reserve imprisonment for a few violent inmates who must (demonstrably) be isolated from the community?"

One fly in the expert's ointment is that parole studies show that most ex-inmates are not traumatized by their prison experience. The inmates' memory for the adversities of prison seems short-lived, and for many there emerges (with time) a disquietingly carefree view, which does not saliently include the fear of incarceration (Irwin,

---

*Excerpted from *Federal Probation Quarterly*, June 1981, and reprinted with permission.

1970; Glaser, 1964). The same personal resilience characterizes inmate reactions to their daily life in the average prison. Though some prisoners experience tangible stress, which is destructive and disabling for them, most somehow adapt to prison, and remain comparatively healthy and sane behind walls. And while it is true that prisons harbor a disproportionate share of predatory and dangerous citizens, the danger of getting hurt in most prisons is not disproportionate to the chances of being injured in the neighborhoods from which the inmates derive (Bowker, 1980, Sylvester et al., 1977). There is also no evidence that prisons are "schools of crime," nor that they in some other way warp, incapacitate or destroy people. A wholesale indictment of the system is therefore unsupported by hard data we have at hand.

This does not mean, of course, that prisons get a clean bill of mental health. There is appreciable inmate self insulation in the shape of self-requested "lock-ins." There are many inmates who are despondent, who live in fear, or who fight "no win" battles with staff. Other adverse indicators include degenerating relationships with loved ones and "in-house" crimes, such as narcotics trafficking and gambling.

The one feature of these undesirable facts which is critical in terms of their practical implications is that most problems affect a limited, vulnerable or problematic group of inmates. This fact is important, because where institutional problems are circumscribed, the most parsimonious solutions involve pointed reforms, rather than the dismantling of institutions. We do not close universities in which professors like myself are boring, graduates illiterate, or administrators autocratic. We keep universities open, because we harbor the forlorn hope that universities can be reformed (by firing "deadwood," tightening standards, and democratizing governance). The same logic applies, in varying degrees, to the prison.

Differential adaptation

Assume, for argument's sake, that five offenders have held up gas stations in the same area and stolen the day's take. Assume that each man is tried and convicted (or plea-bargained) and receives the same five-year sentence for his offense. We visit the inmates within one year, and discover the following scenarios:

(1) Our first felon, Meo Culpa, is employed in the officers' mess, and is unqualifiedly esteemed by peers and staff. Culpa's esteem by peers is reinforced by his periodic receipt (through unspecified channels) of exhilarating drugs. Staff acceptance makes searches of Culpa's person and habitation cursory, and permits Culpa to eat six meals a day, and to share an occasional sandwich with friends, in exchange for suitable consideration.

(2) Inmate Capone distributes towels in the prison gymnasium. As a hobby, he teaches boxing to other inmates, including unwilling disciples who are not very talented and cannot box back. These boxing lessons are designed to inspire acts of sodomy in the shower room, and donations that supplement Capone's commissary funds.

(3) Capone's Number One shower room victim and donor of lunch money is Inmate Rusticus, a retiring former mental patient. Rusticus spends his day attempting to evade Capone and two other inmates with predilections for taking communal

showers. Rusticus has lately taken to spending all day in his cell, with a blanket draped over his head. He has been overheard conversing with his radiator.

(4) Inmate Romeo comes from a close family, and has been cheered by regular mail from home. One day (a) his wife writes of an irresistible passion involving Romeo's best friend, and broaches the notion of an early divorce, and (b) news arrives that Romeo's eldest son has emulated his father by holding up a gas station. Following receipt of these and related communications, Romeo turns from extrovert to introvert, and acquires the nickname "Zombie."

(5) Inmate Jones works in the prison's license plate factory. His involvement is part-time because Jones spends most of his term in disciplinary segregation, where he occupies himself pounding the walls and cutting his wrists. Jones' behavior and accompanying verbalizations make it clear that he does not like segregation, but this does not deter him from promoting the displeasure of custodial staff by addressing them as "pigs" and subjecting them to colorful expletives. Jones is also suspected of distributing sharpened spoons, and there is talk of prosecuting him on charges of advocating riots.

Prison aficionados will recognize these portraits as retouched, but their subjects as real. The implications at minimum include the following points:

- Not only is prison existence much harder for some inmates than others, but it can be also much easier, in the sense of yielding secondary benefits.

- For some, punishment is particularly cruel. The cruelty is a product of special hardships experienced by special inmates. The point holds in reverse for punishment that is converted (by other special inmates) into a sinecure. Unequal distribution of pains and perquisites of imprisonment are produced by consequences emanating from corollaries of imprisonment (fellow-inmates, custodial regimes, significant others outside prison) which impinge unequally on inmates.

- Mental health is not an attribute of the person or a product of situational pressures. It is an intersection of personal susceptibilities and impingements. Mental illness may flare up in prison when specific prison stressors hit inmates who are susceptible to them. Some such prison stress is predictable from data about susceptibilities of the inmate and from knowledge about situations the inmate is likely to encounter where he is sent.

- Prisons provide opportunities and temptations for new felonious conduct. Such conduct sometimes escalates punishment, but often does not. Some prisoners become in-house criminals, others consumers of illegal services, and still others, victims.

I have not outlined these facts because I feel they are deplorable but because I think they are preventable. Prevention can include diversion from prison. However, I think there are lesser options available where imprisonment is inevitable.

Classification reform

Judges send felons to prison, but prison systems allocate felons to institutions, and assign them to accommodations and programs within institutions. This disaggregation process was itself a reform. It was first instituted to separate men from women, and (presumably tender) boys from (presumably hard-bitten) men. As institutions became differentiated in terms of physical attributes — meaning that we acquired tower-equipped prison fortresses and quonset huts surrounded by barbed wire — the emphasis shifted to what is known as "security grading." This type of procedure involves sorting inmates with very exaggerated caution into institutions designed to keep them from escaping. As in sentencing, the inmate's offense was the main piece of data used to decide how much escape risk he represented.

The advent of social work added new dimensions to information-gathering in assessment, which included social history-taking and the administration of all sorts of tests, inventories, and questionnaires. Such facts are ritualistically harvested, but tend to affect the inmate's assignment only insofar as they reveal blatant educational, physical, or vocational deficits (Chapter 14). Inmates who are emotionally disturbed and those who are flagrantly disabled may be flagged, and may be recommended for placement in special settings (mental health units, programs for addicts or mentally deficient inmates) in the few systems that have special settings available (Chapter 8). It is only after the inmate arrives at the prison that a classification committee determines his precise fate, subject to later reassignment. Some prisons deploy a second round of interviewing and testing, which increases the size of the inmate folder, but has little impact on his fate. Classification becomes a reflexive routine, though decisions can in practice lead to fateful miscalculations or corollaries that are at best thoughtless, and at worst callous. For example:

- Classifiers typically press their maximum security button when they encounter either an inmate who is vulnerable or one who is a predator, because both need to be watched. Unfortunately this often sends sheep (victim-prone inmates) and wolves (tougher inmates) into the same types of prisons.

- Inmates with suicidal histories tend to be placed where suicide can be "prevented," which often means segregated settings, in which self-destructive ruminations are apt to flourish.

- Educational programs are aimed at youths who have educational deficits because they hate school. Some such youths hate institutional schooling as well, and may create an environment antithetical to learning.

In theory, the indoctrination of new inmates includes an orientation to the prison conditions they are liable to encounter. In practice, most inmates are given a rule book and counseled to behave. The average inmate's first experience with the system involves the protracted inactivity of a classification center. His or her second experience may be with stressful "entry level" menial jobs — such as kitchen assignments — that are often reserved for new inmates.

Prison subenvironments

If a mega-prison is viewed as a mass of humanity surrounded by walls and guard towers, it is an inflexible, unresponsive jungle, of necessity uninviting to its inmates and staff. But most large institutions — including prisons — are seldom what they seem. Cities are conglomerates of neighborhoods whose denizens know each other, and in which life is geographically and psychologically circumscribed. Citizens, more often than not, have a penchant for sticking close to home. In most settings, even the most cosmopolitan of us have our circles of intimates and our established habits.

Large prisons are enclaves of environments, comprising groups of staff and inmates. These environments consist of segments of yards and sections of dining rooms, shops, offices, daytime cell blocs, and all sorts of places in which people work, study, play, exercise or congregate. One feature of environments, such as the ethnic neighborhoods of cities, is the fact that people gravitate to them in search of the congenial and the familiar, including people and facilities they are used to. In prisons, such "natural" self-selection is circumscribed, and classification is its substitute.

To be sure, there are times when inmates select their own places in prison by gravitating to them or pressing the staff button that obtains them preferred assignments. However, this sort of activity is happenstance, and it often subserves non-meritorious criteria, such as racial chauvinism, membership in street gangs, and availability of fringe benefits. More constructive is the type of intervention that occurs where a guard arranges a transfer for a victim-prone inmate to a tier in which tough inmates are not prominently represented, or secures a protective lockup for a prisoner who "needs to get away for awhile."

The most ambitious subdivision program in corrections is that of the Federal Bureau of Prisons, which we have described in Chapter 4. Of most surprise to experts was the Bureau's discovery that architecture is not an obstacle, that "walls do not a prison make." This followed from an experience showing that a fortress built in the 1930s — complete with nine guard towers and three-tier cell blocs — could be functionally subdivided, and that 15,000 inmates in such a fortress could be relocated without adverse repercussions (Lansing, Bogan and Karacki, 1977; Smith and Fenton, 1978).

An interesting outcome of the federal experience is that the sorting into groups helped produce congenial units for tougher and for more vulnerable inmates without creating jungles and kiddielands. There are data available that showed reductions in incident rates and favorable climate ratings by inmates (Trickett and Moos, 1972; Marrero, 1977).

Therapeutic communities?

Let us imagine an inmate, Norman Smith, who has low self-esteem and is easily intimidated. In the streets, Smith lives with his mother, and seldom leaves his home. Whenever Smith goes out, however, he is led into criminal mischief by tough young men whom he envies and respects. In prison, fellow-inmates discover Smith's susceptibility, and take turns threatening to harm him. Smith becomes afraid and makes his fear sufficiently obvious to invite cruel jokes, extortion, and rape attempts.

As Smith reaches a point where he cannot take more of this, he confides his problem to a staff member, who transfers him to a setting populated by prisoners with "mental histories," suicide attempts, and recorded propensities for being victimized.

Assume that you have been appointed to run this unit, and must define its mission. Is yours a sanctuary or a refuge from the prison-at-large? Do you confine yourself to the custodial goal of reducing destructive incidents? Do you feel you should provide supportive help (say, counseling) to tide your inmates over until they are released? Do you feel you should build inmates up (a more long-term concern) to help them face the prison, and to increase their chances of coping with life generally?

Deciding this question of goals is more than an academic exercise because the inmate-changing or ego-building option happens to be non-custodial, and subscribing to it brings you close to running a therapeutic community (TC), which is a special sort of milieu (see Chapter 4).

Therapeutic communities partly originated in mental hospital wards designed to approximate intensive community living. The idea was that in such settings the residents could learn how to properly interact with each other and with the staff, and that this could lead to healthier and more effective functioning in the free world (Jones et al., 1953; Jones, 1962). A second tradition, initiated by religious advocates of self-purging, has come down through Alcoholics Anonymous, Synanon, and a variety of "self help" groups using peer confrontation techniques to induce confession and reform. This tradition survives in settings for substance abusers.

Other therapeutic techniques, such as cognitive and behavioral approaches, have been used as adjuncts to experiments in community living. Smith, for example, could be readily seen as potentially benefiting from assertive training, tied-down experiences of success, or feedback as to his role in groups. He could be seen to require emotional support, or graduated exercises in independence. He may find it useful to inquire into the origins of his diffidence. Ultimately, however, what one does with Smith depends on the availability of resources. If Smith needs more help than one has available, it may be best to make sure no one physically harms him, and to leave him otherwise alone. It is important to keep in mind that help can harm, and that more of the wrong help can harm more.

A process most like that of the reformed mental hospital model, where no special techniques are added, is least likely to damage people, because its emphasis is on "here and now" experiences of working and living with others. The model would differ from other prison settings in that the relationship between staff and inmates would be informal, and because lower level staff, such as prison guards, would be seen as members of a treatment team. What people did in the settings — how they related to each other while living and working side by side — would be subject to scrutiny, with a view to understanding the roles people play, and studying their impact on others. Such analysis need not be deep, but conflicts and other interpersonal problems would be talked through. The principle is that of "social learning," which means learning from one's dealings with others in a noncontrived context (Chapter 12; also see, Jones, 1979).

A system of checks and balances

What every prison ideally needs are powerful persons who are sensitive to inmate concerns, and who cannot be humored or ignored when they translate and represent these concerns. Such roles can be exercised by humanistic administrators, or by ombudsmen, prison staff (chaplains, counselors) and outsiders (Denenberg, 1975). Unfortunately, in prisons as elsewhere, squeaky wheels tend to monopolize attention. Rarely do prisoner partisans or representatives directly and effectively represent the "silent majority" or problem inmates, who waste away within shooting distance from potentially available resources.

It is also important for the effective prison reformer to work *with* the system (and want to improve it) rather than using inmates — and abusing prison hospitality — by leveling nonconstructive criticisms and antagonizing prison staff.

A neglected means of ensuring decency is to be decent. Standards of ethical and professional work exist in all phases of corrections. Such norms can be unambivalently attended to, welcomed, and implemented. In doing so, one must avoid catering to groups with narrow compositions or special interest representation (such as guards, architects or equipment salesmen). These are groups that may dominate a field, but do not represent its "conscience." There is no substitute for humanistic thinking as an ameliorative counterforce on prison matters. This function is compatible with accepting the prison as a sad-but-real given, and it can be exercised by persons who are part of the system as well as outsiders. It is a function intrinsically compatible with impact, credibility, and reform.

6

If de Tocqueville were with us Today...*

IN 1831, Gustave de Beaumont and Alexis de Tocqueville arrived on American shores to inspect our penitentiaries. After casing the joints, so to speak, the young Frenchmen published a celebrated monograph, *On the Penitentiary System in the United States and its Application in France.* Among other observations, Beaumont and de Tocqueville reported that:

> There are in the United States a certain number of philosophical minds, who, full of theories and systems, are impatient to put them into practice; and if they had the power themselves to make the law of the land, they would efface with one dash, all the old customs, and supplant them by the creations of their genius, and the decrees of their wisdom. Whether right or wrong the people do not move so quickly. They consent to changes, but they wish to see them progressive and partial. This prudent and reserved reform, effected by a whole nation, all of whose customs are practical, is, perhaps, more beneficial than the precipitated trials which would result, had the enthusiasm of ardent minds and enticing theories free play.

---

*A modified version of this chapter was delivered at the Conference "Prisons After the Building Boom: Where Do We Go From Here?" at Sam Houston State University, (1995) and published in *The Prison Journal*, December, 1996; adapted and reprinted by permission of Sage Publications.

Beaumont and de Tocqueville concluded that:

> Whatever may be the difficulties yet to be overcome, we do not hesitate to declare that the cause of reform and progress in the United States, seem to us certain and safe (Beaumont and De Tocqueville, 1964, p. 52).

Students of corrections today who are latter-day philosophical minds are reconciled to the fact that the enthusiasm of their ardent minds and enticing theories does not have free play.

The philosophical minds are not alone in their assessment. 17 October, 1994, *Newsweek* entitled a story, "Back to the Chain Gang?"—which is as prudent and reserved as reform can get. *Newsweek* pointed out that "from Albany to Sacramento, lawmakers have discovered that bashing prison inmates is this season's easiest and most disingenuous way to exploit voters' anti-crime sentiment" (p. 87). The actions *Newsweek* referred to involve stripping prisons of all conceivable amenities, privileges, activities, and opportunities that could be defined as ameliorations of existence. In the types of prisons thus envisaged, Beaumont and de Tocqueville and their contemporaries would have felt very much at home.

One revealing target of prison critics has been that of educational programs for inmates—with Congress leading the charge in 1994 federal crime legislation. A philosophical mind who was acutely disturbed by this movement was George Beto, former head of the Texas Prison System, who argued strongly for the opposite trend. Beto explained to the American Correctional Association in 1989 that:

> The state has "a compelling interest" to provide a first-class educational program for the functional illiterates and the dropouts. If Jefferson was correct—and I believe that he was—when he asserted that a democracy can survive only if the electorate is informed, then that state interest in education becomes even more compelling in the case of prison inmates. For it can be empirically shown that a good educational program in a controlled prison environment can accomplish more in a shorter time than can the school "on the streets." The year 2012 should witness in America's prisons superior educational programs ranging from literacy classes through the baccalaureate degree, programs increasing the skills, enlarging the vision, and enhancing the hope of prisoners.

If Texas followed George Beto's recommendations, it would increasingly diverge from states which had resolved to fire prison teachers to save money. Texas and New York, for example, might go distinctly separate ways. Such divergent developments were the focus of Beaumont and de Tocqueville's observations about American corrections. Beaumont and de Tocqueville indicated that one would expect uniformity of practice in any country, and wrote that "there is, however, nothing like that in the United States.... We have spoken of nine states which have adopted a new system of prisons; there are fifteen more which have as yet made no change" (p. 48).

As cases in point, Beaumont and de Tocqueville cited several examples. They wrote:

> By the side of one state, the penitentiaries of which might serve as a model, we find another, whose jails present the example of everything which ought to be avoided. Thus the State of New York is without contradiction one of the most advanced in the

path of reform, while New Jersey, which is separated from it but by a river, has retained all the vices of the ancient system.

Ohio, which possesses a penal code remarkable for the mildness and humanity of its provisions, has barbarous prisons. We have deeply sighed when at Cincinnati, visiting the prison. We found half of the imprisoned charged with irons, and the rest plunged into an infected dungeon; and are unable to describe the painful impression which we experienced, when, examining the prison of New Orleans, we found men together with hogs, in the midst of all odors and nuisances. In locking up the criminals, nobody thinks of rendering them better, but only of taming their malice; they are put in chains like ferocious beasts; and instead of being corrected, they are rendered brutal (pp. 48-49).

Beaumont and de Tocqueville saw advantages in a system which, they noted, provides unfettered opportunities for local ingenuity, initiative and creativity (p. 50). They advanced the further presumption that progressive developments would be enviously emulated elsewhere. In the words of the French duo:

The impulse of improvement is given. Those states which have as yet done nothing, are conscious of their deficiency; they envy those which have preceded them in this career, and are impatient to imitate them (p. 52).

There is no provision in this type of dissemination scheme for a domino effect in which states might imitate other states that set up chain gangs or that decided to save money (or garner votes) by firing teachers or selling off gymnasium equipment.[1] Moreover, one could thus anticipate a situation in which foreign observers would be surveying American prisons to inventory things their countries must try to avoid.

Another problem not anticipated by DeTocqueville was the effect on prisons of contemporary social policy. The United States, for example, is currently embarked on welfare reform, which entails insistence that able-bodied recipients find jobs that largely do not exist. Once welfare nonrecipients discover that they cannot find legitimate work, it almost follows that many will join the underground economy, which is the target of the drug raids that are congesting prisons.

The war on drugs is a development DeTocqueville could never have predicted. He could not have anticipated the degree to which the future of prisons today hinges on the extent to which individual states escalate or de-escalate the war on drugs, and respond to public concerns about street violence and recidivistic violent offending.

These latter concerns are related to the principal development that DeTocqueville could not have predicted, which is the prevalence of persons serving extremely long prison sentences today, of a magnitude inconceivable in DeTocqueville's day.

One wonders what DeTocqueville could have suggested we do with very long-term prisoners. Since De Tocqueville was a humanist, one would suspect that his views would be congruent with those of George Beto, who said in his speech that "to tell a young man in his mid-twenties, full of the juices of life, that regardless of his behavior, he must spend the next twenty or more years of his life in prison, not only removes hope but creates a serious management problem." It would no doubt make sense to De Tocqueville that we try, in Beto's words, not to make long prison sentences hope-destroying.

Today, long-term prisoners *live* in the prison. Portions of prison life can in theory offer hope and fulfillment, in the same sense in which portions of life are experienced by the rest of us (Chapter 15). Careers presuppose advancement, progression, planful continuity, choice points, and valued achievements along the way.

Can careers in this sense be engendered in the prison? I suspect that they can, and in my capacity as a DeTocqueville-equivalent I have observed a prison system that has approximated the career model and is refining it. Essential elements, as I saw them, are the following:

1. The career model presupposes that prisoners have case managers who help them plan their careers. A staff member of the prison must work with the prisoner to formulate short-term and long-term plans that are congruent with the prisoner's interests. Such plans ought to include activities that yield meaningful products, and develop skills that can subsequently be rehearsed. Case managers would arrange for placements through which plans can be implemented. This includes mobilizing resources and services, and relevant learning opportunities, and keeping in touch with the inmate and those who work with the inmate. It also includes keeping a cumulative record, which assures continuity as the torch is passed from case manager to case manager.

2. The model presupposes opportunities for consultation and choice. The prisoner must be able to review his or her career to date, and decide whether to continue on a given path or explore new and different options. Choice points should occur at the inception of confinement, at the transition from early career to mid-career segments, and as the prisoner moves from mid-career to a late-career or pre-release stage. Choice points should also occur if and when the prisoner is transferred from one institution to another.

3. The model presupposes a sequence of settings that is congruent with phases of the prisoner's career. The Scottish Prison Service, in which the scheme I referred to is being developed, has introduced an orientation setting for long-term prisoners. The system also has mid-career settings, and permeable institutions for prisoners approaching release. It also has provisions for prisoners with special needs, who have difficulties coping with mainline settings.

4. Some jurisdictions in the US have an information system that makes it possible to keep track of prisoners individually and in the aggregate (Colorado Department of Corrections). Such data are invaluable for career planning. One can, for example, schedule services and programs over time, wait-listing prisoners for their next set of involvements. At the press of a key, inmates and case managers can resuscitate past decisions and review their next options. If a plan is entered, resources can be co-opted. Matching demands with supply allows for flexible resource allocation and planning.

5. New kinds of reward systems are called for by a career-oriented model (Chapter 7). Inmates' achievements must be recognized, and constructive contributions the prisoner makes must be valued. The inmate must know that being in prison does not foreclose the opportunity for demonstrating competence, being creative, or becoming useful to society.

6. Another desirable requisite is the chance for citizenship (Chapters 9 and 10).

Being a citizen means that one can affect the environment in which one lives. Prisoners might even try to help prison staff improve prison conditions to the benefit of both parties. Beaumont and de Tocqueville talked glowingly about inmate governance in 1831. "Nothing is more grave," they wrote about residents in the Boston House of Reformation, "than the manner in which these electors and jurymen of tender years discharge their functions" (p. 147). Long-term prisoners, who spend their lives in prison, might be even more serious, if provided the opportunity.

Resistance to this idea can, of course, be expected. In 1960, the Warden's Association of America "went on record as being in opposition to the idea of inmate self-government" (Baker, 1964, p. 47). There is no evidence that the resolution was ever rescinded.

Resistance to the other elements of the scheme can similarly be expected. Prisons are not attuned to long-term planning. Programs for inmates tend to be delivered as modules. Joint staff-prisoner decision-making is rare in programming decisions. Case management is usually confined to record keeping, and information systems in most prisons are primitive.

But I still think that career planning is the obvious alternative to long-term storage of prisoners in warehouses with walls. I know of no one in corrections who wants to run such institutions, and no one who would want us to run them, if we became so inclined.

Notes

1. Chain gangs were first revived by the state of Alabama; the idea then spread to Arizona, Florida, Iowa, Wisconsin, and to detention systems run by politically-conscious county sheriffs.While this dissemination occurred, the American Correctional Association condemned the practice as "harsh and mean-spirited." The American Correctional Association is a national organization. Federal prisons (a post-de Tocquevile development) have been able to play constructive roles, spearheading reforms such as classification (Chapter 14) and functional unit management (Chapter 4). Innovations—including units—often have gravitated from the state level to that of county or municipal jails (Zupan, 1991).

7

Rewarding Convicted Offenders*

ONE OF the most neglected subjects in criminal justice is that of the rationale and/or the criteria for distributing rewards to offenders. This oversight is understandable, since the system is presumably in the business of dispensing punishments, which at first glance appears inconsistent with the opposing business of allocating rewards. This appearance, as it happens, is deceptive, because (among other things) punishments are subject to modification, which means that they can be de-escalated, suspended, and discontinued in response to sterling — or, at least, improved — behavior. Consider the following sample scenarios:

> The parole board explains to inmate Jones why it has decided to release him. "At our last meeting with you," notes the Chairman, "we advised you to show concern about your drinking problem. We see you now coordinate the prison AA program, and we hope you will follow through in the community."
>
> The probation office has reduced Smith's schedule for office visits. "You are

---

*Reprinted, by permission, from *Federal Probation Quarterly*, June, 1988.

married and have a steady job," explains the probation officer. "We can see you somewhat less frequently."

The good time review committee has restored the time allowance inmate Sylvester has lost through prison disciplinary violations. "We recommend restoring good time," explains the board, "because this inmate's behavior has been exemplary for two years."

Resident Endicott is transferred to the Honors Cottage. She comes highly recommended by work supervisors, and has moved from illiteracy to a high school equivalence diploma.

Junctures such as these have two attributes in common: (1) they de-escalate the onerousness of the offender's treatment, and (2) they respond to behavior deemed meritorious by corrections staff. The combination fits the dictionary definition of a reward as "something . . . that is offered or given for some service or attainment."

Other developments in an offender's life may also have a rewarding effect, without it being planned for by staff. Such junctures meet the first element of the definition but they lack the second, because there is no desire to reward the offender when his conditions of punishment are mitigated. Examples include the following:

The inmate is given a work assignment in the officers' mess. "Good deal!" he exclaims. "An unlimited supply of snacks!"

A detainee is recommended for commitment, but a psychiatrist demurs: "This man is a malingerer," he argues. "He prizes the hospital as a respite from confinement."

An offender is segregated for a disciplinary violation. "I've made it into the Big Leagues," he tells friends, "and my creditors cannot get to me in the hole."

A graduated reward system in corrections

A conception that is of distinguished vintage envisages progress in the correctional system as a sequence of earned rewards or de-escalated punishments. The inception of this idea rests with Captain Alexander Maconochie, who became warden of the Norfolk Island colony in 1840 and promulgated a roster of prison regulations which is still breathtaking. This document proposes that an inmate's sentence be translated from time-to-be-served to a commensurate obligation to make positive contributions, which Maconochie called "tasks." Productivity and good conduct were to be rewarded, using a fixed scale of "marks of commendation," which were to be allocated on a daily basis. The minimum inmate wage was to be ten marks a day with provisions for overtime. For five marks the inmate could treat himself to the Australian version of a three-star meal (regular food cost three marks; bread and water were free). Accumulated marks could buy time reduction at the rate of ten marks for each day of good time.

All inmates in the system were to earn their progress from tightly supervised prison experiences through seven-man team membership to a community-based reentry stage in which inmates lived in cottages and owned sheep. (Barry, 1956; Barry, 1958).[1]

From 1854 to 1862, a student of Maconochie's, Sir Walter Crofton, ran a derivative regime in Ireland, which has been called the "intermediate system." The regime derives its appellation from a middle (intermediate) stage in a sequence of graduated freedom. This intermediate stage involved residence in a halfway house on work release.

Crofton influenced the New York Prison Association and inspired the wardens and reformers who shaped the Declaration of Principles of the 1870 American Prison Congress. This declaration recommends a "system of rewards" for inmates, "a gradual withdrawal of state restraints" and "constantly increased privileges... earned by good conduct." The fifth of the declaration's principles emphasizes that "the prisoner's destiny, during his incarceration, should be placed, measurably, in his own hands" (*Transactions*, 1871, pp. 1-8).

The advocates of systematically graduated rewards for inmates argued for this reform in 1840 and could still argue for it, on the following grounds:

(1) Rewards for good conduct provide hope: The availability of graduated improvements in the offender's conditions of punishment gives him something to look forward to. He can face his situation with greater equanimity, knowing that his fate can become less onerous in the foreseeable future.

(2) Rewards provide incentive: The offender in a graduated system knows that there is something he can do to improve his own condition. This gives him a reason to participate in constructive endeavors. Once a person has some reason for self-improvement, he may evolve other reasons, such as love of learning or pride in products of work.

(3) Such a system empowers the client: If performance leads to rewards, the person in fact controls his future, in that he can generate improvements through his own efforts. Conversely, he can decide not to buy into the reward system, assuming he is willing to accept the consequences of nonparticipation.

(4) The sequence is ultimately reintegrative: As punishments are mitigated, environmental conditions get to approximate life in the community, where the offender must operate free of restrictions. The sequence provides an opportunity for the rehearsal of prosocial behavior under regimes involving decreasing surveillance. Reward systems also are reintegrative because they resemble career ladders in the free world, in which advancement is presumed to hinge on performance. Lastly, there is value in learning that decent behavior is occasionally profitable.

Critics' objections to a reward system in corrections

Though one might suppose that objections (if any) to reward sequences built into corrections would originate with conservative critics, the loudest protests in fact derive from strongly felt concerns of liberal or radical students of the system. These observers argue that reward systems in corrections are inhumane and undesirable, on the following grounds:

(1) Reward systems are self-serving: The goal of corrections officials is envisaged as one of institutional behavior-control, meaning that the objective is to induce inmates to conform to rules that benefit the system rather than the inmate. The

historian David Rothman describes parole, for example, as "a disciplinary mechanism far more potent than the lash" (Rothman, 1980, p. 74). He also tells us that prison privileges exist because they can be withheld "to the ends of discipline" (p. 151). In other words, rewards become a gambit, a way to achieve prisoner obedience, and a means to discourage manifestations of autonomy by offenders.

(2) Rewards induce hypocrisy: If offenders come to participate in programs because program participation is rewarded, they can be presumed not to be interested in program content. The process is sometimes described as one of blackmail which inspires undignified pretense and reduces the effectiveness of programming.

The authors of *Struggle for Justice* (American Friends Service Committee, 1971) thus contend that inmates are made cynical about prison programs, that "programs are regarded as phony and that the motivation for participation is to manipulate the parole process" (p. 88). With regard to rewards, the authors of this report note:

> In rehabilitative prisons the person's release may be effected by the quantity and quality of his participation in "treatment programs." Since he knows that this is true, he is greatly influenced to enter these programs not simply to help himself, but in order to manipulate the release system. In doing so he usually corrupts the treatment value of the programs (p. 98).

David Fogel goes so far as to suggest that prison programs are often (at best) unnecessary and would decay if they could not drum up business by relying on rewards. Fogel (1979) asks, for example, "We wonder, in an atmosphere of real choice (in the sense of 'free enterprise'), how many prison clinical programs would survive if survival turned merely on attendance and inmates were assured immunity for absence" (p. 263).

(3) The administration of reward systems is inevitably capricious: The right to make decisions about who gets rewarded confers wide discretion upon those who make such decisions. This fact places a great deal of power into the hands of officials, who can punish offenders against whom they are prejudiced by withholding rewards.

In relation to parole, for example, Fogel writes that:

> It is in this process that prison staff decision-making fades into unbridled, low visibility discretion. If at first blush discretion looks like power, in prison it also produces an arena in which indecisiveness, favoritism, racism, suppression and lawlessness are acted out daily (pp. 200-201).[2]

(4) Rewards can be unjust: Tampering with a fairly arrived-at sanction can devalue a system which has the obligation to stick to its guns. If one must not add penalties in midstream, the same consideration applies to the dilution of penalties. Von Hirsch (1976) comments that:

> The reverse situation — releasing an offender early on rehabilitative grounds — presents much the same questions as releasing him early on the basis of a prediction that he is not dangerous . . . Releasing him as soon as he completes his cure — like releasing him immediately if he is predicted not to offend again — remains objectionable as disproportionately lenient in relation to the gravity of the crime for which he was convicted (p. 129).

A related argument is that a prison sentence should be punishment, prison activities should be rehabilitative, and the twain should not meet as parole decisions. Morris (1974) thus deplores "the corrupting link between time and treatment, which creates a further corrupting link between coercion and cure" (p. 14). Morris does not object to other rewards, however, such as the provision of enriched milieus to inmates willing to consider self-improvement.

(5) Rewards endanger civil rights: As some see it, reward systems turn offender rights into privileges and convert offenders into recipients of amenities to which they should be entitled. This means that the offender has reduced bargaining power with staff members, who can retaliate more easily if they feel challenged. Moreover, enterprises such as counseling and education are contaminated when staff who are supposed to work with offenders can also determine their fate. One student of the system has even suggested that "as long as prison therapists feed data and recommendations to decision makers, there is little point in maintaining that they can do therapy" (Toch, 1981, p. 338).[3]

A sequence of nondiscretionary benefits

Close reading shows that most critics do not object to improving the offender's fate but profoundly mistrust the judgment of officials who would decide that improvement is warranted. This means that most critics would have no problem with routinized increments of privileges which automatically accrue to the offender at predetermined junctures, with the burden placed on officials to justify denials of benefit, subject to challenges and appeals.

The irony is that under a system thus envisaged, one can punish an offender by withholding a benefit, but one cannot reward him by conferring it. This view also generates expectations that invite rancor and bitterness: For example, it makes parole boards ratifiers of a sentence that the inmate should serve; the board must therefore release any given inmate unless it decides to deliberately injure him by denying him parole, which is added punishment. Good time credit gets similarly taken for granted. The fact that good time is often routinely awarded in practice may assist such expectations, but the view has nothing to do with probabilities of award. If parole is a presumed right, a parole board which turns down most inmates at first appearance would evoke expectations no different from one that releases them, though the bitterness such a board invites would increase. This is so because of the view that the board retains people whom it could release, rather than releasing people whom it could retain.

The perspective may strike us as presumptuous, but it approximates a good deal of "real" (outside of criminal justice) life. As we shall see (Chapter 8), it particularly resembles seniority-based career systems, such as civil service. In such systems there may be talk of merited progression, but actual benefits (the analogues of good time and parole) become available as a function of time served, barring exceptional, and usually embarrassing, circumstances.

Defensible strategies of reform

No one — including radical critics — would regard a "time serving" paradigm outside a prison as a model we should aspire to or emulate. Such a system implies passivity rather than citizenship, provides no incentive or recognition, has little integrity, and fosters bureaucratic survival. The problem is that given the obsession with capricious exercises of power by officials, it is hard to envisage systems other than time-doing that mistrustful observers would find acceptable.

This point becomes quickly obvious when we consider some suggested — and occasionally essayed approaches:

(1) Circumscribing decisions with rules: A popular approach is to use guidelines or point systems to make decisions more reliable. Hypothetically, the link between performance and rewards can be similarly prespecified; the result can thus become more predictable, though one can never get around the fact that the offender's performance is in the first place assessed by someone whose judgments become data that are fed into the actuarial system.

Judgments, of course, can be idiosyncratic, but less so if they are pooled or reviewed, which reduces arbitrariness. John Barry notes that Maconochie was aware of the need for reliability checks. Maconochie "contemplated that marks should be affixed daily by various goal officials, acting separately, for various aspects of a prisoner's conduct and labor. In this way he considered that the dangers of abuse of discretion would be lessened" (Barry, 1956, p. 159).

Another desideratum is to have publicized criteria and rules about how behavior is to be rated. Again, according to Barry:

> Maconochie's emphasis was always upon the desirability of a prisoner's knowing where he stood, and what he had to do to gain his liberty. I do not think he would have cared for a system where the time of release depends, not upon a prisoner's own efforts, but on a tribunal's estimate of the significance of those efforts, and of various other considerations which may not be known or disclosed to him (p. 160).

(2) Demonstrating inmate-centered concerns: Some critics envisage a zero sum model which has it that behavior that benefits the prison by definition cannot assist the inmate, and vice versa. If we take this grotesque formula seriously we cannot encourage inmate achievements, no matter how laudable and profitable for the inmate, unless these achievements increase the inmate's nuisance value to staff. The bottom line is that no incentive systems could ever be instituted because any improvement of conduct can make an inmate more congenial or easier to manage, which can be adjudged "convenient" to staff if one wants to impugn their motives.

An incentive system of integrity can be best created by ignoring prison benefits and advancing prescriptions that envisage results beneficial to offenders. A prescription might read, for example, "demonstrably illiterate persons entering the system will receive encouragement and credit if they partake of remedial education programs until they achieve reading and writing proficiency," or "certifiably addicted persons will be rewarded if they participate in substance abuse programs" (presuming such are available). If educated or rehabilitated inmates demonstrate behavioral improvements, this fact would be welcome but irrelevant.

(3) Engendering inmate participation: One pet presupposition of critics is that rewards are constraining, meaning that if anyone is rewarded for doing something this compromises the free exercise of his or her volition. Speaking for a blue ribbon committee, for example, Von Hirsch (1976) proclaimed that "we stress that offenders should be free to decide whether or not to participate: If a person is subject to penalties if he refuses to join (or promised more lenient treatment if he does), the program is no longer voluntary" (p. 116).

Such reasoning about the constraining effects of rewards is never applied to higher wage scales in prison industry, which most critics favor. Nor is it applied outside of prison, such as to the well-rewarded careers of legal scholars who make such arguments. The fact is that "constraint" and "voluntariness" are mostly in the eyes of the beholder, but this does not mean that we need not be concerned about the relationship, and it is obviously important that program involvement be as spontaneous and enthusiastic as possible.

One established way of promoting inmate participation is to offer to negotiate contracts in which the prisoners agree to behavior goals whose attainment will be rewarded. It is true that one can point to power imbalances in such contracts between staff and clients who sign them. Limited choice, however, is better than no choice, and volition that is exercised in the absence of all constraints or incentives is rarely encountered anywhere.

Finally, offenders could volunteer to participate in a reward system and might be permitted to do so, with nonvolunteers undergoing routine, fair, and standardized processing. This, however, creates a two tier arrangement which invites being seen as a way of punishing the noncompliant under the guise of rewarding those seeking to achieve.

Rediscovering incentives

It should be obvious at this point that almost any solution one can think of invites objections from persons who feel that the power to reward is a license to punish. In a system that accommodates such objections, only routine benefits could be provided; some intrinsic rewards (including the joy of winning law suits against officials) would also be available. The idea would be that motivated offenders could achieve goals of their choosing and unmotivated offenders could contentedly desist. The system could obviously continue to punish destructive behavior, given due process, but it could not encourage what it deems desirable behavior, using rewards.

This "hands off" position is not currently in the ascendance. It is not favored by officials who want to expedite the program participation of inmates in crowded prisons so as to enhance their readiness for release.[4] It is also not favored by reformers outside the system with parallel concerns, who are legislating innovations such as performance-based presumptive parole.[5] The view, however, contaminates our thinking about both parole and institutional practices to a surprising extent and partly helps explain the timidity with which we customarily approach the realm of prisoner achievements. For example:

(1) Information in most offender files prolifically highlights lapses of behavior and litigations, but provides few details about personal effort, activities, and achievements that deserve encouragement and support.

(2) Classification systems only secondarily specify programming needs, such as areas in which developmental possibilities and offender interests converge. Unincluded, moreover, are inventories of conditions (such as types of assignments) the offender indicates he would find rewarding and would be willing to work toward.

(3) Reward options in the system remain uninventoried, except in general terms. We have ballpark norms about penalties assigned to types of infractions, but no equivalent norms about graduated rewards (such as increments of time reduction) commensurate with magnitudes of accomplishment. Our awareness of rewarding milieu attributes of different prisons in a system, such as the level of freedom they offer, is similarly vague, so that conditions cannot be systematically improved.

(4) Amenities are serendipitously distributed, as where a prison job happens to bring improvements of living conditions. This supports the presumption that institutional needs always take precedence; it also permits amenity-seekers to gravitate to assignments for inappropriate reasons, particularly where squeaky wheels (persons who file requests) get selective attention.

(5) Eligibility requirements governing access to opportunities in the system frequently emphasize time-related and offense-centered considerations, rather than personal achievements. An offender who is close to release date, or one who has committed a nonviolent offense, may get precedence for a rewarding transfer (such as one closer to home) over an offender with a commendable record of institutional accomplishments.

(6) Reward systems are least available under conditions such as punitive or administrative segregation where hope is at a premium, living conditions deplorable, and motivation low. (Progress can be built into all prison settings, including those most likely to invite resentment and bitterness.)

(7) Long-term planning for clients rarely takes place; most programming and referrals specify short-term objectives, such as placement in a prison course or a job. Sequences of experiences that could involve progressions or promotions are not considered, though the proportion of long-term confinees in the system is steadily growing (Chapters 6 and 15).

(8) There is little concern about elementary learning theory principles, such as those that point up the value of arranging short-term rewards at the inception of learning or the need for consistency if rewards are to be effective.

The above picture holds despite the fact that most corrections systems offer types and degrees of amenity that can be inventoried and used and others that can be instituted through variations of the regime, provided one does not feel that standardization of treatment is a self-evident desideratum.

The behavior modification specter

Does any self-conscious use of rewards verge on behavior modification? The answer is not clear at first glance. Behavior modification as a procedure systematically applies behavioral learning principles. Maconochie only missed being a behavior modificationist by accident of birth, because his prescription was a model of what learning theorists prescribe. By the same token, self-styled psychological interventions in prison — such as the infamous Project Start — violated fundamental tenets of applied learning theory, starting with its definition of goals, which, in the words of an authoritative source, must "facilitate improved self-control by expanding individuals' skills, abilities and independence (Brown et al., 1975, p. 1).

Project Start was a behavior modification program for disruptive inmates which relied on involuntary recruitment and contingent restraints consisting of indefinite segregation. At least one psychologist associated with the program defended this practice as necessary because "a voluntary program could be expected to be used by those prisoners who find themselves distressed by their situation, not by those who are causing extreme distress to others but are little inconvenienced themselves." (Scheckenbach, 1974, p. 468)

The psychologist's rejection of the criterion "distressed by their situation" is particularly troublesome, because the understanding in behavior modification circles is that the interventionist supplies the technology (such as a reward schedule) but the client supplies the goals. In fact, over three years before the inception of Project Start, the leading authority on behavior modification, Albert Bandura (1969), underlined and emphasized this principle. He wrote that "though the change agent determines the means by which specified outcomes can be achieved, the client should play a major role in determining the directions in which his behavior is to be modified" (p. 101); Bandura also pointed out that to the extent to which this distinction is observed "the frequently voiced concerns about human manipulation become essentially pseudo issues" (p. 112).

Not to consider the reduction of inmate suffering as a goal of intervention feeds the objection of critics to other goals, such as improved deportment and rehabilitation, which can appear to disregard the needs of inmates. This connotation of inhumaneness has also given the concept of behavior modification unsavory connotations, particularly in prisons. As a result, prison administrators are probably well advised not to invoke the concept in designing rewards and incentives for inmate self-improvement.

Amenities and necessities

In thinking about implementing reward systems, it becomes essential to distinguish between commodities that any civilized regime should furnish to its clients, conditions that must be furnished because a client needs them, and those that can be deployed as rewards because they transcend civilized entitlements or personal requirements.

Failure to draw such distinctions not only invites well-deserved lawsuits (such as those that nowadays shape permissible behavior modification experiments)[6] but confuses reward systems with systems that punish or injure under the guise of rewarding. This issue is relatively straightforward when one thinks about amenities which must be made universally available, because not to make them available creates substandard conditions. It is more complex with respect to milieus that must be created in response to special needs, setting aside any reward levels that might be built into such assignments.

To be defensible, the principle governing allocations must be that personal needs must take precedence over other claims to amenities. Given two inmates who are in line for a porter's job, for instance, the person whose mental health or social adjustment can be improved through solitude must get preference over the person who wants (but does not need) the job, though this person has assiduously "earned" the assignment. By the same token, it is inappropriate, and inexcusably cynical, to highlight improvements of living conditions that are attendant upon needed conditions, such as a hospital assignment. If a person is both vulnerable and a con man, the former fact must be considered relevant and the latter irrelevant, even where it is obvious that an assignment (e.g., a hospital ward) is the person's idea of nirvana.

These and similar considerations place reward systems for offenders in appropriate and defensible contexts. They make it obvious that for a reward system to thrive and withstand criticism it must never supplant a civilized regime, but must supplement it. The criteria for allocating resources must place entitlements in the foreground and expand the residual so as to multiply incentives available for rewarding achievement.

In formulating the priorities in this way, I do not imply that currently prevailing practices are wildly divergent from my formulation. The point is not to create a different system for allocating benefits (such as introducing token economy programs), but to find ways of enhancing the use of existing performance-based criteria of allocation. My contention is not that we must change course, but that we can do more than we are doing to demonstrate to offenders that we welcome any efforts they make at self-improvement, and are prepared to buttress such efforts.

The move seems timely, on two important counts: First, it has become axiomatic that we must uncongest prisons, and performance-based criteria are a more flexible way of selecting candidates for release than an offender's past history, which none of us — including the offender — can change. Second, the reward strategy furthers rehabilitation if we reward an offender's resocializing moves, but it also accommodates just desert since the logic that dictates that we must punish transgressions allows for its corollary, which is that we reward contributions that benefit the society that offenders have harmed.

Notes

1. During the four years of Maconochie's tenure and in its aftermath, 1,450 Tasmanian convicts were released; the recidivism rate of this group was less than three per cent, despite the fact that two-thirds of the group (950 men) had been classified as unreformable.
2. One of the authors of *Struggle for Justice* (David Greenberg) takes an even stronger stance. He ruminates:

> What if the prison staff and officials, as well as the government of which they are a part, are not merely stern and corrupt but murderous? These disturbing questions have been shown to be more than academic by the events in the last 15 years. Revelations of the killing of prisoners by guards, of confinement, beatings and

enforced transfers of militant prisoners have left us with a more sinister view of penal administrators (Greenberg, 1977, p. 11).

The report itself takes a more tempered position. It concludes that "today the evils of discretion far outweigh conceivable benefits, but this might not always be true (p. 143).

3. One other concern relates to the potential of corruption, as in some prison systems that have been declared unconstitutional, in which inmates were formally or informally rewarded for keeping fellow-inmates "in line" by brutalizing them.
4. A Canadian news item, for example, reads: "The Solicitor General has announced that the National Parole Board will consider participation in a literacy program when deciding on parole. 'Perhaps this more than anything else will help inmates to understand the importance of literacy skills in functioning successfully on the outside,' Mr. Kelleher noted" (*Liaison*, March 1987).
5. One variant on presumptive parole is a New York program incorporated in the legislature's (1987) Omnibus Prison Bill. Inmates who participate in this program receive a Certificate of Earned Eligibility upon completion of individually designed treatment and work assignments which presage "successful transitions" to law abiding careers. The Certificate offers each inmate the probability of release at the expiration of his minimum sentence unless the parole authorities find a "reasonable probability that if (the inmate) is released he would not live and remain at liberty without violating the law, and that his release is not compatible with the welfare of society." (See Part 2100, Earned Eligibility Program, Title 7, NY Official Compilation of Codes, Rules and Regulations)
6. Court decisions relating to law suits have held that amenities to which all institutionalized clients are entitled cannot be used as rewards, to be purchased with tokens.

8

Enhancing the Quality of Survival in Prison*

IN THE real, or possibly the unreal world, we often enhance the quality of our lives in a way that reflects our privileged condition. We may do so by juggling luxuries to which we have somehow been accustomed. *Time* magazine of 5 March 1984 referred to two life-enhancing residents of Texas. One was a Dallas socialite who complained that "If you polled every woman in the US, you would find not one who has enough closet space." The lady had remedied her own problem with a "two-room super sanctum" that had fully marbled floors, skylights, a fireplace, and a conveyer rack for dresses which occupied 1,000 square feet. The other Texan was a lady with a six-room closet for her "$750,000 plus" wardrobe. Meanwhile, in nearby Austin, an attorney had been preparing to defend the state of Texas against a suit centering on the routine double-ceiling of its prison inmates (*Ruiz vs. Estelle* 1982). The issue for this lawyer — and for those who were suing him — did not center on "quality of life" in closet space, but on "quality of survival" in cell space.

---

*This chapter is excerpted from a contribution to *Coping and Caring*, a colloquium report edited by A. Rosenblatt and W. Ilchman. It is here reprinted by permission from Rockefeller Institute of Public Affairs of the State University of New York (Albany, NY).

"Quality of survival" is different from "quality of life," because we must "survive" before quality of life becomes an issue (Maslow 1954). The relationship is one of figure that is derived from obfuscating ground, in the sense that survival-related concerns are concerns which we who are surviving have forgotten or repressed or never faced. This distinction does not imply that the world is eventless or joyless for those who are by necessity concerned with survival, but that the satisfactions that surviving entails are commodities that we would never think of as satisfactions, because we take their availability for granted.

Let no one tell you, for example, that there is no pleasure in prison. Imagine yourself an inmate on an errand through a half-empty prison yard. Your breath fearfully suspended, you note that no guards are in sight and that the gate you have left recedes as you quicken your pace. Your heart sinks as you see a group of prison bullies — men who have been teasing and threatening you — swagger into view. You assume that these men will notice you, but they are miraculously distracted by someone or something behind them. There is pleasure, indeed, or at least exquisite relief, in your respite from humiliation. There is accomplishment in the crossing and there is a miracle in the moment of invulnerability it buys.

For most of us who cross yards, doorways, roads, and parks with unself-conscious impunity, survival awareness and satisfaction are unavailable to consciousness. We never know how much it can mean to experience relative noiselessness (say, at bedtime), to get a postcard or a furtive cup of coffee. We are even less capable of visualizing how much one can prize brief respites from obsessive rumination or discomfort.

The other side of the coin is that life loses something for those who must struggle to survive. Those who grapple with basics find that the enterprise is a consuming one (Maslow 1954). Such persons can spare little time or energy for "higher" goals, and the effete concerns of the outer world look unreal to them. This fact matters. It matters in hospices, for example, where survival is all one can hope for, but it matters even more wherever a future life is possible.

Helping prisoners to survive

In civilized societies we are asked to address survival issues as a societal moral obligation. Humanists accept the premise that we have no right to reduce offenders — no matter how reprehensible they might be — to a life limited to the avoidance of pain. This issue can be addressed across the board, or selectively for those who suffer the most (Chapter 5). Prison or any other environment that can offer flexibility reduces the need for special or supplementary settings. An educationally handicapped youngster, for example, needs no special classroom if his teachers can accommodate his deficits and can prevent his peers from the sort of unself-conscious sadism that casts him as a scapegoat. The option at issue is not a cold turkey, take-your-chances mainstreaming, but rather, the availability of mainline settings with special provisions (such as personal attention and medication) that accommodate deviant needs.

The assumption that such provisions exist or can be built in must be tested. A prison official once assumed that his prisons could easily absorb inmates of marginal intelligence who had been quartered in a special unit. When he disbanded the unit, most of its clients found their way to other special settings for marginal copers. Luckily for the inmates, the executive left the prison system before he had disbanded all special settings, which served variegated needs.

We have noted in Chapter 2 that when one multiplies prison stressors one can push inmates over various brinks, such as those defining the limits of their social, emotional and disciplinary equilibria. Unfortunately, breakdowns in stressful circumstances tend to become less visible when they multiply sufficiently because we accommodate degenerating climates by lowering our expectations. The rebellious inmate of yesterday becomes the surly inmate of today. A suicide attempt gets pejoratively characterized as a "superficial scratch" or as "manipulative." Such judgments are the jaundiced fruits of cynicism-producing experience.

Prison systems become less hospitable when they are forced into a survival orientation in which attending to symptoms of stress seems unimportant. But they attend to one consequence of stress, which is that of assaultiveness, violence, and general disruption (DeWolfe and DeWolfe, 1979). One hears a great deal in crowded prisons about increasing numbers of disruptive inmates, and maxi-maxi settings mark the failure of what has heretofor been an adequate range of environments to accommodate an expanding range of problems. "Getting rid of trouble makers" is often a way of pretending concern for individuals when the real issue is convenience for the system, as when a teachers' union president proclaimed:

> ALTERNATIVE CLASSROOM SETTINGS MUST BE ESTABLISHED FOR DISRUPTIVE STUDENTS. Many students view suspension and/or expulsion as a "free pass" from a school that they didn't want to be in anyway. *As educators, we have a responsibility to provide an environment where the educational and emotional problems of these students can be dealt with.* There is no benefit gained by turning these young people loose on society just as there is no benefit gained from allowing them to continue as a disruptive force in a normal classroom situation (Hobart 1984, emphasis added).

The beneficiaries of such settings — if any — are the non-residents who are protected from the residents, or are deterred from joining them. Other system-serving options address (but do not solve) logistic problems. They are storage depots or holding pens for inmates yet-to-be-absorbed, transferred, released, or otherwise processed. Other settings are places for inmates who fall between cracks, and serve as makeshift solutions at best.

Sanctuaries and oases

Inmate-centered settings solve problems. They include what John Seymour and I have called 'niches' (Toch 1977; Hagel-Seymour 1982; see Chapter 25). These range from places of refuge to settings where inmates can grow, develop, and change. Formal niches are those described in prison brochures. Some are explicitly ameliorative and are reserved for inmates who are non-resilient, handicapped, or vulnerable. These settings render a service by physically sequestering inmates and surrounding them with non-stressful peers. Beyond this function, these niches can provide remedial or other services, up to and including rehabilitative services. There are also settings that are oases. They are reserved for meritorious inmates and feature a relaxed, privileged, and less institutionalized regime.

Sanctuaries and oases in prison have existed since time immemorial. Keeping the concepts separate has not been a problem: Protective settings have always been sterile settings, and inmates have had to swallow their pride to secure protection. This stigmatization of non-resilience is still rampant in prisons today, though an inmate has to make fewer trade-offs today in exchange for protection. One reason is the recognition — mostly by judges — that it is unfair to penalize those who are forced to seek refuge.

Whatever the reason, some sanctuaries in prison are now also oases. This means that superficially relevant features of such environments can attract some wrong inmates for wrong reasons and reduce the availability of survival-relevant slots. More seriously, the supposition that a sanctuary offers some fringe benefits makes its custodians (the staff) more cynical and suspicious of inmate motives. This disquieting propensity acquires spurious documentation from reductions in deprivations that can be features of niches that such inmates need.

Informal niches are unrecorded highlights, and the staff responsible for their creation are unsung heroes of correctional sagas. An informal niche can arise in almost any mundane-looking setting: A shop, tier, dormitory, classroom, boiler room, or office. Such a setting becomes a niche when inmates are selectively assigned to it or selectively gravitate to it in order to survive. In other words, niches are niches because of inmates who are excluded or included in them, because of staff who run them, and because of the climate that the inmates and staff create.

Formal niches can serve a group of prisons or they can be prison-specific. Informal niches are always prison niches, which means that the prison can use the niche to blunt the edges of its milieu, or can use it to attend to vulnerabilities of inmates or to serve sub-populations whose needs are urgent but unprovided for. Local niches can be immensely effective because the staff who assign inmates to these niches often know the inmates personally, and know the settings and the personnel who run them. By contrast, system niches can be deployed by staff who must depend on formal descriptions of the settings, and may know an inmate only from his or her file (Chapter 14). System niches also are visible targets at which prisons can aim their misfits. This fact, and the resulting fighting off of undesired candidates, can lead to unseemly and demoralizing games, sometimes called "ping ponging."

Settings that are used as dumping grounds lose potency when they are faced with groups of prisoners for which they were not designed. System-wide settings can also be seen as guests of prisons and may be made to feel unwelcome by their hosts. At worst, they may be rejected as alien implants (Studt, Messinger, and Wilson 1968). Moreover, crowding endangers almost any special setting. A bed is a bed, and invitingly beckons as administrators desperately seek space.

Inaugurating a special setting

Special settings must be special, both for staff and for inmates. Staff who gravitate toward such settings as a sinecure, as a stepping stone to advancement, or as a place of semi-retirement can neutralize their benefits. To attract the right staff, one must emphasize the risks, challenges, and complexities of assignments. The foreground of job announcements must be the work and its inmate-centered core. Union contracts and civil service provisions can constrain, because unions are committed to protecting seniority. But the opportunity to try out a job might self-select dedicated, idealistic, inmate-oriented staff. Short-term immersion, given an intense regime featuring continuous interactions with staff and inmates, might send the requisite message to the indolent.

Training can screen trainees if it demands hard work and hard thinking and insists on meaningful quality participation. And in new settings, training can double as planning of the details that must be resolved before the first inmate arrives. Routines, programming, and individualized treatment regimes can be worked out by groups of staff trainees.

Folders of inmate candidates for special settings make great training and planning content: What are the inmate's coping difficulties? What will be his or her impact on other inmates? What behavioral problems will the inmate most likely present? How should interpersonal difficulties be addressed? How can one help the inmate negotiate challenges? What are the inmate's special concerns and interests, strengths and weaknesses? How can he or she gain competence in dealing with the prison and life outside the prison? As a bonus, in a training cycle of this kind supervisors can pick a cadre of subordinates who show insight, sensitivity, competence, and involvement, though some interpersonal competencies will only emerge (or submerge) when staff deal with inmates in vivo.

Case-centered training has the virtue of being less ivy-covered. Officers who care about their jobs may resent the seeming irrelevance of general lectures on human relations or abnormal psychology. (The non-dedicated officer may not object to such experiences, because classrooms provide a respite from inmate contacts.) Inmate-oriented officers want to learn to better assist inmates or to respond more appropriately to their enigmatic behaviors. They are concerned with incidents that present dilemmas, and academic disquisitions about human behavior in general terms do not help resolve such dilemmas.

The development of an inmate cadre for any new stress-reducing setting is also an inestimable luxury (Toch 1980). Properly inducted, an inmate cadre can build a unit culture that is antithetical or tangential to other inmate cultures (Vorrath and Brendthro 1974). Involvement of inmates in planning can build their loyalty to the results, and inmates who feel secure in a setting can ease the entry shock and risk for subsequent arrivals. An inmate core can allow staff to cast promising individuals as group leaders, co-therapists, and other central roles.

To make a unit different from the prison yard can be easier than introducing selective, piecemeal reform. The paradox is highlighted by Margaret Mead, who cited a study by Leon Festinger. Festinger's study had shown that new and different food

Enhancing the quality of survival in prison

containers were accepted by customers when the food they contained was also new and different. Mead herself had observed culture changes abroad in which "the culture had in fact been transformed into another culture, rather than having suffered from extreme changes in some parts, no changes or partial changes in others, of the type which accomplish slower and less conscious social change" (Mead 1983). In culture building, Mead said, more can be easier. Another asset of culture change was that "the group of people who had made the change had made it all together" (p. 178).

It is probably impossible to create an enthusiastic staff culture if one insists that it function as a cog in a larger bureaucracy. Though "bottom line" prison rules have to be adhered to, this is no reason why a niche cannot define its residual mission in its own way. A niche, for instance, can control its admissions and discharge, and do some disciplining of its residents. Such arrangements may look less than neat in organizational charts, but the increased *esprit de corps* and job satisfaction they inspire would justify the tradeoffs.

Running a survival-oriented prison

The most basic mission of prisons is of course to incapacitate convicts. This fact makes it inviting to confuse custody with the restricted task of sequestering inmates. But custody means more. In prisons, as in schools, custody prevents and controls in-house deviance. This is a far from inconsequential job, because prison clients (thanks to selection criteria) have fairly low temptation thresholds for alcohol or narcotics addiction, and in some instances have clear-cut predatory propensities, volatile dispositions, and less-than-perfect respect for the sanctity of property. This point, needless to say, applies also to some schools.

Schools at risk can reduce crime without becoming custodial settings. Custody in the form of behavior rules, disciplinary procedures, proctors, and locks is no doubt helpful, but obsession with such a custody strategy can backfire, and lower student and teacher morale. Schools successfully rely on their non-custodial attributes — on curricular and extracurricular involvements — to harness student energy, entice interest, cement loyalty, and build community (Grant and Capeil 1983). Prisons can similarly mobilize activities and programs to achieve "dynamic" security, and they can rely on custody ("static" security) to take the remaining slack (Ellis 1982). The assumption is that the more effective the former, the less need for the latter.

Postscript

To run prisons humanely means to generate a climate of trust among inmates, correctional professionals, the public, and the courts. One contributor to such a climate is the demonstrated concern for the reduction of inmate suffering, in the shape of provisions for prisoners whose survival may be at risk. Such survival provisions for vulnerable inmates must never be confused with the exercise of custodial power in prisons — meaning power that hurts and restricts. The point must be made that power can be misused by not being used, because the worst abuse of power may be the failure to intervene to neutralize adversity among those who are entrusted to us, including inmates who cannot help themselves.

9

Democratizing Prisons*

IN 1924, a town in West Virginia wanted to become the site of the first federal reformatory for women. To attract this prize the town donated 202 acres of prime pasture adjoining a river, a railroad, and neighboring farm that had become available at distress prices.

The Alderson Reformatory opened on 22 February 1928, and on that date its 200 inmates adopted a constitution setting up what they called "cooperative clubs" in each of the prison's fourteen cottages. The constitution said that the inmates resolved "to improve the life of our cottages, thence [of] the whole institution, and finally [of] the families and communities to which we hope to return." The inmates also declared that they would show themselves "capable of taking responsibility" and earning "the trust reposed in us" (Harris, 1936, pp. 344-345).

The way the Alderson co-operative clubs worked is illustrated by the minutes of a typical session, which read, in part, as follows:

Our meeting of the Co-operative Club was held Monday, 19 October 1931, with

---

*This chapter is a revised version of an address at the Scottish Prison Service College, Polmont, 24 June, 1993. It appeared in *The Prison Journal*, March, 1994, and is here republished with permission from Sage Publications.

66

Lulu chairman and Carrie secretary, and was opened with the Sentence Prayer in concert. We took in six new members who were: Mary, Virginia, Charity, Georgia, Maude, and Willie.

Our Secretary, Carrie, read the pledge to them and each signed it, and it was witnessed by our Warder [correction officer]. The minutes of the last meeting were read, and stood approved.

The opening of business was to elect a new Committee girl. When the votes were counted, Annie had the most and was made our new Committee girl. She thanked the Club and said she would do her best in every way she could.

As several of the girls had gone home, new ones had to be put on the different assignments as follows:

1.	Lights	Lulu and Blanche
2.	Promptness	Carrie
3.	Courtesy	Mabel
4.	Cleanliness	Blanche
5.	Librarian	Elizabeth
6.	Entertainment	Annie

Also, the Fire Drill was reorganized . . . .

Reports were asked from the different Committee assignments; there were no complaints . . . .We talked of the Hallowe'en party, and Annie was given the assignment for Entertainment. No further business, the meeting was voted adjourned (*Ibid.*, pp. 348-349).

These inmates at Alderson willingly undertook civic obligations, and farmed out assignments to each other. They made decisions about the running of their cottage, and expended effort to implement these decisions. They elected representatives to groups concerned with activities in the institution as a whole, and staged events that made for highlights in the daily regime of the prison.

A second valued innovation that was taken seriously at the Alderson Reformatory was the Classification Committee, which met two mornings of each week. The concept of the Classification Committee had been imported from another institution, but Alderson's version was self-consciously democratic. In the words of the warden of the prison:

> An important departure from the procedure followed [elsewhere] is the inclusion in our classification meetings of the warder of the cottage where the inmate under consideration is living. In our small units the head of the cottage comes to know her group intimately, and the fact that she is expected to make a verbal report on the personal peculiarities and difficulties of her charges at these formal meetings undoubtedly tends to sharpen her observation and quicken her interest. She cannot confine her attention to a few even if she would lean in that direction, for she has a pride in being able to answer the searching questions asked about the progress or retrogression of all her wards.
>
> Unquestionably these classification meetings are exceedingly educational for all who participate in them. Several warders attend each meeting and not only hear

their own cases discussed, but learn how other warders are facing the common problems successfully. They become familiar with the significance of the physician's and the psychologist's reports and asks questions if matters are not clear. When a new medical term occurs, I ask the doctor to tell us what it means, and frequently she gives us a short account of the symptoms and remedies of the ailment mentioned. This clinic [case conference], for such it is, is far more educational for the staff than formal courses could ever be. When a new warder comes, one of the first things we have her do is to attend a classification meeting. All members of the staff, whether they deal directly with inmates or not, get a better understanding of what it is all about if they attend these meetings occasionally (p. 329).

Alderson's classification process was not only a training experience and an exercise in staff involvement, but also a way to do participatory sentence planning for the prisoners, including an opportunity for the prisoners to express their desires, interests, and preferences, and to ventilate their grievances. The warden (Mary Harris) testified that:

The women are always asked at these meetings if they wish to continue with their work assignments; if not, why. When possible, adjustments and changes, if they seem reasonable, are made. When they cannot be made, an explanation is given of the situation. These fixed dates for reconsideration are almost without exception kept to the day, and everyone knows that she is going to be given a hearing at a definite time. If at that time she does not ask for a change, she gets no sympathy from her mates when she complains afterwards. They say: "You were up for classification. Why didn't you ask for a change?" It is the recognized clearing house for complaints and dissatisfactions (p. 332).

To put this story in perspective, one must re-emphasize that the account refers to procedures that were followed between 1928 and 1935, and that the institution later became a more conventional prison (Giallombardo, 1966). One must also note that both staff and inmates were the objects or targets of innovations.[1]

Experimenting with organizational democracy

Prisons in theory are susceptible to any trends and fashions in organizational reform that are prevalent in the private or public sector. In other words, when administrators outside prisons have found a better way of running things, their ideas and experiments can carry implications for the prison. The obverse also holds, of course: Alderson's Co-operative Clubs and Classification Committees, for example, could have been adopted by schools or hospitals.

It is not *a priori* obvious, of course, whether democratization or participatory trends in society are relevant to prisons, or whether prisons can afford to ignore them. Some otherwise progressive countries have chosen the second path. That course of action was adopted in Yugoslavia, for instance, before the country fragmented. There, industrial enterprises were in theory self-managed, with workers making production decisions and allocating budgets (Blumberg, 1973; Zwerdling, 1980). Apartment complexes were run by tenants. Health decisions were made in municipal conclaves of providers and consumers. But prisons were run with paramilitary staff hierarchies.

Democratizing Prisons

There were inmate groups, but they were regarded as vehicles for gripe sessions.

Different societies have advanced different reasons for promoting participation in organizations. In the US, the goal has fit most neatly under a heading such as human resource management (Likert, 1967). One premise of this approach is that people work more effectively when they are involved in making decisions that govern their work, and that organizations are more effective when they deploy the intelligence, wisdom and judgment of all of their members — particularly those on the front lines of the organization. A second premise is that involvement brings a sense of ownership, and buys loyalty, dedication and commitment.

Another way of stating the human resource argument is that the classic hierarchical, top down management model may have outlived its day, even on the assembly lines where it was born (Special Task Force, 1973; Morse and Reimer, 1956). A recent version of this argument sees organizational democracy as the only means to achieve quality of products or services. Companies that claim to produce quality cars thus advertise in commercials that their assembly line workers are involved in the quality control process.[2]

Extending democracy to criminal justice agencies

If one can improve quality by democratizing assembly lines, the question arises how one can pretend to do quality social work, nursing, teaching, police work or corrections with managers attempting to second-guess the decisions that professional employees make, or subjecting them to detailed prescriptions and instructions. A second question is how one can expect such workers to carry out policies which offer implementation problems that supervisors might not be able to anticipate.

Some human service managers can of course be expected to argue, "We manage workers who make fateful decisions about people, and we have to protect people from the damage these workers could do, and ourselves from the law suits that could eventuate from their mistakes." Teachers might not cover their lessons, nurses might poison patients, police might administer street punishment to suspects, and correction officers might brutalize inmates. How can we prevent these sorts of contingencies other than through eternal vigilance, painstaking monitoring, and unsparing discipline?

Ironically, my own experience with participatory involvement began against the backdrop of this concern, in a police department that had problems with uses of force by officers against civilians, and was getting an exceedingly bad press. Some colleagues and I confirmed that a minority of officers were involved in repeated violent encounters, and saw themselves doing excellent police work in the process. The officers recounted incident after horrifying incident with evident pride, while I shuddered at what they were describing to me (Toch, 1969). The aggressive officers were also, as a group, productive officers, and had many arrests to their credit. In one sense, they would never have been missed, but in another sense, the organization might have hated to lose them.

What we did in response to this situation was to set groups of violence-involved officers to work addressing the police violence problem. The groups advanced a number of useful ideas, but their most innovative and influential solution was a peer review panel for officers who were recurrently involved in incidents, run by other experienced officers. The peer review panels in short order retrained scores of officers and gathered the statistics to prove it (Toch and Grant, 1991). Their outcome statistics suggested that the officers had succeeded where management had failed, and had done so because they were close enough to the problem to understand its nuances, and because they carried credibility with other officers. It also no doubt helped that the prescription they implemented was their prescription, to whose success they were dedicated.

In another participatory project we worked with groups of correction officers in four large prisons. Each group drafted proposals for prison reform — two designed for their own institution, and two for the system at large. The ideas for these proposals evolved after systematic dissection of the problems the officers thought needed solution. But though some of the ideas were adopted, in only two cases did officers get credit for their contributions (Toch and Grant, 1982).

Job enrichment

Related to participation is the notion of job enrichment (Herzberg, Mausner and Snyderman, 1993). The assumption is that it is work itself that can motivate, provided that it is interesting, and that it offers variety, complexity, feedback and a sense of completion when it is done — that a person can go home at the end of a long day and say, "I have accomplished something which has contributed modestly to human betterment. I get a sense of satisfaction from these accomplishments." The presumption in corrections is that the tasks of guarding, counting and escorting people may not provide such satisfaction, and that one may have to supplement traditional custody tasks by introducing other tasks, such as assessing prisoners, or helping to rehabilitate them.

Some prison systems have followed the enrichment route, but not across the board: they have enriched some of their custody jobs, but not others; they sometimes have ended up with two kinds of officers, only one of which is the enriched variety. This arrangement can work, but also can become seriously problematic.

A case in point is that of the Norfolk (Massachusetts) Prison Colony, founded by Howard Gill in 1931. According to an article in *Corrections Magazine* (Serill, 1982), Norfolk was "the best hope of a whole generation of prison reformers" (p. 25). *Corrections Magazine* pointed out that "The State Prison Colony at Norfolk was the crucible in which many treatment and other programs were tested — the casework approach, the inmate council, the simulation of 'normal' society behind prison walls. The documents associated with Norfolk . . . are full of observations that seem as applicable today as they did in 1931" (Serill, 1982, p. 32).

Unfortunately, these documents make clear that Gill saw one set of his officers as the core of his enterprise and another as ancillary, or as a necessary evil. His core staff were called House Officers, and according to Gill's Manual, they "live with the men throughout the twenty-four hours of every day while they eat, sleep, work and play, (and) their influence upon the inmate is the most constant and influential factor in

Democratizing Prisons

maintaining morale and in promoting constructive, wholesome attitudes and adjustments to the institution and to life in general" (Commons, 1940, p. 32).

Gill's other guards made up a Custodial Division, which (according to the same Manual), "is operated under a semimilitary type of organization, with periodic drill and instruction periods, and its regulations provide for continuous observation and frequent periodic, systematic checking of all inmates and their activities throughout the entire 24-hour day" (p. 22). The custodial officers had no meaningful inmate contacts, and their views were disregarded or disrespected, even on matters of prisoner discipline. These officers came to resent what they saw as unbridled anarchy, and delighted in feeding examples of licentiousness to legislators and newspaper reporters. Gill also imported professional classification personnel, who sat in resplendent architectural isolation and second-guessed the opinions of the housing officers. This created another destructive rift in his staff.

Prisoner participation

In general, inmate representative governance has had a checkered and, to date, unpromising history. The standard complaint has been that the wrong inmates arrange to get themselves elected, and that they advance selfish and parochial interests to the detriment of the common good (DiIulio, 1987). Another concern is about the impact on staff of what we do with inmates. It is axiomatic that prisoner participation in the absence of staff participation lowers morale. There are few complaints as plaintive as that of an officer who can say "the Inmate Council regularly meets with the warden, but he does not listen to our views, and I cannot get to see him."

Several types of participation are possible in prisons. One approach is to involve inmates in the day-to-day running of small institutions and small subdivisions of large institutions. The second is involvement of prisoners in specialized groups that are concerned with some aspect of prison administration. Such groups can consist of inmate-staff task forces that deal with problems of topical interest. The third approach is to have prisoners individually participate in their own management, sharing critical decisions along the way, and reviewing their progress at key junctures in their careers. Needless to say, these approaches are combinable, and a prison system can aspire to offer variegated avenues of participation.

One important conception that achieved popularity in the sixties saw democracy as a vehicle of "social therapy" (Jones, 1968). Social therapists believed that one can learn to govern oneself through involvement in governance. As one learns, one assists others to learn, and is assisted by others in doing so. Some social therapists (including Jones) argued that inmate learning and staff development should always go hand in hand in institutional settings.

There are many examples of programs such as the Alderson classification teams in which staff acquire new responsibilities that permit them to provide new services which benefit inmates. Staff develop, because they learn and exercise new skills. Prisoners acquire new roles, new ways of interacting with each other and with staff. Such social learning benefits are available even where they are not explicit, as in groups concerned with bread and butter issues, or issues of governance or policy, in which prisoners and staff can interact around shared or intersecting concerns.

One can orchestrate groups to achieve desired intersections: A group that deals with issues of visitation, for example, could contain inmates and staff with very large families, or others who have recently married. The presumption would be that custodial and inmate perspectives could be softened by shared concerns about the maintenance of family ties, which would be a common goal for the group. The problem-solving exercise would be meaningful and consequential, and it could lead to further cooperation if inmates and staff were charged with coordinating modified visitation arrangements, or were invited to monitor the impact of innovations in visitation.

Problems can be addressed proactively, before they arise or culminate in disruptive crises. Institutional violence prevention, as example, can be a subject of concern to staff and inmates. As in the police example, prisoners who in the past have been sources of problems could become members of violence prevention task forces, and their "expertise" could be invoked. Past incidents of violence can be reviewed for lessons they may convey about future incidents. Prisoners and officers could meet separately and report to each other, or to plenary sessions. Groups from different institutions could interact, and pool suggestions.

Special skills and interests can be exploited in selecting participants in governance bodies. An advisory group to the prison kitchen, for example, could contain persons who have worked in restaurants, grown vegetables, or become famous because of the amount of food they consume. Former accountants could be enlisted to review budget decisions. (A budget may seem an unlikely subject for inmate participation, but at least one prison warden routinely presents his budget to prisoners, and asks them if they would prefer to repair broken windows or buy television sets, given budgetary constraints.)

Prisoners as consumers

Service consumption can become a passive or an active enterprise, and the latter is preferable to the former. A passive consumer can be forced into a regressive, dependent stance, which some students have described as a "gimme" posture (Fogel, 1975). Such a person's role becomes that of a mendicant, who is fond of whining and who tends to grouse and complain. An active consumer exercises options among available alternatives, or invents options, given existing resources.

Gradations of consumer activism (or active consumerism) can be envisaged in prisons. Inmates can be afforded choices of services, or combinations of services. Such choices can involve mindfully trading off something one would like, to attain something else one would like, within existing constraints: A program one might want, for example, can be available at a relatively distant location, or require that one arise at dawn, or that one live in substandard accommodations. Choices can also be subject to review: An inmate may agree to try a program for size, with the explicit provision that he can opt out of it after a reasonable time (Morris, 1974).

The most common form of active consumerism is a *quid pro quo* arrangement, in which the prisoner agrees to participate in a set of experiences staff feels he can use

Democratizing Prisons

in exchange for actions staff promise to take on his behalf. Contracts can also provide for admission into a desired program after completion of a less-desired one, or conditional increments in quality of life (Chapter 17). The common denominator of such arrangements is that the prisoner has mindful control over the sequence of events, in negotiation with staff members.[3]

More active participation involves the creation of new options, as in consumer cooperatives. A staff role in such arrangement can be one of sponsorship or facilitation. Staff members might arrange adjoining housing, for example, to permit a group of inmates to engage in some shared constructive activity or to create a social milieu that affords a commodity (such as privacy) the inmates might want (Toch, 1977). Or staff may provide modest funds or facilities so that prisoners can engage in self-educational pursuits not otherwise available in the prison.

Active consumerism involves adult-to-adult transactions between prisoners and staff. It requires prisoners to do something to get something. And it lets prisoners engage in assessment, deliberation and planning in determining their future. This process gives prisoners an enhanced stake in the outcome, and motivates them to validate the choices they have made. The prison remains physically confining, but becomes psychologically liberating, to a limited degree. The experience is also one that prepares prisoners for more responsible participation in the opportunity structures of society at large.

Notes

1. Alderson was not the first effort at prison democracy, but is unique in its concern about staff members in the design of the experiment. The best known early democratizing venture was that of Thomas Matt Osborne at Sing Sing prison, which was a radical experiment in inmate self-governance. Osborne's Mutual Welfare League was initiated at the Auburn Penitentiary in 1914 as the Good Conduct League. In Sing Sing, it survived Osborne's tenure, and was abolished — after a riot — in 1929 (Tannenbaum, 1933).
2. The most recent approach to human resource management — which is called Total Quality Management (TQM) — was introduced to Japan after World War II by W E . Deming (1986), and re-exported to the US. TQM advocates worker team involvement in policy decisions and input from consumers in the definition of qualitative production goals. The approach has been experimentally introduced in government agencies (see, for example, National Governors' Association, 1992 and Keehley, 1992), including some correctional bureaucracies.
3. The importance of mindful control in prison adjustment is discussed in detail by Goodstein, MacKenzie, and Shotland (1984). See also Chapter 18, p.143.

10

Inmate Involvement in Prison Governance*

FEW OXYMORONS sound to most people as silly and naive as that of prison democracy — and with reason — in fact, with two opposite reasons. For one, one wants offenders punished, and democracy sounds like a reward. For another, few citizens are enchanted with what passes for democracy elsewhere, and one can conceive of the liabilities of representative governance enhanced, corrupted and caricatured in prison settings.

How do we see democracy misfiring?

- We may feel the wrong people dependably get elected.
- To get elected, we see them making promises that we believe are not seriously intended.
- We feel that when political candidates get elected they start looking out for

---

*This chapter is based on a presentation at the 12th Annual Conference of the New Jersey Chapter, American Correctional Association, 24 October, 1994, published in *Federal Probation* 1995, 95, 34-39, and reprinted by permission. I am grateful to the protagonists in the experiment I describe in this paper—to John Pearce and Ed Wozniak of the Scottish Prison Service; Hamish Ross, Governor of Penningham Prison; Governor Dan Gunn and Principal Officer Derek Watt of Greenock Prison.

themselves and their sponsors instead of those who elected them.
- These perceptions make many of us cynical about politics.[1]
- And as people lose interest they stop participating, which one suspects makes it easier for the wrong people to get themselves elected.

Time and again, prison politicians have been blamed for the demise of prison governance experiments, and with unseemly delight. Carefully documented worst-case scenarios have made it possible for penologists to indulge in 20/20 hindsight and discouraging extrapolations. Their jaundiced accounts, of course, are only one side of the story, since history can supply scenarios which show that prisoner involvement can work[2] — that it need not create vehicles for the ascendance of self-appointed sub-cultural spokespersons who are oily, smooth and psychopathic, or loud and angry and unconstructively obnoxious, nor that participatory management needs to widen the gap between prisoners and staff or corrections and the public.

But there is a third side to this story. Prisoner involvement, constructively envisaged, can be the very opposite of cynicism-enhancing game playing. It can be about prisoners having sound and practical ideas about improving life in the prison, about proposing these ideas, and working hard to implement them (Chapter 9). It can be about staff and prisoners working together to solve problems. And it can be about enhancing prison regimes by reducing the dependency of dependent prisoners, the alienation of alienated ones, and the ambivalence to authority of most others.

Commitment and trust

Prisons gain from prison democracy when prisoners become committed to the improvement of prisons. The development of this commitment in turn hinges on the degree to which we can provide the prisoners with opportunities for involvement that make sense to them from their perspective, as well as making sense to us from ours.

Commitment also varies with the degree to which we can provide opportunities that permit each prisoner to successfully display and rehearse skills along areas of his or her interest. Humanists assume that for all participants — including prisoners — mindful activity is preferable to mindless activity, and that it is satisfying to do something that one feels qualified to do. The same holds for the benefit of collaborative activity. Working with others allows for the exercise of interpersonal skills, and can enhance one's competence in the exercise of these skills. This, many prisoners and staff find useful. Collaborative activity also provides a respectable setting for people to interact with people they would ordinarily avoid. One can sneak up on offenders and subject them to constructive staff and peer influence. Persons who are sources of prison problems can even be enlisted in this way in the solution of prison problems (Grant, 1968). At minimum we can expect that those who have been enlisted to help solve a problem will be less likely to resist the implementation of solutions. Where prisoners and staff collaborate, problems can be solved in ways that are acceptable to prisoners and staff, and the resulting actions can make sense to prisoners and staff.

But no one can argue that any of this is easy. There are many difficulties, but the principal impediment to initiating any experiment in prisoner involvement is the "them vs. us" culture of prisons, which is shared — or rather, reciprocated — by prisoners and staff. Where a group of prisoners is convoked to consider involvement, one hears variations on themes such as "They don't trust us," and "We don't trust (expletives to taste)," and "We don't trust them to let us do anything," meaning, to trust us. Counterpart issues for staff are "Can we trust offenders to behave responsibly without constant monitoring and supervision?"

Trust issues are related to the fact that even in the most benevolent prisons — and there are such institutions — transactions between staff and prisoners are essentially parental. Prisoners request, demand or protest. Staff concede or refuse, circumscribe, delimit, monitor, and order prisoners about (Chapter 9).

The transition from these sorts of transactions to adult-adult transactions is unbelievably difficult and strangely painful for both prisoners and staff. Among other things:

- Prisoners must give up structure, the support inherent in dependence, and the luxury of blaming staff for every conceivable adversity, and;
- Staff must give up structure, and prized assumptions about the immaturity, incapacity and intrinsic untrustworthiness of prisoners.

To threaten to violate these vested assumptions of prisoners and staff invites expressions of anxiety from both groups to varying degrees. Anxiety is also evoked by the prospect of unknown challenges with which one feels one might be unable to cope. And then, there is the prospect of hard work, which may not be unambivalently welcomed by some.

Anxiety, unfortunately, can be expressed in a variety of ways, and none of these is delicate, civilized or attractive. This is especially true where anxiety translates into anger, and the change agent is at the receiving end of this anger. Such are stormy seas, and interventionists must reliably weather them at early stages of implementation. They must also deal with the next stage of the process, where staff and prisoners wake up in the cold light of morning from their initial commitment, and ask, "How can we undo this?"

A prison constitutional convention

In the remainder of this chapter I shall summarize efforts to stimulate the inception of democracy in two Scottish prisons. One of these interventions was an intensive two-day convocation in an open prison, a prison without walls for prisoners who are on the last lap of long sentences. The prison contained some 70 prisoners and 37 staff.

The person who designed the convocation in this prison was the Regional Director of the Scottish Prison Service responsible for the region in which the prison is located. Also involved was the prison's warden. Half the prisoners in the institution were present for the two-day meeting and participated in it. So did some twelve staff members — mostly uniformed officers.

The first day opened with a session in which the results of an opinion survey of staff and prisoners were presented to the group (Chapter 26). A discussion of these findings was led by the head of the Research Branch of the Scottish Prison Service. The discussion highlighted perceived problems in the prison that could hypothetically

Inmate involvement in prison governance

benefit from remedial action. It also pointed up the fact that the climate of the prison was seen as a relaxed one which would make it conducive to collaborative relationships.

The convocation was subdivided into task forces after a second presentation by the Regional Director about the Prison Service's commitment to empowerment of officers and prisoners (Pearce, 1994). The Director stressed the opportunity offered to the prison to become a pioneering experiment in self-governance, in subservience to this philosophy.

A staff group and three prisoner groups were then formed around the issue of assigning and taking responsibility. The officers dealt with the question, "What do we do that *they* can and should do for themselves?" while the prisoners considered, "What do they do that *we* can/should do for ourselves?"

During an ensuing plenary session, spokespersons for the groups explicated their suggestions, which decorated the front of a dining hall, and varied considerably in legibility. The reports also varied in content. The staff manifesto ranged from justificatory statements (such as "Why all the boundary rules? [Answer:] Protection of residents") through cautious bids (such as, "Don't you trust us? [Answer] Yes — given trust") and concessions varying in generosity from making residents responsible for cleanliness and tidiness to letting them allocate the recreation budget and coordinate visiting arrangements.

One prisoner group brought a roster of requests for autonomy or discretion, and a second included new privileges in a laundry list. The third group, by contrast, offered several detailed, constructive proposals, some of which implied a strongly task-oriented outlook and an uncompromising commitment to the Protestant ethic.

The group suggested that "educational trips be organized by prisoners' committees." It proposed "a meeting between a town committee and a prisoners' committee every month to improve relationships between prisoners and town folk with a view to enhancing [work and volunteer activity] placement schemes." It recommended a system of "work allocation [for work on prison grounds] by a prisoners' committee made up of skilled or experienced prisoners." The group also asked that "people with work or recreation skills [be] given the opportunity to pass on experience to others who are interested," and that "prisoners be consulted about job creation within the prison." They requested that prisoners be permitted "to organize [their] own lunches for [outside] placements by given budget for [each] week," to "organize and supervise their own visits — again, by committee" and that they be allowed to run the inmate canteen "with accounts available for inspection at all times."

The prisoners emphasized that "all committees [would have to] be democratically elected," and added a proposal for "an open day for town folk, to visit the prison and talk to prisoners and staff about the aim of the prison to improve relations," with the possibility of "having town folk visit any time to see the jail working."

An idiosyncratic element in the report was mention of a vote of no confidence in the prison social worker, but not much was made of this passing reference in the discussion of the group's report. A concluding talk — by myself — dealt with the need for meticulous detail and careful documentation in proposals to be drafted.

The second day

The second day opened with a speech by the prison's warden, who emphasized his receptivity to responsible proposals. The warden extended this offer to include proposals for the allocation of portions of the prison budget. The Regional Director also spoke, enjoining the group to be productive, and offering support.

The next set of subgroups were asked to consider "the other side's" perspective, with officers considering the prisoners' views, and prisoners those of staff.

The officers responded valiantly to this mandate, reviewing the impact on the inmates of minor rules and redundant security rituals, and discussing the need for greater flexibility and open communication. Several of the staff showed remarkable empathy in characterizing prisoner reactions to frustrating prison routines.

No such empathy was forthcoming from the three prisoner groups, whose summarized reports were discursive and off the point. The discussion was similarly tangential, and degenerated into attacks on the prison social worker. The rest of the reporting period was taken up with demands that the social worker be fired, and the Director's rejection of this demand. This dialogue sounded like a parent-child exchange in which limits are tested, and parents have to react, to set boundaries.

The juncture proved to be a turning point in the intervention: A transmutation into attentiveness to business occurred in the next session, during which prisoners and staff dealt with the question, "What's in it for us?" presuming that the program were implemented.

The group of officers indicated that if they were freed of surveillance obligations and permitted to expand human service activities this would make their jobs more interesting and worthwhile. They welcomed the opportunity of changing from a custody role to a facilitator-counseling role, and of enhanced "opportunity for interaction." They also recognized that their jobs would become more demanding, and that training might be in order to ensure that they were qualified to do what was expected of them.

The officers discussed the risks and benefits of the impending changes for themselves as a group. To participate in a pioneering venture could advance one's career, but less so if the institution were seen as wildly divergent. Officers in other prisons might subject one to derision, and the public might become concerned about safety issues. A single escape could work to damage the program.

In response to the question, "What is in it for us?" the officers listed:
Job satisfaction.
Free the staff to do other more worthwhile productive tasks.
The opportunity for more interaction.
A more demanding role for staff.
"Because it is a pioneering project (it can) further your career."
Gives staff opportunity to change from conventional role.

One of the prisoner groups answered the same question with a counterpart list of benefits:
The chance to get rid of the them-and-us attitude.
More relaxed community atmosphere.

Inmate involvement in prison governance

> More integration with staff, i.e., joint ventures with staff. One example could be the football team, i.e., any staff want to join in, as in driver to the games they should be allowed on team.
> Less boredom.
> Less paranoia about release.
> More rehabilitation factor.
> Less bitterness against system on release.
> Learning to be more responsible for ourselves and each other.
> More problems for us to deal with through which we are given the opportunity to prove ourselves able to cope.
> More family contact.

It is obvious that the roster reflects commitment to collaborative activity and reintegration. The prisoners said they wanted to multiply joint activities with staff, including recreational activities. They saw the possibility of a useful bridging experience from the prison to the community. They saw activities as a way to reduce boredom and acquire and rehearse coping skills. The groups also saw value in improving the prison for future generations of prisoners.

Creating an organization

To this point we had experienced dramatic movement, which included all-night debates in prisoners' dormitories. It now remained to capitalize on this enthusiasm by designing the structure of the new governance machinery. To this end, prisoner groups were tasked with listing desired interest groups or committees; a mixed prisoner-staff group was asked to deal with the overall organization and structure of governance.

The products of the groups turned out to be remarkably congruent. Joint staff-inmate committees were envisaged by the prisoners, except for groups representing housing units. These committees were envisaged as carrying responsibility for various functions, such as advising on culinary matters, running the commissary, coordinating visiting arrangements and disbursing recreational funds. Each drafting group also suggested setting up a public relations committee to cement relations between the prison and the public.

In the overall structure, the committees were seen as reporting to a council of six officers and four inmates, who in turn were to report to a managerial group comprising the warden and two senior officers. This system was set up to deal with budgetary and policy decisions at various levels. Also envisaged was a monthly community meeting including all prisoners and staff of the institution.[3]

The convocation ended with the appointment of a prisoner-staff coordinating group charged with the implementation of the design, which was to begin work at once. The prisoner representatives to this group were chosen among those who had played leading roles in the convocation.

The coordinating group went on to define its mission to include drafting a constitution. In this constitution the prisoners and staff streamlined the organization that had been suggested, consolidating proposals from the various groups. The constitution also spelled out procedures for elections and committee deliberations. Excerpts from the document read as follows:

1) The community council will consist of one executive committee and four sub-committees. The executive committee will be known as the council committee and will consist of four residents, one senior officer and one officer, who have been duly elected to serve.

The four sub-committees will be known as: 1) House-committee 2) Visits and Family Welfare Committee 3) Sports and Recreation Committee 4) Public Relations Committee

Each sub-committee will consist of two residents and one officer who have been duly elected to serve. The executives reserve the right to increase the size of any sub-committee to look into different aspects of any changes or problems which may arise, and also to co-opt anyone who has specialized knowledge to help to solve problems in their field.

Sub-committees

Each sub-committee will meet at least once per week. Relevant time to be allowed.

Any issues that cannot be resolved at sub-committee level will be forwarded to the council committee.

It will be the responsibility of each sub-committee to put forward reasoned arguments backed by relevant documentation where appropriate, when forwarding issues to the council committee.

Council committee

It will be the duty of the council committee to review all proposals put forward by the sub-committees and to try to resolve all issues at council level. Any issues that cannot be resolved at council level will be forward to the Governor [Warden].

The council committee will elect a chairman at each meeting who will have the power of a casting vote where required. All decisions must be substantiated.

The council committee will have access to relevant documentation, stationary and equipment in order to put forward properly formulated issues to the Governor. The council committee will meet once every two weeks to discuss and resolve any issues put forward by the sub-committees.

The council committee will meet once per month with the Governor to update him on any relevant decisions taken, and to put forward to him any issues they could not resolve.

Election of committee

All officers and residents will be eligible to serve on the council committee or any of the four sub-committees.

Notice of forthcoming elections and for willing candidates will be posted on the notice board at least seven days prior to the election. Anyone interested will put their name on the posted sheet. All candidates will be subject to a ballot with those attaining the highest number of votes being elected into office. If any positions are not filled from the notice board then proposals will be accepted from the body of the hall. All officers and residents are eligible to vote.

All committee members will serve for a period of three months when they will be subject to re-election. If, during a term of office anyone decides to drop out, the candidate with the next highest vote (relevant to the specific committee) will be co-

Inmate involvement in prison governance

opted on till the end of that term.

Any alterations or additions to the constitution can only be passed by a majority vote at an election.

The council committee will have the right to call an extra-ordinary election by giving the appropriate notice.

Co-ordinator/record keeper

It was decided at the inaugural meeting that an election should take place for a co-ordinator/record keeper, whose post will include the duties of keeping the flow of information between the various sub-committees and the council. And also be responsible to the council for the preparation of proposals from all the committees to the Governor. And of course the keeping of records, and decisions made for future reference.

The post will be on the same terms as the posts on the council and sub-committees.

A month later the prison's newsletter reported results of elections to the committees and the Council. The paper reported that "the Community Council held their first meeting last week," and pointed out that "the sub-committees meet every week and report to the Council who assemble on a fortnightly basis.... Minutes of each meeting are taken, then submitted to the coordinator who will keep a record of them."

Of course, this type of first step does not end the change process, and problems can still develop. The governance structure can be deemed superfluous and become under-utilized. Fresh trust tests can be posed, in the shape of proposals and demands that invite rejection. Personality conflicts can also arise that preempt serious business.

New political entities in prisons are at first vulnerable, and they must be monitored and nurtured to ensure their survival.

A grass roots mission statement

It remains for me to describe a briefer experiment, which proved instructive but less conclusive. The target in this instance was a prison cell block in a multi-purpose prison, which functioned as detention facility for the west coast of Scotland. The cell block contained long-term inmates and lifers in the mid-stage of their careers, and was relatively new.

Twenty prisoners and three staff participated in an afternoon meeting presided over by the principal officer of the cell block who was serving as its acting warden. This officer was a respected staff member who volunteers as coordinator for a prison religious fellowship, and has a loyal following among inmates.

Given the time available for the intervention, I proposed that the group draft a mission statement for the cell block. Mission statements are taken seriously in Scotland, where quality management strategies are popular. The Prison Service has a mission statement, as do all prisons and autonomous special units. But no cell block — in Scotland or elsewhere — has drafted a mission statement, and none has originated with a group of prisoners and officers.

I started the session noting that mission statements had traditionally been vapid public relations ploys, but that they have in recent times become embodiments of the central concerns of organizations, which guide and inform what they do and serve as reminders of what they stand for. This proved to become a problem when I cited the Prison Service mission statement, and the prisoners questioned whether this statement guided the agency's actions. (Rumors had circulated about impending cutbacks in furlough arrangements.)

Other objections from the group took familiar forms. One inmate reviewed a long and checkered prison career to document his reluctance to place trust in new initiatives. Another prisoner cited societal and systemic constraints to make a case for the proposition that local reform was futile. Other prisoners opined that mission statements should be drafted after more fundamental concerns had been addressed.

Eventually, the discussion drifted to mission statement planks that appeared to have some group support. Among these, one dealt with the desire to have the cell block operate as a community; another dealt with the involvement of prisoners in decisions; a third suggested that rules be enforced with "flexible consistency"; a fourth proposed that a climate be created to make family visits pleasant and profitable; others dealt with the use of time, the planning of prison careers and the control of serious drugs in the prison. This topic proved especially controversial, and sparked a spirited debate.

The debate next turned to issues of a housekeeping nature, and focused on assignments to double and single cells. The ostensible issue was the prioritizing of single-cell assignment, but the concern revolved around a specific individual and his assignment, with pressure to exact a decision in this matter becoming quite intense. The senior officer resisted the concerted campaign to force this issue, which presupposed the eviction of an inmate who was not present at the meeting.

At this stage the mission statement had to be tabled, but group members expressed satisfaction at the opportunity for what they saw as an open and honest exchange. This satisfaction was somewhat tempered when the prisoner on whose behalf cell-assignment pressure had been exercised exploded in anger and left the meeting in a huff. It was subsequently resolved that the mission statement project be resuscitated at a more strategic juncture.

I relay the second account with the first to point up the difficulties one encounters in pursuing the task of making prisons more normalized, humane and participatory environments. Inmate cultures — and sometimes staff cultures — are obdurate, and persons who have learned to fear, resent and mistrust members of other groups are apt to respond to trust bids with reluctant misgivings. The process of facing, surfacing and disarming such resistances is slow, painful and emotionally laden. But given skilled and committed allies, such as my friends in the Scottish Prison Service, reform can eventually be achieved, and prisoners and officers can learn to work together to improve the settings in which they live and work.

Postscript

Whether American corrections is ready for participatory reforms is a difficult question. US prisons are larger than those in Scotland. Our public appears more retributive (Chapter 1). But inmate councils exist in American jurisdictions, and their role can be expanded. So can the involvement of prison staff in working with inmate

Inmate involvement in prison governance

councils. And in the US functional prison units exist (Chapter 4), which can serve as settings in which community can be fostered.

Both American and Scottish correctional philosophies presuppose that offenders can be challenged to take responsibility for their lives upon release.[4] This challenge — if it is taken seriously — is better met if prisoners are provided with opportunities to undertake responsibilities while in prison than if they are deprived of such opportunities. The point is that one must find acceptable ways for prisoners to shoulder and discharge responsibilities in the prison.

Notes

1. A recent news story, for example, was headlined "Voters disgusted with politicians as election nears." The writer reported that "voters are profoundly alienated from their powerlessness and pessimism over the future of the nation . . . Disgust with congress is near the recorded high." An even more recent newspaper story detailed results of a nationwide survey of 237,700 college students, concluding that "something about the 1994 political campaigns seems to have soured an already embittered and indifferent younger generation. The one-year drop in interest from the previous year's already low levels was nothing short of 'remarkable,' said [the] survey director" (Albany *Times Union*, 9 January, 1995).
2. See Murton (1976). An example of an innovative prison democracy experiment is provided in Doering (1940). For earlier examples, see Harris (1936) and Tannenbaum (1933). An encomium to early experiments with prisoner governance appears in the monograph *On the Penitentiary System in the United States and its Application in France* (Chapter 6). Beaumont and de Tocqueville (1964) visited houses of refuge for young delinquents, which they said were "a medium between a school and a prison" (p. 139). In one institution, in Boston, they witnessed an inmate election, and reported that "each time that it becomes necessary to elect among them an officer or monitor, the little community meets, proceeds to the election, and the candidate having the most votes is proclaimed president." (pp. 146-147). They add that they hope "the reader will pardon us for having dwelt so long on this system, and for having pointed out its minutest details," and conclude (by way of justification), that "the impressions of childhood and the early use of liberty, contribute, perhaps, at a later period, to make the young delinquents more obedient to the laws. And without considering this possible political result, it is certain, that such a system is powerful as a means of moral education (p. 147).
3. A large room was subsequently refurbished for this purpose. It is called the Hans Toch Room.
4. The basic policy document of the Scottish Prison Service is called *Opportunity and Responsibility* (1990). The authors of this document postulated that "we should regard the offender *as a person who is responsible*, despite the fact that he or she may have acted irresponsibly many times over in the past, and that we should try to relate to the prisoner in ways which would encourage him or her to accept responsibility for the actions, by providing him or her with opportunities for responsible choice, personal development and self improvement" (p. 30, emphasis in the original).

Part Three

Reforming Prisoners

CORRECTIONAL rehabilitation as a goal is supposedly "dead," but arguments about whether rehabilitation is dead or alive simplify the issue of what it means to work with prisoners. It makes little sense to argue that we should ignore the change impact of constructive actions we take relating to prisoners, individually or collectively. If a teacher, a chaplain or a corrections officer positively affects a prisoner, or if a setting in which a group of inmates is placed promotes cooperation or encourages prosocial behavior such effects must be acknowledged and valued in a correctional system. The fact that impact can be achieved by prison staff who are not formally designated as "rehabilitators" does not diminish the value of their actions (Chapters 12 and 13), and may even enhance it.

Almost any programs can improve prisoners who take them seriously, because of the chances for learning new skills or prosocial attitudes that are potentially deployable. The outcome measure for programs is positive change, which is a defensible end, even if the offender reoffends. Recidivism reduction becomes an issue for programs that address offense-related behavior, which presupposes forearming the person against pressures and temptations in the community. Recidivism-related programs are best scheduled shortly before the person is released, when the issue of community adjustment is most real and alive. By the same token, programs that promote prison adjustment are best placed at the inception of a long-term prisoner's sentence (Chapter 15).

A point to keep in mind in thinking about the term "rehabilitation" is the obvious fact that we deal with the offender in a prison. This fact has been translated into dicta such as "you can't teach a man to fly in a submarine." In other words, prisons—at least, today—are a far cry from communities, and therefore a poor place to rehearse community adjustment. But prisons are settings in which people live with each other, as are submarines. The task of assisting a person to get along with other persons in the prison is therefore a legitimate end. If a prisoner is destructive or predatory, inept or self-destructive, this is not only a liability for the prison and prison staff, but harmful to the prisoner and other inmates who must live with the prisoner. If improving prison behavior makes a person a better citizen this is a desirable but inessential byproduct of psychological treatment in prisons.

A final point is that prisons and prison systems are composites of environments which differently affect different people. One way in which constructive impact can be maximized and destructive impact reduced is to "match" (or enhance congruence) between the person and the setting in which he or she is placed, and to reduce "mismatches" (or incompatibility) between person and setting (Chapter 14). This process must take place when the person first comes into prison, but also over time, especially with long-term prisoners (Chapter 15). Such prisoners must be reassessed not only because they may change (hopefully, some may mature), but also because life should offer progression. Not all prisoners, moreover, are equally tough and resilient; low-pressure settings must be available, especially for those who cannot manage the jungle-like world of the yard.

11

Correctional Rehabilitation*

SEVERAL YEARS ago, I addressed a meeting of mental health workers in Kansas City, Missouri. The audience contained staff members of the federal prison system, and representatives of the US Disciplinary Barracks at Fort Leavenworth.[1]

My talk was entitled "Reinventing Offender Rehabilitation." It was premised on the hope that one could envisage a renewed thrust in correctional rehabilitation. But I pointed out that rehabilitative endeavors had been relevant before, and suggested that one must attend to a dictum that says that those who ignore history are fated to reinvent the wheel.

I then regaled the mental health workers in the audience with a war story, drawn from a period spent defending the beaches of San Diego. I recalled that I had the distinction of being the only sailor in the Navy with a Ph.D., though there were several other draftees who had advanced degrees. This fact made it incumbent on the Navy to provide us intellectuals with proper stimulation, which resulted in two educational field trips. One consisted of a day spent on a mine sweeper, where I discovered that

---

* This essay was originally published as a "News of the Future" column in *Federal Probation* (September, 1993). Reprinted, with modifications, by permission.

Correctional Rehabilitation

mine sweepers make you sea sick. The second expedition was a trip to the Naval Retraining Command, Camp Elliott. *Time* magazine visited Camp Elliott around the same period (1955), and described it as "high wire fences (that) take in 40 square miles of desert scrublands northeast of San Diego, and keep in 885 gray-uniformed men." They characterized Camp Elliott as a "military purgatory" in which marines and sailors "run through a routine of work details, formations, exercise and orientation lectures."

The representatives of *Time* and our group went to Camp Elliott to see what had become known as the Camp Elliott Experiment, which was run by J. Douglas Grant. *Time* described Grant as "a burly, six-foot Stanford graduate, with an infectious grin and a saddle-tanned bald head." But our group did not get to see J. Douglas Grant. After the usual welcome by a braided officer, we were hosted by a Marine sergeant. The sergeant told us he was on Grant's staff. He worked with court martialled offenders, some of who were also on Grant's staff. It developed that Grant's sergeants spent six to nine weeks eating, sleeping, working, recreating and frequently meeting with offenders in closed Living Groups of twenty. Each group had a consulting psychologist, who worked with the men individually and in group sessions.

I had not envisaged anything like this happening in the military—or, for that matter, in prisons. But the psychiatrist Maxwell Jones had heard of it. He wrote about Camp Elliott that:

> The introduction of a role for prisoners (or psychiatric patients) which involves active collaboration with trained staff personnel in an attempt to better social understanding and circumstances (or treatment) is the distinctive quality of a therapeutic community. The prisoners (or patients) now become actively involved in studies and tasks usually limited to trained personnel; and in the process renounce the more passive recipient role of the conventional prison (or hospital) (Jones, 1957, p. 308).

For Jones to say that the Navy had therapeutic communities was the equivalent of the Pope certifying a person as a Catholic. But the Camp Elliott Experiment was innovative in many ways. J. Douglas Grant wrote that his Living Groups were "an attempt to create in a correctional situation a program which would produce in the subjects a challenging uncomfortableness without rigidifying panic"(Grant and Grant, 1959, p. 129). The uncomfortableness arose from having to deal with others in a close, intimate setting in which everything was up for scrutiny. The scrutiny was more intensive than in other therapeutic communities. The Experiment was committed to the concept of self-study, and to systematic inquiry, including research. Inmates studied their personalities, and those of other inmates. Custody studied custody. Grant (1957) recalled that:

> Three times a week, three professional members of the staff meet separately with three maximum security groups (which include all maximum security prisoners), for an hour and a half discussion. The custodial staff are included in these discussion groups. Once a week the maximum security custodial staff meet with the three professional staff members and a research representative for self-inquiry discussions concerning their maximum custody work (p. 304).

Grant's group evolved a differential treatment approach. Inmates were classified by the sort of interventions they could tolerate and benefit from, treatment staff (including nonprofessional treatment staff) by the sort of approach they felt comfortable using and were good at using. This made it possible to pair intervention agents and targets in ways that were effective and congruent with each inmate's stage of development. The inmate who needed structure and benevolent control got structure and benevolent control. The high-anxiety, conflict-ridden inmate received all the empathy and insightful exploration he could use. Grant referred to drill sergeants who had that sort of capability as "junior psychiatrists." The behavior modifiers he called "coaches."

Camp Elliott was an exciting place and those who worked there found it exciting, because they learned a great deal and felt they were making a difference. Over half of the Camp Elliott graduates were successfully restored to duty. This outcome was particularly valued in wartime. In 1942, rehabilitation centers were established in nine service commands. Between 1940 and 1946, 84,245 new commitments arrived in these institutions; of the 70,000 who graduated by 1946, 42,373 were restored to duty—the equivalent of three infantry divisions (Gray, 1970, p. 112). At the time of our visit, Camp Elliott could man two large aircraft carriers with a nine-year cohort of its alumnae. The military took rehabilitation seriously, because—as John Morris Gray put it—"manpower was our most precious resource during the war years, and every possible effort was expended to rehabilitate the maximum number of general prisoners." (Gray, 1970, p. 111)

Studies showed that military corrections could point to successes in the aggregate and in individual cases. Gray contacted military unit commanders and received rave reviews about corrections graduates. Most of these were standard military commendations, but some were encomia to rehabilitation. One officer, for example, described a soldier as "an excellent example of a man who has rehabilitated himself through his own determination" (p. 121). He might have added, "with help from dedicated staff."

The early history of US prisons

The history of military corrections and the federal prison system is intertwined. The first federal prison was the United States Penitentiary at Leavenworth, which physically occupied the grounds of Fort Leavenworth, on loan from the Army. This happened in 1895, and in the late twenties civilian authorities repossessed Fort Leavenworth, and used it to hold narcotics offenders. They also built two specialized reformatories, one for women in Alderson, West Virginia (Chapter 9), and one for youthful offenders in Chillicothe, Ohio. Both institutions emphasized rehabilitation and education, and thus presaged the pre-eminence that the "feds" subsequently achieved in offender rehabilitation.

The formula that evolved was an interesting one: Classify the prisoners in treatment-relevant terms, and sort them into homogeneous enclaves that would be run by teams of congruent staff members (Chapter 4). In each enclave, offenders would present comparable problems: Some could be predatory men, for instance, and others, young mothers with infants. Inmate needs would be accommodated with tailor-made regimes, including specialized services. The staff teams would get to know their inmates, and each other. They would be supported by modern resources, such as vocational and training facilities.

Enlightened correctionists had also begun to worry about the need to attend to the opportunities, pressures and temptations in the environment to which the offender returned. The seventies marked the birth of Community Corrections, which extended the notion of treatment to encompass changes in settings. California — and J. Douglas Grant — stood in the forefront of this supplementation of the rehabilitative ideal. The federal system also touted community treatment as an extension of rehabilitative goals: No conceptual revolution was thus contemplated, though progress in thinking had occurred.

But at some juncture it was advertised that there had been a transmutation of corrections from a rehabilitation-oriented philosophy to a management-oriented one. A discussion of this shift occurred at a 1991 conference on the history of the Bureau of Prisons (Roberts, 1990). This landmark conference featured a panel of directors of the Bureau of Prisons, who were asked to discuss the end of the so-called "medical model." Director Alexander—whose model it supposedly was—pointed out that "I never heard it called the Medical Model until after I retired. We simply called it 'training/management classification.'" Director Carlson—who presided over the demise of the alleged Model—talked of the discovery "that we in corrections could not coerce change," and said:

> We could facilitate change, certainly, and we had that obligation. But somehow the notion had escaped many people that we just could not force people to change their behavior.... We can offer assistance and guidance, and we can provide programs, but it is up to the individual offender himself or herself to take advantage of those programs if they are to have any meaningful impact on their lives.

The next Director, J. Michael Quinlan, added that "the responsibility of corrections agencies is to provide solid programs," but "prisoners have a responsibility, too" and "the prisoner is going to make the ultimate decisions when he or she is released."

If one takes such statements seriously, it becomes hard to see what the disengagement from rehabilitation consisted of, since no rehabilitators see their job as "coercing change," and rehabilitators who think they are in the disease-curing business exist only in sociology texts. As a final piece of irony we have noted (in Chapters 1 and 7) that prisoner program involvements such as drug education, remedial reading and work assignments are increasingly being tied to peremptory incentives, which constrain prisoner voluntariness.

Given these facts, did we have a sea change in corrections, as advertised? Had we deleted offender change as our goal? If we did this, might the pendulum swing again? And might the time come for new Camp Elliotts?

Notes

1. The occasion was the 1993 Mental Health in Corrections symposium held in Kansas City, Missouri, 9-11 June, 1993.

12

Psychological Treatment of Imprisoned Offenders*

TODAY, everyone accepts the assumption that prisoners must be imprisoned as punishment, though it may be defensible to provide even dangerous inmates with such remedial services as filling their cavities, giving them sleeping pills, supplying prevocational training, and maintaining links to the outside.[1] There is also allowance made for hard-core psychiatric attention, provided an offender is psychotic, and as long as he or she is psychotic. If an inmate has the good fortune of periodically going into remission, it is customary for a shuttle to convey him from a mental health setting to the prison yard and back, as the occasion demands. The inmate may also be sequestered in an outpatient capacity, and maintained on medication.

Some time ago, Sykes (1958), whose prison book is still an undisputed classic, wrote that "allegiance to the goal of rehabilitation remains at the verbal level, an expression of hope for public consumption rather than a coherent program with an integrated professional staff" (p. 34). Where clinicians have operated in prisons, theirs has usually been an ill-defined or circumscribed goal. Clinicians also often felt that the

---

*This chapter is abstracted from a contribution to the Twelfth Annual Symposium of the Texas Research Institute of Mental Science (1979), published in *Violence and the Violent Individual*, edited by J R Mays, T K Roberts and K S Solway.

sharp break between formal therapy, organizational climate and routine processing of offenders foredoomed any possible impact their therapeutic ministrations might have had. Mental health interventions were usually casually and inappropriately targeted, with therapists doing whatever they had learned in graduate school to a hopelessly misdiagnosed group of clients, most of who reacted indifferently, while some relieved their boredom by baiting, mimicking, or otherwise humoring their therapists.

Even this portrait is deceptive, however, and can be overdrawn. Most inmates live and function in an environment that demands a pretense of cynicism from persons who are more vulnerable than they admit (Toch, 1975). Prison is a milieu of "pluralistic ignorance" (Chapter 16), and in our context this means that inmates labor under the mistaken assumption that aloof posturing and antistaff facades are required of them. This is the same point we could make if we were talking about slum schools or about any setting in which everyone thinks that everyone else is tough, inviolate, and hostile to whoever is their keeper, while privately admitting that there is much to be said for the warmth, support, recognition, and assistance that institutional custodians (whoever they may be) could provide.

Goffman (1961) has described the fact that "typically, the inmate when with fellow inmates will support the counter-mores and conceal from them how tractably he acts when alone with the staff." According to Goffman, mental hospital patients who felt themselves heavily involved in therapy "tended to present their favorable view of psychotherapy only to the members of their immediate clique" (Goffman, 1961, p. 65). The same point has been made for incarcerated soldiers by Cloward (1956), who saw these soldiers as privately thirsting for rehabilitation, while publicly contemptuous of it. Hard data that are supportive of this portrait are provided by Wheeler (1961), who found that inmates favored therapeutic encounters while laboring under the impression that their peers held antistaff norms.[2]

The antistaff theme and the vulnerability theme are separable, though both work in the same direction. The antistaff issue relates to assumptions that are prevalent in prison about appropriate social distance. They have to do with the fact that inmates and staff each assume that their peers demand a staff-inmate chasm, which many (at some level) personally deplore. The vulnerability issue has to do with the perceived need for a cool, inviolate facade. This stance has been diagnosed by Redl among delinquents, and he writes that "admitting value sensitivity, just like admitting hunger for love, is quite face-losing in our youngsters" (Redl, 1959: p. 45).

Vulnerability is built into prisons — as it is built into hospitals — by the fact that such institutions promote childlike behavior in their clients (Goffman, 1961). Sykes (1958) pointed out that typical prison regimes pose "a profound threat to the prisoner's self-image because they reduce the prisoner to the weak, helpless, dependent status of childhood.... For the adult who has escaped such helplessness with the passage of years, to be thrust back into childhood's helplessness is ... painful, and the inmate of the prison must somehow find a means of coping with this issue" (pp. 75-76).

What is "treatment"?

The essence of treatment is its goal, which is the achievement of personal growth or of constructive change in people. This goal may be stated negatively, by stressing the change-resistant experiences whose impact we try to neutralize; it may also be stated positively, by highlighting various regenerative or growth-producing experiences we furnish through our treatment strategies. Realistically, psychotherapy must achieve both positive and negative ends; it must disconfirm residues of a destructive past, and it must buttress, rebuild, and provide its clients with new attitudes, values, and skills.

The goal of treatment is always change. Since procedures must be designed and targeted to achieve change, we may define treatment as planned individual change. In this sense, the closest ally of psychological intervention is probably the field of education. To be more accurate, our ally (particularly with adult offenders) is the field of re-education which, as noted by Freud, "is something quite different from education of the immature" (Freud, 1925).

The psychological perspective that is most applicable to prisoner re-education is the social learning perspective, in the sense in which it has been discussed by Albert Bandura. Bandura has listed the practical implication of his views for therapy as follows:

> Change programs based upon social learning principles differ from those relying heavily on conversational methods in the content, the locus, and the agents of treatment. With regard to content, treatment procedures are mainly applied to the actual problem behaviors requiring modification, instead of to verbal reports of troubles. Change agents, therefore, devote the major portion of their time to altering the social conditions governing behavior rather than conversing about them.
>
> To enhance successful results, treatment is typically carried out in the natural settings in which the problems arise. It may be conducted in the home, in schools, in work situations, or in the larger community, depending on the source of the critical determinants....
>
> The third factor which partly determines the success of a change program is concerned with who implements the corrective practices. Social learning approaches do not regard professionals as the exclusive dispensers of treatments. Professionals have expertise to identify the determinants of behavior and to specify the optimal conditions for producing desired changes. But the most beneficial treatments are generally carried out under professional guidance by persons who have intensive contact with the clients and can therefore serve as powerful mediators of change. They are the ones who exercise substantial influence over the very conditions that govern the behavior to be modified. Unless they too alter their practices, any changes, whether produced by professionals or otherwise, may not endure for long (Bandura, personal communication).

It is difficult to argue that change efforts of the kind Bandura refers to are not occurring in prison. Even if we expect no behavior modification impact from prison reward structures (Chapter 7), we are left with numerous daily staff-inmate contacts in scores of prisons that in theory could be inventoried and studied and harnessed to good effect.[3]

Fritz Redl speaks with more authority than I do when he writes, "We are... deeply impressed with the great opportunities that the closeness to daily life, daily conflicts and mistakes offers the clinician, in contrast to the traditional seclusion of the action-remote interview techniques" (Redl, 1951: p. 144). "Some things can be talked down," Redl notes, "others can be listened down. There are a few that have to be lived down, or they will not budge" (p. 137).

The context of change-relevant encounters must be "respectable" in the client's everyday world if this is at all possible. Beside the bureaucratization and rigidity of helping professions, their artificiality is one reason that being classified as a counselor or some such can become a liability to the exercise of a therapeutic role. In fact, the formal role can become the kiss of death if the role incumbent keeps public records and makes decisions or recommendations about his or her clients, since gatekeeping hopelessly contaminates therapy, no matter where it occurs.

Research such as Glaser's (1964) and inferences from social learning theory suggest that significant impact or change may occur in custodial settings, provided that:

1. The place where change occurs has dominant or salient work to be done (such as plumbing, carpentry, running Sunday school, or clerking for a guard) which frames a relationship that can be a vehicle for change.
2. If possible, a legitimizing peer in-group develops which approves of staff/inmate links, and/or
3. The staff and inmate(s) are ecologically insulated from pressures that emanate from the prison-at-large.
4. Staff-inmate links shift from instrumental task orientation to relationships featuring supportiveness, warmth and loyalty, permitting modeling, emulation, and spontaneous influence.

The social learning process

In his view of social learning, Bandura (1977) highlights the importance of modeling. The perspective also assumes that there must be incentives and rewards for learning, and a substantive cognitive component, which means (in part) that what is learned must be perceived as useful by the person who is learning it. The three conditions implicit here are a credible change agent, a satisfying learning experience, and useful or meaningful learning content. To put the matter even more simplistically, the person to be changed must learn through tangible success in a supportive climate that fosters internalization of change content. Maxwell Jones (1962, 1979) uses the social learning concept somewhat differently. The process as he envisages it involves modeling, but the change agent is also a catalyst of group process. Change requires feedback, with the accent on revealed feelings and latent agendas in behavior. The juiciest experiences are interpersonal difficulties or (even better) crises. Social learning occurs in failure experiences, provided these are analyzed and their lessons internalized in a supportive context.

I do not mean to undersell the common elements in the two views. Jones and Bandura both prize real-life learning experiences, and prefer "natural" change agents to artificial influences. Both value the "here and now" experiences of persons-to-be-changed as learning (hence, as "treatment") laboratories. Both Jones and Bandura would see learner activity as a requisite to change. Jones refers to "living-learning" in describing this link, and Bandura talks of the person exploring new opportunities that his natural environment affords. In referring to the therapeutic community inmate, Jones writes:

> If his interest can be obtained in some simple and familiar work, and particularly if the occupational therapist can enter into a supportive relationship with him, even the most elementary occupation may be therapeutic; it may bring out and direct constructively a variety of emotions which have been denied outlet, and it may do something to offset the restrictions of the mental-hospital regime.... (an effectively utilized constructive work group) is capable of leading to better contact with reality, to behavior more in accordance with social standards, and to the foundations of self-esteem (Jones et al., 1956, p. 343).

Not surprisingly, this brings us back to considering supervised activities as rehabilitative experiences in the prison. Here, one problem we discover is that our plumbing foremen may not see themselves as rehabilitation agents, and this suggests that their influence (as differentiated from their plumbing) may be unsystematic, unplanned, and haphazard. This spontaneity is a feature that any respectable social learning theorist may have to deplore. On close inspection, in fact, the average influential staff member is mainly an unself-conscious source of genuineness, benevolence, and personal interest. He claims no change technology or skill as group catalyst.

He is described as a "good Joe," a "decent guy" who inspires respect, shows integrity and cares. At best, he sounds like a part-time Rogerian, but violates this description by giving homespun advice, drawing on his experiences as husband and grandfather.

Worse, everyone sees the treatment influence as extracurricular, with the foreground occupied by shared activities or work problems. Issues of group dynamics tend to be clumsily mediated, and any transparent "father-offspring" transference is matter-of-factly accepted as a corollary of age differences.

The foreman's influence strikes one nevertheless as potent because it is transactionally framed, in the sense that the inmate determines the extent and quality of the influence. The sticky issue of "consent" does not arise with respect to job assignment and group membership. The genuineness of the changer-as-model is also enhanced by the foreman's unselfconsciousness, which reduces social distance and deletes any potential credibility gap.

What the offender may learn from his foreman (beside plumbing) is law-abiding citizenship, constructive interpersonal dealings and acquired work habits. Such content is communicable through a wide range of experiences, provided these include partnership in work, benevolent conflict resolutions, demonstrations of personal and work-related competence, and a model who is visibly content with a noncriminal life style.

What must be unlearned by the inmate includes dependency problems that show up in unhealthy expectations of, and relationships to, authority; childhood traumas that enhance the attractiveness of peer groups that value pre-adolescent goals (or worse), highlighting physical combativeness and short-term hedonism or displays of impulsivity; a consistently alienated perspective, which views the world as a dog-eat-dog place in which violence and expropriation are plausible means to desired ends; and developmental deficits, such as complete insensitivity to the perspectives of other people. Such dispositions and frames of reference are developed through cumulative long-term experience, much of which is redundant and self-engineered. Positive influence must *disconfirm* such experiences. This, to say the least, is no mean task, but our foreman, because of his lack of sophistication, is apt to be oblivious to the odds. If he lives up to his billing, he consistently and disarmingly becomes the dependable, nurturing, and empathetic parental figure that was absent in the lives of his charges. He disconfirms authority-related expectations by disregarding (and hence, extinguishing) behavior that is based on subcultural norms; he counters inmate cynicism with naive optimism and disarming faith. He connects and welds pipes, blissfully ignorant of the syllogism that only shortcuts produce success. What is worse, he indiscriminately praises his charges (a prized reinforcement) for modest advances to long-term goals.

This Meek-but-Sturdy Proletarian Healer of the Disaffected is an ideal portrait, and one may exaggerate its import. My point is not that prison foremen shall inherit the therapeutic world, but that they can form part of it. What Glaser (1964) has told us is that some inmates ascribed critical influences to some supervisors. Such transactions make psychological sense, and the paradigm is worth emulating.

Support systems

Other key players are prison chaplains, whose influence, says Glaser (1964), transcends their numbers.[4] As a treatment agent, the chaplain enjoys diplomatic immunity. For one, he offers confidentiality, and his primary loyalties are disaffiliated from the source of his paycheck. Though a chaplain can overidentify with secular authorities (one is reputed to have led a charge in a riot), such instances are mercifully rare (Shaw, 1995). Chaplains are potential links to the community, and offenders are permitted vulnerability lacunae in relation to significant others in the free world.

The ambiguity of the chaplain's role is a clear asset. No matter how many diplomas or certificates in pastoral counseling a chaplain may display, his contacts with parishioners occur under higher auspices than Carl Rogers'. Moreover, religious participation (like welding) is activity that has nontherapeutic content. And though the normative system of the Real Man in prison proscribes trust in others, it is not clear that this proscription includes chaplains. A final point relates to change content: The chaplain's sphere includes concerns with morality and ethics, which (in translation) permits frontal attacks on impulsivity; it allows the skilled chaplain to aid the inmate in shoring up control functions of his ego and superego. Along the same psychoanalytic lines, one recalls that the chaplain's role is quasiparental by definition; it permits transference but has some built-in protection against countertransference.

Despite the chaplain's assets, some chaplains are more likely to be therapeutic than others, while inmates differ in their susceptibility to religiously tinged interventions. As a modality, chaplains' special attributes probably lie in the assistance they may offer to conflicted inmates, and in the support they mobilize for those who feel lonely and abandoned.

The chaplain is primarily a psychological support system, and his rehabilitative impact is a testimonial to the now unfashionable link between neurosis, vulnerability, and criminal activity. There is a widespread tendency to equate seriousness and chronicity of offenses with portraits of professional, subcultural, or psychopathic offenders, despite the fact that the assumption that penny-ante offenders may be confused and weak, while hardened criminals are sturdy and self-sufficient, has for decades been an obstacle to the appropriate targeting of prison interventions.

The prevalent view satisfyingly but often wrongly highlights offense history as a measure of the offender's intentional dangerousness, which is then reacted to through the length of the prison sentence. This view is buttressed by the public's classification of offenders in terms of the danger they allegedly pose. Lastly, for serious offenders the perspective is face-saving, because anyone would prefer to be seen as professional, vicious, and loyal than as conflicted or vulnerable.

Stress and coping

Since everyone agrees that prisons should not be personally destructive, we find less resistance to stress-reducing interventions than to measures addressed to the cementing of resources. The permissive stance to crisis intervention is undergirded by the prison's sensitivity to suits charging staff with negligence. It is negligent, for example, to ignore despondency that may signify suicide potential, or to set aside an inmate's claims that he is in danger. As a result, "protective" settings are populated by inmates whose problems (examined in the light of day) include demonstrably long-term inabilities to cope (Toch, 1975, 1977).

In this connection, the correctional officer's role, both as diagnostician and rehabilitation agent, becomes relevant. This is the case because officers see the inmate more continuously and more frequently than anybody else. They also talk with inmates, although in the past officer-inmate conversation was frowned upon. Even where anti-conversational taboos may persist among inmates and officers, the officer is the target of many inmate requests, because he mediates services to inmates.

The guard's surveillance of inmates also supplies him with rich data. Guards see inmates interact, and they view them at work and at play, at rest and active, eating and fasting. The range of information obtained in such contacts is substantial, and the patterning can be dramatic. Unavoidably, each officer encounters mood changes, developing behavioral trends and chronicity of habit that are of clinical import. The officer sees inmates withdraw into shells, or watches them as they become irritable, obsessed, or panic-stricken.

Faced with such data, the officer may ignore what he sees. He has every right to ignore it (unless he infers violence potential) because he has not been sanctified as a "shrink." Moreover, the officer's superiors see him as a walking burglar alarm and human conveyor belt.

Ironically, many officers ignore their job-impoverished role definitions and react humanely to their charges' plights. They may react by invoking institutional resources on behalf of inmates, relaxing and modulating rules to reduce stressors, helping define problems in quasi-counseling sessions, encouraging peers to be available to the inmate, arranging transfers to more congenial settings, and pressing medical or mental health personnel to consider inmates as a mental health problem (Toch, 1978).

Although the officers' concerns are usually short-term, this does not preclude an inmate's experiencing long-term benefits. One way in which impact occurs is by freeing persons who are in crisis from impediments to self-regeneration. If this statement seems ludicrous, it is well to remember that the most salient finding in therapeutic research is that control group members tend to improve. The line between treatment and nontreatment must be drawn around interventions that work in partnership with self-restorative forces where these exist.

A second feature of what guards do is that they manipulate such environmental features as inmate work, solitude, recreation, and official information. This approach is much less drastic than its counterpart, the use of medication to rearrange *people* so they can face their *environment*. By knowing himself not to be a "shrink," the officer must treat his inmates as if they were normal but upset. Though this strategy has limits, it may work better than do interventions based on the saliency of symptomatology, with their relative lack of respect for the forces of ego which, Freud tells us, are the allies of therapy.

Exceptionally dramatic incidents involving guard impact are of a different order. They involve young inmates who are usually extreme discipline problems, and who have an "arrangement" with authorities involving recurring cycles of acting out and punishment. These cycles are redundant because they confirm interlocking expectations. The authorities know that the inmate is a troublemaker, and the inmate knows, as he has known since childhood, that adults are arbitrary, cruel, and malevolent.

But this game is not half as congenial as it looks, because it is an ineffective management strategy and leaves the inmate with thwarted dependency needs. Possibly as a result of ambivalence, there are occasional instances of "conversion" and behavior change when the cycle is broken through disconfirmation. Such incidents generally involve a guard who refuses to label an inmate, overlooks insubordination, and tries to form relationships with his charges. The potency of such encounters can be documented by reviewing the subsequent career of the officer's client, which is often trouble-free.

Peer Influence

Inmates and juvenile judges have spread tales of callow youths who acquire or cement criminal values and skills while they are incarcerated at the knees, so to speak, of seasoned offenders. These sagas are largely misleading on at least two counts: Statistically, younger inmates have much more disruptive and destructive impact on older inmates than vice versa (Chapter 15); and whatever influence older, more mature inmates have on younger inmates, and on each other, is more stabilizing than it is crime inducing. Older prison inmates, particularly prison senior citizens, may have one or two select friends with whom they engage in reciprocal crisis intervention when the occasion demands it; some older inmates also do amateur counseling with younger inmates (Glaser, 1964).

Spontaneous constructive peer influence can be exploited, harnessed, and upgraded, as has been demonstrated by innovators in residential treatment programming for youth. In guided group interaction and its variants, peer pressures have their polarities "reversed" (Vorrath and Brendthro, 1974) so that gang norms can evolve that support and promote non-toughness, sensitivity, collaborative behavior, and self knowledge.

In the hands of skillful catalysts, a group culture may be created, preferably in a small institution or a protected unit — such that inmates may explore their own (and each other's) patterns of antisocial conduct, and design solutions to life problems that do not involve addictive behavior, stealing, exploiting, and exploding. Through the use of techniques such as sociodrama (Jones, 1949) such new solutions may be tested or rehearsed despite the artificiality of the prison environment. Other rehearsal opportunities can be provided through innovative deployment of furloughs (Toch, 1967) and of contacts with significant others in the outside world.

Notes

1. Among those who draw this distinction are Morris and Hawkins (1977), who write:

    The cage is not a sensible place in which to cure the criminal.... But this does not mean that such treatment programs as we now have in prisons should be abandoned; quite the contrary, they urgently need expansion. No one of any sensitivity can visit any of our mega-prisons without recognizing that they contain, as in all countries, populations that are disproportionately illiterate, unemployed, vocationally untrained, undereducated, psychologically disturbed, and socially isolated. It is both in the prisoners' and the community's best interest to help them remedy these deficiencies.

    Nevertheless, it should be recognized that rehabilitative programs to that end are not the purpose or even one purpose of imprisonment.... There is a sharp distinction between the purposes of imprisonment and the opportunities for the training and assistance of prisoners that may be properly pursued within those purposes (pp. 67-68).

2. "Pluralistic ignorance" was a term coined by the psychologist, F.H.Allport in the 1930s. Extreme pluralistic ignorance is defined by Krech and Crutchfield (1948) as a state in which "no one believes, but in which everyone believes that everyone else believes" (p. 389).

3. Wheeler (1961) reports that "a larger proportion of custody than of treatment staff members felt that treatment programs could be successful for 'the great majority of inmates,' and that most inmates 'desire to improve themselves' while in the institution" (p. 243, footnote 11).

4. Like other prison staff, the chaplain can ensure his lack of impact by defining himself as a specialist. The chaplain whose role definition is formally religious or ministerial is equivalent to the purely custodial guard.

13

Regenerating Prisoners through Education*

THOSE WHO value educational programs for offenders usually argue for them on pedagogical grounds, emphasizing the benefit to the offender of remedied deficits or acquired skills. This perspective is no different from the instrumental view of education for nonoffenders, where schooling is seen as a means to goals such as vocational success.

We often undersell intrinsic — or at least direct and immediate — functions of education, which can be unexpectedly tangible. These functions have to do with the personal impact of educational experiences and involvement in educational pursuits. This fact particularly matters in settings such as prisons, where we find persons who have long and discouraging careers of maladaptive behavior which continue in confinement.

In this chapter, I shall explore the role of education as a regenerative experience for maladaptive prisoners. I shall begin this exploration by relating short narratives of

---

*This article is a modified version of a keynote address delivered at the New York Department of Correctional Services Library Division Conference, May, 1987. It was published in *Federal Probation*, September 1987, and is republished by permission.

the careers of three clients of a state prison system. The implications of these career segments will be essayed in the latter part of this chapter.

If not love, attention

Jones (not his real name) was a prison inmate confined for burglarizing a home and damaging a car. There is a notation on Jones' dossier that he had absconded from a juvenile home and tried to escape from a jail. Jones had been institutionalized at a very early age after authorities had done a great deal of soul searching about what to do with him. According to his parole officer, "he was referred to the school psychologist because he was unable to cope with first grade work, very nervous, appeared afraid of admitting to be wrong, stubborn." Jones' teachers write that "the most outstanding feature of his difficulties in school was his continual clowning to get the attention of his peers.'" One teacher reports that:

> He seems to be totally unable to stop talking. He will stand up in the middle of a class and do something quite distracting, for instance tell a dirty joke, make an off-color remark to another classmate, etc. Today in the middle of a lesson he was playing with a leather bracelet. He unzipped his pants, put the bracelet almost inside and ran around the room saying, "What does this look like?" Since this is a mixed class, I believe this act was a definite offense to the girls in the class.

Efforts to discipline Jones prove unsuccessful. He responds to the injunctions of a teacher by entering the man's office and having a bowel movement in his wastebasket. He similarly reacts to disciplinary efforts in his home by running away and wandering about town. He then enlists a sidekick (age 15) and goes on a crime spree, estimating that he has perpetrated "about 55 burglaries." He also claims that he would welcome assignment to a camp for youthful offenders because "it will be better than staying here [home]. I hate it here." He subsequently changes his mind, and escapes from the juvenile institution. This escape nets him an indeterminate sentence to prison.

In the prison Jones gains visibility by escalating an incident in which he has been asked to pick up a piece of bread he has dropped on the floor. He is charged with "riot and disturbance" because the incident ends with a confrontation that pits Jones against an officer and all of the other inmates in the mess hall. Most remaining difficulties in Jones' early prison term revolve around conflicts with other inmates and have to do with his propensity to accumulate debts that he cannot repay, requiring his placement in protection at his request. He later has other problems with his peers to which he responds by drawing custodial attention to himself. According to one incident report:

> The inmate had turned his bed upside-down. His mattress was under the bed, the inmate under the mattress, when found by the officers. He had covered his body with red dye. He claims that inmates are trying to kill him and he wished to be placed in protective custody.

Jones commits a burglary and steals a car one month after being paroled from this first prison term. His only defense is "I'm a criminal," but he also blames the parole board, who he feels should have realized that he "was not ready to be released." In a more positive vein, he "claims that he is a magician and that his nickname is Houdini. He believes he could escape from any situation if he wished."

The inmate's self-proclaimed escape artistry proves a liability which nets him 60 days of segregation and six months loss of good time credit after he has supplied toothed blades to fellow inmates to help them saw through the cell bars of their windows. After this incident, Jones' violations are mainly confined to accusations that he engages in horseplay and fights, that he refuses orders, and fails to participate in programs. Such incidents are frequent, however, and earn Jones a transfer to a tougher prison where he signs himself into protective custody (probably as insurance) ten days before he is paroled.

Jones is reimprisoned for a burglary which is noteworthy in that he has himself called the police, claiming credit as a helpful citizen. Later he escapes from a holding cell but instead of seeking freedom, "walked to the desk and said, 'Hi' to the officers seated behind it."

From the reception center Jones is sent to a program-rich low security institution. His first report records that he "appears to get along well with staff and peers" and "performs duties in an average manner." His second report promotes his custodial adjustment to "outstanding" and points out that Jones is involved in college-level art study and that he is "an intelligent, interested student" who "accepts and completes assignments with minimal supervisions." Jones is also an active participant in a drug and alcohol counseling program.

The story obviously has a happy ending. Though at first glance Jones has doubled his IQ, he has in fact succeeded in a lifelong campaign to earn attention. He started at age six, attempting to obtain the esteem of peers by playing the clown, and has been trying to capture love from his parents by running away, hoping that he would be missed. These efforts boomerang and cement Jones' reputation as an imbecile and "attention seeker." Jones reacts to whatever rejection he invites by resorting to fantasy, which results in his classification as mentally ill. He also operationalizes a fantasy world which consists of a one-person gang with whom he steals and drinks and patronizes amusement parks. Stealing sustains Jones' private world but also invites restraint, which is probably the closest Jones has come to receiving affection.

In prison Jones discovers that fellow inmates associate with him around the gambling table. But he is not very good at gambling and becomes involved in conflicts which he cannot handle. He also discovers that clowning in the prison invites disciplinary charges of horseplay and results in conflicts with officers when they tell him to stop clowning and he disregards their instructions. He additionally discovers that escape fantasies are taken very seriously in the prison.

The situation improves after Jones is assigned to an adult prison where there is no audience for his performances and where the climate is one that demands sobriety. But he has also been brought along by educational programs in the prison which initially demand lower levels of involvement than those in the community. He has thus laid the foundation for more disciplined experiences that he discovers are esteemed. Concurrently, Jones has discovered an interest and aptitude in art. He can now evolve a formula for gaining recognition which centers on conformity and achievement. What he does also yields intrinsic satisfactions, making him less dependent on attention and approval from others.

Fronting tough

Smith (again not his real name) is an obese 17-year-old convicted of an aborted burglary, who experiences entry shock in jail and is placed on suicide watch. He continues to have problems in the reception center, where classification analysts write that "it appears the inmate goes through periods of depression and when he does, he goes off the deep end."

In the prison Smith has difficulties with both staff and peers. He is injured in a fight, in which he reports that "me and the guys were playing around, calling names and [the other inmate] got mad and came at me from behind." Problems with staff include a propensity for snottiness and disobeying orders and refusing to attend program assignments.

Smith is referred to a behavior modification program, and some staff members feel that this changes his outlook. His counselor writes, "I have seen a vast improvement in his general overall attitude about authority figures and rules. His type of tickets aren't as serious as before . . . . His attitude has changed tremendously, from being quite negative to very positive and (to) taking things in stride." Even more dramatic is Smith's response to his program involvements. His counselor reports:

> I have seen some of his art work, which is quite outstanding. He is quite an accomplished artist, has a lot of talent . . . . Since being incarcerated he has learned more skills in commercial art . . . . In art class the teacher has asked him to be her aide due to his advanced talent . . . . [He] can be easily worked with, especially with some positive reinforcement, encouragement and attention.

Smith has been afraid of prison and all the people it contains, including fellow inmates and staff. His fear has at first manifested itself through straightforward anxiety, but he later resorts to bravado, which includes defying officers and demonstrating to peers that he is as tough as the next man (which he is not). For a time the defiance also includes resistance to programming. Smith does recognize that he has a problem, however, and volunteers for the behavior modification program which he feels "helped him a lot."

Smith is probably most substantially influenced by the reinforcement he gets from the civilian staff members who view his artistic contributions with admiration, which they freely and volubly express. As these staff members act the part of benevolent parental figures, Smith acts the part of prodigal son. He occasionally still stages demonstrations of toughness for officers and peers, but finds a niche as teacher's pet and as a counseling client who has a strong reciprocal bond with his counselor. These compensatory experiences reduce pressure on Smith and temper his responses.

"Unrealistic" expectations

The inmate we shall call Sanchez serves a short sentence for a burglary; he is also a drug addict and has a long disciplinary record, mostly of sins of omission. One theme consists of matters of cleanliness and has to do with Sanchez refusing to take care of himself and his surroundings.

Sanchez is a long-term problem. His presentence report notes that at age 14 "a petition was brought by his mother alleging that he was using drugs, stealing money from her, being truant, and was beyond her control." As a result of this petition, Sanchez spends two years in a training school. He later becomes tragically involved in his mother's death in that she suffers a heart attack "precipitated by her attempts to assist [Sanchez] after he had collapsed from an overdose of heroin in the family bathroom."

It is not surprising to find that Sanchez has a tattoo on his arm that reads "Pardon me mother" in Spanish and sports another tattoo inscribed "Born to suffer." The presentence report indicates that Sanchez:

> Seems to think of himself as a little boy. He was very self-pitying during the interview. His attitude toward authority is very childlike. He seems to have no sense of authority as a disciplinary or retributive force, but only as a source of support and forgiveness. This appears to be in line with his very dependent nature and his apparent inability to conceptualize the results of his behavior.

This notation predates Sanchez' first prison stay. His conviction of a second burglary occurs two months after he is paroled from this first sentence. He has received his high school equivalency diploma in prison, and enrolls in a college program during his second stay. After he is once more paroled, he again violates his parole by committing another burglary within two months.

By this time a change has taken place in Sanchez. The presentence report notes that "he appeared in need of psychiatric intervention." Classification analysts in prison report that:

> This individual appears to be experiencing a pre-psychotic state . . . . He is withdrawn . . . . Needs a therapeutic milieu, as he would have difficulty at the present time adjusting to the general population.

In line with this recommendation, Sanchez is placed in a therapeutically oriented program. His first report from the program reads:

> During his tenure in phase one he appeared to be withdrawn and somewhat hostile, especially in a group situation such as orientation. He felt the program "sucked," to use his own words. However, to his benefit he was most cooperative in completing his assignments.

Soon, however, a psychiatrist places Sanchez on medication because he is incoherent and making "illogical statements." By this time Sanchez has accumulated a long roster of misbehavior reports, mainly for being dirty and keeping his cell in a messy condition, but also for occasionally remaining asleep and not going where he is supposed to go.

Sanchez discontinues his medication and the psychiatrist suspects that he is having a tough time. He records that:

> The inmate had a great deal of problems learning the schedule . . . Appears to have difficulty concentrating, his memory functions are not particularly good, and some

of his thoughts are quite illogical. However, he maintains himself in the community by keeping his bizarre thought train to himself.

When Sanchez is subjected to therapeutic efforts, he "spends most of the time staring into space and making quite unrealistic demands." One of the demands Sanchez makes is to be transferred to a college program, which the staff members regard as ludicrous given the man's level of functioning. Staff members write:

> He presently requires that the building officers supervise his personal hygiene to control his impetigo (a skin condition). Basically he is experiencing difficulty in meeting the minimum requirements for following the schedule, maintaining reality contact, obeying the rules and his personal hygiene.

Staff members summarize the disciplinary record by noting that "to date he has 24 misbehavior reports for failing to follow his program, not attending his work assignments, sleeping through mandatory meals and poor hygiene." They note that "to reasonably approach the problem, a highly structured and supervised program was designed for the inmate," but regard the effort as unsuccessful, and conclude that Sanchez has become "a poor example for other community members and a source of discord on the therapeutic community."

They make the point that Sanchez' smelly, dirty exterior and his repulsive skin condition make him unattractive to peers, and that his behavior is a source of tension. They also insist that the requests Sanchez has kept making about having himself enrolled in a college program are unrealistic, although everyone would appreciate it if he were transferred out of the unit. They write that "this inmate appears to understand only what he wishes to." As evidence they point out that "he is fixated on an unattainable goal and has displayed a great deal of zealousness in its pursuit." In other words, Sanchez wants to be transferred to a higher education program and has sent letters to everybody in the system stating these demands.

Sanchez, meanwhile, "appears conveniently bewildered," and receives reports for refusing to do things such as go to breakfast and tuck in his shirt. The custody staff complain that "every form of corrective measure available has been tried to no avail." However, when Sanchez goes to segregation he is often reported to do well. He reads, draws, and exercises in his cell and has no discernible problems.

At this juncture Sanchez is released and convicted of another burglary. While awaiting trial, he is again characterized as "seriously disturbed mentally." However, on this occasion Sanchez is enrolled in a college program after he arrives in prison. His evaluations in this program are very satisfactory, and his disciplinary record is described as "outstanding," with only one minor incident being filed in a period of 19 to 20 months. Sanchez not only does well in college courses but also has a work assignment in a relatively isolated setting as a porter and is adjudged a very good worker.

If one were to confine one's assessment of Sanchez to his third prison sentence, one would be depicting a person who keeps some sort of equilibrium by trying to simplify his world as much as possible, which requires not only avoiding meals, program assignments and showers, but which makes taking care of his elementary needs too taxing an enterprise. This period, however, is sandwiched between two relatively successful periods, each of which shows Sanchez engaged in an educational experience to which he responds and which he is able to master.

Did Sanchez suffer a bout of disabling mental disorder and subsequently recover? Onsets and remissions of psychosis are by no means unusual, but discontinuities need not be radical, and Sanchez contends that his disability is more apparent than real. In this connection, Sanchez intuits that his obtuseness is a panic reaction, which dissipates when stimulation is reduced, such as in solitary segregation. He also knows that he has substantial capacity for involvement and concentration when challenged by books (which do not threaten him) rather than people (who do).

Mobilizing regenerative impact of education experiences

In reviewing prison success stories in which education plays a role, two prototypical sequences emerge. The first is a sequence in which the inmate as student becomes enticed by educational content or subject matter, which provokes curiosity or furnishes satisfying activity, and ultimately may provide a sense of growing competence and expertise.

The second (more frequent) sequence is through the establishment of a relationship with a supportive staff member which makes a program attractive, at first as a way of maintaining what has become a significant relationship and, later, for its own sake. There are also obviously instances in which an inmate's approach to programs is superficial or exploitive, but he becomes gradually involved against his own inclinations, increasing his investment while decreasing his investment in prison underworld involvements.

In reviewing the genesis of our three turnabouts in inmates' careers, a number of guidelines or principles suggest themselves. These include the following:

1. *One must assume as a working premise that one can find a point of intersection with the inmate.* The task for the educator in the prison is to find some ignitable spark that kindles interest in education or (as some would put it) a "button to press." The search for an opening requires establishment of acquaintanceship with the inmate and presupposes an optimistic (possibly utopian) stance, as well as confidence in one's acumen and sensitivity. The enterprise involves taking risks, which means that failures must be routinely expected. Rewards are substantial, however, when a success is achieved in defiance of probabilities.

2. *Success must not be measured in terms of postprison adjustment or rehabilitation, or contribution to a person's career, but in terms of helping the inmate to cope or giving him something positive or meaningful around which to organize his life.* The "here and now" emphasis is essential in prison education because it provides the educator with a "product" he can experience and yields a sense of completion. It also deletes distracting criteria such as "marketability" or deployability of knowledge. Instead, learning experiences can be arranged to provide the inmate with stability and a sense of purpose and disciplined progress. In some instances there is value in educational experiences that do no more than keep a disturbed individual afloat, which may require providing him with a quiet, relaxed, and tolerant setting in which

to function. In this connection, it is important to recall that:

3. *Respite from destructive or distracting influences can be a requisite for change.* A young inmate who responds adversely to the temptations of a youth prison may relax amidst an older population or under a stricter regime. An inmate who appears limited or disturbed can blossom where lower levels of stimulation or demand free energies from unsuccessful efforts to cope with life generally and permit the prisoner to channel energies into task-oriented pursuits. Such instances alert the educator to the fact that contextual factors can advance or defeat his or her efforts to exercise constructive influence. The prescriptive implication is that the educator must be concerned with the prison situation in which the inmate finds himself outside the classroom.

4. *Facades are sometimes permeable.* Part of the educator's acumen to which I have referred implies that he or she knows that one cannot be overly concerned with the hospitality or inhospitality of the inmate's demeanor. Antiauthoritarianism — especially among the young — can mean that authority figures matter. The stance also means that what a young person expects, based on experience, is that he will be disapproved of, rejected, and disrespected. To challenge such assumptions is difficult when a person works hard to ensure that he will be disciplined or rebuffed — but a success along this line can be a powerful unfreezing experience, and a rebellious inmate may show (after some testing) surprising and disarming loyalty.

5. *Timing matters.* A California corrections expert has noted that it is axiomatic that no one in prison is reprehensible and antisocial all of the time. Another way of putting this dictum is that no inmate is impervious to intervention all of the time, and this means that if the "right" overture happens to intersect with the "right" intermission or crisis in even a discouraging personal chronology, the inmate is likely to resonate and respond.

Prison educators also do not operate in a vacuum, and correctional administrators can do a great deal to assist them to regenerate inmates, provided the enterprise strikes them as worthwhile. While making an impact on a seemingly inhospitable client itself is rewarding, recognition of the achievement can increase the reward. A prison administrator who prizes humaneness can advance his or her goals by expressing admiration and gratitude to those who engage inmates, involve them in meaningful pursuits, and increase their coping skills.

14

Inmate Classification as a Transaction*

ELEVEN YEARS ago, in one of the symposium papers I deliver at ten-year intervals, I talked about taxonomies and typologies of offenders (Toch, 1970). At the time, I suggested that it does not matter what classifications we use as an aid to our thinking — including my classifications and my thinking — but that I saw problems arising where categorizations "lead to sorting and dispositions." I still worry about sorting-assignment problems today, although I know that classifications have fewer consequences now than they did a decade ago. What I mean is that fewer dispositions in life (including in correctional life) are based on classifications. Among the reasons for this trend are shrinking resources, which narrow the spectrum of the clientele we can set side for differential dispositions (Chapters 2 and 4). This point holds both where clients and facilities are scarce. For instance, where student applicants become scanty, even prestigious centers of learning are less concerned about psychometric predictors; as asylum admissions are discouraged, only the most disturbed among us become

---

*This article was adapted from a presentation at the annual convention of the American Psychological Association, Montreal, Canada in September, 1980. Reproduced, with permission, from *Criminal Justice and Behavior*, Vol. 8 No. 1 (March 1981).

candidates for hospitalization, while the rest must pack our sleeping bags and move to nonobtrusive rooming houses.

With some exceptions, prison systems today assign inmates on the basis of space that has just become available (Chapter 2). As inmates arrive, they are placed into slightly warm beds that are being vacated, and the richness of data in prisoner folders becomes understandably inconsequential. I exclude criminal history from this recitation, because this variable mostly bears on security or custody grading. Such sorting always remains a priority, but is done mechanistically and carries few psychological implications. A state with 75 per cent maximum security spaces will classify 75 per cent of its intake population as maximum security, to reduce its risk to a minimum. The classification problem is to reliably sort offenders with the most impressive offense records to reach the system's threshold level. The process is homeostatic, and the classifier is usually a cog in the homeostat, and no more.

Psychologically relevant classification in prison has traditionally been a self-contained phase of inmate processing, which has neither benefited nor harmed the average inmate. The information accumulated during classification is meaningful to the classifiers, but people who make decisions about inmates are a different breed and speak a different language. As I have pointed out elsewhere (Toch, 1977), "information used in making assignments is more often the experience accumulated by staff through previous assignments than the recommendation of classifiers.... And, while classification-diagnostic personnel go about their task of filling folders, and [local prison] staff juggle slots to accommodate warm bodies, the hope lingers that somewhere, sometime, the twain will meet" (p. 287).

I think the most urgent problem is to enhance the probability that "the twain will meet" — assuming that crowding decreases to the point that classification-relevant assignments can be made for the average inmate. In the interim, the twain must meet in relation to "special needs" inmates who require intensive services to help them remedy deficiencies, recover their sanity, survive in prison, or work through personal crises (Chapter 8). In New York State's Downstate Center for the reception of inmates, this process is called "extended classification" or "specialized offender classification." The concept presupposes a triage process which sets aside some inmates as nonroutine. For such inmates, information must be gathered that spells out for prison staff how special needs can be met. The logic of this process dictates that the information must be consumable, meaning that it must differentiate between appropriate and inappropriate interventions, and must help staff who assign the inmates and who work with them after they are placed.

Interstaff communication enters this process early in the game. Department documents tell us that "when the need for specialized psychological classification becomes evident to staff during the classification process.... the inmate, *and staff with whom he has been in contact*, will be interviewed by a psychologist. If there is sufficient evidence to indicate the desirability of more in-depth, specialized classification, the inmate will be transferred to a center for extended classification services" (DOCS, 1980, emphasis added).

The phrase "staff with whom [the inmate] has been in contact" is more important

Inmate Classification as a Transaction

than it sounds. Where classification proceeds sequentially through a series of stages, staff members who are in charge of successive stages must be in personal touch, or the people assembly line turns into an obstacle course. In such gauntlets, the phrases that appear on paper may be reliable, but the meanings that are assigned to these phrases as they pass from hand to hand are discontinuous. To avoid this contingency, staff members at earlier stages must be told what they must do to be listened to and to provide usable information. The New York Department of Correctional Services (1980) design for its extended classification complex comprises this requirement. One key paragraph describes the center as "an opportunity to initiate programming at an initial stage of incarceration." It refers to transfers from the center to regular correctional facilities, and stresses that:

> Transfer in this manner will require that the classification staff . . . become extraordinarily familiar with specialized facilities within various departmental facilities. It will serve to build a base of expertise within a select group of classification professionals at the entry point to the system and also provide the oasis for a communication network between classification and facility staff. Thus, feedback concerning appropriate assessment of inmates with special needs can be sought and reviewed on a regular basis.

Two objectives are implied in this paragraph. The first requires that classifiers know assignment options, and forces them to be specific about which option they invoke for each inmate. This requirement sounds modest but isn't, because assignment options can change in subtle but important ways from day to day. Thus, a setting for older inmates today may be a younger and wilder place tomorrow, and staff turnover can change supervision levels and other critical features of prison subenvironments. Classification options may become fictitious, dead, or emergent. New options may have to be invented to accommodate groups of offenders whose needs are currently unmet.

This caveat attaches to any organization where people are sorted. An unforgivable source of stultifying mindset is to assume that our range of options is given and that our task is to force people into existing slots. Ideally, sensitively assessing and grouping people alerts us to gaps in our programming spectrum, and offers cues as to what is needed but does not exist.[1] This is the point made by Robert Hackman (1974) about workers in industry when he writes that "work redesign can help managers move toward the view that both the pegs and the holes are fair game for change in trying to achieve the best fit between the organization and the people who carry out the work."

The second requirement mentioned in the New York document is that assignments be monitored by classifiers, which gives them continuing responsibility for programming over time. As needs change, their prescriptions for programming must change.[2] As I have emphasized previously:

> Wherever we engineer environmental transactions we must conscientiously hedge our bets and check our hunches. At this stage of our knowledge it is unthinkable for us to place people in settings without carefully ascertaining how they fare there. We must observe our clients, talk to them, and keep contact with the custodians of their milieus in order to verify or to disconfirm our assumptions about our clients'

personal needs and about our responsiveness to these needs.

Even if we have achieved a good fit or congruent transaction, we must be sensitive to changes that may be taking place in people or in settings. Reviews or reclassifications are vital, particularly where people have career patterns, where settings are dynamic, or where people stay in the same milieus over long periods of time (Toch, 1977, p 296).

The term "transaction" in the above and in the title of this chapter requires some comment. The word means that classifications are seen as predictions about the way individuals will adjust to settings. For instance, some categories in offender classifications imply that offenders thus classified will adjust poorly to most settings or some settings. "Poor" adjustment can mean that the offender is likely to break down, act up, or both. The other side of the classification equation consists of hypothetical settings presumed to be optimal for offender adjustment. These are living arrangements, activities, staffing patterns, and social milieus that we expect will help the offender to cope in the setting itself or build his or her capacity to cope elsewhere.

In describing classification in this fashion, I am not attacking conventional views of the process. My point is that classification in practice always implies predictions about the way people will adjust to environments, and that this context must be made explicit for the benefit of classification consumers. If I must house or care for a schizophrenic, the diagnosis *per se* does not tell me how to keep my charge from vegetating or exploding, nor does it warn me that this individual may upset other people by mumbling incoherently or declaiming obscenities. If I am assigned a "mental defective," it helps to know that this individual is able to tie his or her shoelaces, but is liable to be victimized by predatory peers.

Neither "dynamic" nor actuarial classifications are independent or self-sufficient. The former help me to understand my clients but not to anticipate what they will do. The latter may predict, but do not tell me why the person does what he or she does, which makes it hard to affect or modify behavior. Classification consumers are minimally entitled to two categories of information:

1. They must be told in plain, uncluttered English what sort of person to expect, so as to give them a "feel" for individual problems.
2. They must be apprised of their clients' probable reactions to management strategies, and to key features of their environment.

The classification target is similarly entitled. This means we must communicate with the offender in plain English; it means sharing what we perceive; it means speculating as to the "why" of it, and it means projecting future conduct as a corollary of documented past behavior which may (or may not) change. The offenders must be told why they are being assigned where they are being assigned, and what they can expect there. This involves describing the distinguishing attributes of the setting, including physical features, human services and social milieu. Future reclassifications can then be discussed on a contingency basis, so the individuals know that when they are no longer victim-prone, or depressed, or illiterate, or explosive, or beset by nightmares, or manipulative and predatory, they may (if possible) be reassigned.

Such — as I see it — are the minimal requisites of classification-in-use, but there are other attributes that strike me as desirable. One such attribute is the involvement of front line staff in the process; the other relates to offender participation. In the usual classification transaction, what the inmates and staff supply are raw material (data) and what they receive are manufactured products (conclusions from processed data). This process makes classifiers "experts" and relegates inmates and staff to the far less challenging roles of being data sources and data consumers. I objected to this arrangement decades ago (Toch, 1970), and have found no grounds to change my mind.

A key function classification analysts must perform is to collate information. This does not imply that they should have a monopoly on the drawing of inferences, judgments and evaluations. In some offender classification systems, including a typological scheme deployed in the federal prison system (Quay, 1984), staff are asked to rate inmates, and these ratings are taken seriously. Other strategies involve teaming. US prison system officials acknowledge that "the decisions of a conventional classification committee are reactions to developments that are reported to it, whereas the decisions of the treatment team are reactions to developments about which the team has intimate knowledge and perhaps has had a direct role in manipulating" (Hagan and Campbell, 1968, p. 4). Beyond better classification, there are payoffs for staff in a well implemented team approach. A Missouri study assures us that "an actualized team classification procedure may be promoting a more favorable work environment among staff, especially those custody staff who seldom are in a position to participate in routine decisions affecting inmates and who do not usually meet with and become familiar with noncustody staff" (Hepburn and Albonetti, 1978, p. 71).

Teaming describes arrangements in which assessment merges with programming because people who work with inmates are parties to classification. The key issue is the integration of staff expertise in the process of assessing offenders and making decisions about them. This feature is important because information can be a weapon of conflict in corrections, where people who need information often cannot find out what they must know, and those who are best informed cannot contribute what they can. Unsurprisingly, resistance develops. This is not only predictable, but in my estimation, legitimate. Resistance is also predictable and legitimate where there is no inmate involvement in the classification process. Offender self ratings, as in the Quay typology and in a Prison Preference Inventory (PPI) that has been used in the New York system, constitute minimal input.[3]

The ideal classification vehicle would be the sort of interview in which the offenders' past experiences could be explored — particularly their experiences with prisons and similar environments — and in which the offenders' coping strengths and weaknesses, their affinities, habits and phobias, positive and negative valuations, affective reactions, satisfactions and dissatisfactions, stresses, problems, and accomplishments, could be described, and in which we could consider (collaboratively with the offender) the implications of the information for prison programming. The key point is the choice that is afforded to the inmate: The opportunity to enter into the classification equation in a way that can be taken into account and accommodated.

Where clinical judgments and projective and/or psychometric instruments are deployed, complementary provision could be made for inmate input. Objective indicators can be supplemented by the results of inmate-staff conferences that let inmates function as expert informants, consultants, negotiators, or contractual parties. Inmates who disbelieve inferences from psychometric measures may accept recommendations that follow from such inferences if staff simultaneously consider inmate preferences.

Offender classifications usually result in assignments that are buttressed by clout and accepted on faith, and such assignments often work. We can match inmates and staff who don't know how we reach our decisions, and these inmates and staff may accept our word for classification formulas that make programs fit the needs of clients. In such a system, we may learn (within limits) from our successes and failures, but no one else can learn. In fact, the parallel to a privileged priestly caste becomes increasingly too close for comfort. The system is also unstable, because it rests on compliance, which in turn rests on power. Inmates who do not see the point of what to us are plausible sortings may demand transfers, and may get them from staff who do not see the point either. Staff who must supply feedback without getting information in return may sensibly discover that they have pressing obligations that are more urgent than filling out computer-coded forms.

Foot-dragging and turf-protecting are mild versions of process disjunctures. A more radical and effective gambit is to operate duplicate classification systems at every prison, or even in settings within prisons. In most organizations, staff proposes and line imperfectly disposes; criteria that are most often "pulled" on classifiers invoke administrative reality which originates in burning bushes and is graven in stone.

In theory, classification is not a thing unto itself. It is a means for matching people and services, people and settings, people and people. This makes classification the science and practice of arranging decent, meaningful and effective person-environment transactions. In the last analysis, classification itself is a transaction — or at least it can be, and possibly it must be.

Notes

1. Robert B. Levinson sees this function of classification in security grading as well. He writes: "A workable classification system tells management what kind of *security needs* its incoming population requires. As a consequence, new beds at the proper security level can be built or old beds modified." Levinson adds that "the idea of de-securitizing institutions or beds surprises many people." Levinson notes that "the development of program assignments or treatment plans is very complex — To my mind, the latter process should be done at the institution, which will then have the obligation to follow through on its own treatment recommendations. The notion that inmates can have a treatment plan developed at a diagnostic center and then implemented at a regular institution is naive" (Levinson, R B., personal communication).
2. Megargee (1977) agrees. He argues that a useful classification system "should be *dynamic*, so that changes in an individual, such as improvement as a result of correctional treatment, will be reflected by a change in his or her classification" (p 108).
3. The Prison Preference Inventory is described in Toch, (1977). New York refers to the instrument as the "Prison Environment Preference Profile," which yields the acronym PEPP.

15

Dealing with Long-termers and Old-timers*

LIKE OTHER senior citizens, long-term inmates like to indulge in reminiscences. Such inmates tell us that prisons have become jungles populated by unprincipled, predatory "punks" who are at best tactless and at worst violent. In former days, they say, convicts respected each other, "kept their hands out of your pockets," and did their time with discretion. Guards were also dependable and basically nonintrusive; some guards treated you "very fairly," others kept their distance.

These comparisons of the status quo to the "good old days" parallel chronologies by sophisticated observers of prisons (e.g., Irwin, 1970, 1980) but must nevertheless be accepted with caution. One problem is that the stories recur over decades of research, which suggests that one generation's stability becomes another's chaos, and vice versa. Second, the stories are similar to those of inmates in other sorts of institutions. For example, graduate schools tend to be recalled as congenial, and mentors as wise. Mentors, in turn, tended to relay experiences involving rigorous-but-

---

*This chapter is excerpted from an article in *The Prison Journal*, Vol. 80, No. 1, Spring/Summer 1990, pp. 1-8, by permission from Sage Publications.

scintillating apprenticeships.

A common denominator in such accounts is that the narrator's memory has gilded attributes he or she currently values. Progenitors gain stature in ways we now appreciate. Prisons offer commodities — structure and privacy — of the kind older inmates like (Toch, 1977). Younger inmates (including old inmates when young) have predilections that may be quite different. The "young punk" in the senior citizen's story could be the senior citizen when he was carefree and aggressive, loud and invasive, himself.

A sanitized past is also a type of history that is useful to inmates. For one, it helps to validate grievances. When one says "things are lousy but have been improving" this takes the steam out of condemnations. "Prisons were okay, but now they stink" invites sympathy. We expect inmates to hate prisons, because we know that prisons are punitive. But if prisons have always been punitive, it is hard to see what inmates have to complain about at any point in the sequence. Only "things have been getting worse" can attract interest to complaints.

Another contention we find in senior citizen accounts is the refrain, "I am an Old Convict." When an inmate tells us some version of this he means, "I am a product of the system" or "prison has made me what I am." If we believe the inmate's charge, we are invited to see prisons as emasculating people (Cohen & Taylor, 1972), making them violent (Abbott, 1981), or teaching them crime (Bondeson, 1989). We may be impressed because an inmate has declared himself emasculated, violent, or criminal, which looks disarmingly self-effacing. We forget that the attribution in the statement also makes the inmate not responsible for his conduct.

Prisoner accounts may be valid despite such facts, but over time composite reminiscences become suspect. Moreover, when we accept retrospectives that say "prisons are getting worse" and others that say "I used to be decent and normal, but prison has warped me," we are asked to abandon hope for prisons. For if prisons harm people, they harm more people more seriously if they get worse.

Resilience and perceptions

Older inmates prefer different types of prison from younger inmates. A prison that is a good place to do time for senior citizens would bore younger inmates. A prison that is lively enough for the young is much worse. It shows that one group of inmates is capable of destroying the milieu of another group by creating an environment satisfactory to itself.

In other words, some inmates have strong impacts on other inmates, but such impacts are not symmetrical, meaning that some groups can harm other groups more than they can be harmed in turn. A "bad" prison from an outsider's perspective is a prison in which the benefits derived by some are outweighed by the harm they do to others. But what is a "bad" prison from an insider's perspective depends on which side of the fence one is on.

Three facts are relevant to the prisoners' experience of degenerating prisons:

1. One fact is that the more taxed a person is by his environment, the more apt he may be to see that environment as "bad." The more resilient the person, the less

jaundiced his perspective is likely to be.

2. Given a constant environment (no change), increased resilience may inspire a perception of "improvement," but lessened capacity to cope may translate into the conviction that "things are getting worse."

This means that as we learn to cope, we reinterpret our failures and blunders as incursions by the setting in which we learn. A summary statement such as "the place was tough but it loosened up, and now things are fine," suggests an apprenticeship that has been completed. "Things were really rough for a while" denotes a crisis, and it is not clear whether the source lies with us, or with the world.

3. This gets us to our third fact, which is that all of us shape our environments while we experience them. Sometimes we do a lot of shaping, but at other times we come to benefit (or suffer) from the shaping of others. Transitions from shaper to shapee roles are often not consciously perceived but can be attributed to the environment, as in the case of long-term inmates. As researchers we know — but the inmates do not — that:

a. Young long-termers at the inception of their sentence are among the most troublesome inmates in the prison;

b. Old long-termers in the late stages of their sentence are among the best-behaved prisoners; and

c. These two groups are often the same people at two points in time.

Tracking environmental congruence and discordance

As we look at the same people over time, we can see junctures at which the settings in which the people live "fit" them better than at other times. By "fit" we can mean many things, including a fit between aptitudes or skills and the challenges that settings pose. When we get better at negotiating life, we need settings that grow with us, and when we decline, we need a lowering of the pressures that we face. It may be true that when the going gets tough, the tough get going, but it is also true that under the same circumstances the nontough frequently get hurt.

A second point has to do with the fact that settings do consist of people — meaning that in social environments such as prisons, one group is the milieu in which another group functions. The tough who "get going" may be the milieu of the nontough who get shouldered aside, and suffer in consequence. A disjuncture or mismatch would be a situation in which one group thwarts another group's goals, or becomes victimized by them. One aspect of this mismatch is experienced as a "destructive milieu" and the other as a feast. The two perceptions, of course, come hand in hand, depending on the source of the assessment. The scenario of the fox in the henhouse spells Armageddon for hens and a banquet for the fox.

A third point is that resilience and vulnerability may evolve or not evolve. Given two tough groups, the first can stay tough and the other not, creating a mismatch over time. The same mismatch can be created where one group is a succession of toughs or tough cohorts that come and go, while the second is a group that starts tough but mellows and ripens into victimhood. This fate typically befalls our long-term inmates.

Such offenders often start out surrounded by young short-term inmates and continue to be surrounded by them (or their successors) as they age. This process starts as a "match" and becomes a "mismatch" over time. This contingency is even more strongly the case where resilient inmates increase in resilience (i.e., get tougher) and vulnerable inmates gain vulnerability (get nontougher), as is likely to occur where "weakness" feeds on predation in prisons.

Classification over time

In Chapter 14 we dealt with the classification process generally. A different set of prescriptions emerges when we consider the careers of long-term inmates over time. The first proposition would be that:

1. Classification might be a cross-sectional process with short-term inmates, but it must be repeated over time with long-termers, whose changing vulnerabilities one must gauge.

Another way of saying this is that:

2. Static offender attributes have to be superseded as classification criteria where the prisoner and his or her problems change, as they do among most long-term offenders.

And that, instead:

3. Classification adjustments must be made for inmates who experience increases or decreases in (a) capabilities or coping competence and (b) vulnerability or coping deficits.

The goal of this process would be to adjust environmental challenges or pressures so that they keep rough pace with changes in the inmate. An inmate who temporarily undergoes a personal crisis, for example, could be sequestered in a low-pressure setting for a short time (Toch, 1975). An inmate who has acquired new skills (say, through vocational training) could be assigned work in which the skills are utilized. The point being that:

4. Changes of assignment for an inmate should have something to do with changes in the inmate, so that stability of experience becomes an option with accommodation to emerging needs.

Long-term inmates as classification targets

Long-term inmates must be classified and dealt with differently at different stages of their sentence. A young long-term inmate could be grouped with young short-term prisoners, rather than with long-term inmates in the twilight of their careers. This does not mean, of course, that the inmate's length of term is irrelevant. Sentence length is relevant but has different connotations at different junctures of a career. For example, a long-term inmate when he first arrives in prison must invariably deal with the prospect of his term. He may do so by appealing his case, expressing rage, immersing himself in day-by-day living, denial (pretending his sentence does not exist), or becoming depressed. These adjustment strategies each have different implications for the programming of the inmates.

The same point holds throughout the prisoner's term. The inmate at the end of his sentence, for example, may have to digest problems such as those of significant others who are no longer significant, neighborhoods that have become unfamiliar, and strange (if any) job prospects. The inmate at this stage of his career needs pre-release assistance, but such assistance must be different from that provided to short-term prisoners, who have less drastic adjustment problems, and return to a world with which they are familiar.

These are short-term classification concerns, in that they relate to discrete stages of the long-termer's sentence. But to respond to a long prison career in stage-by-stage fashion is like baking a pie one slice at a time. Life is a continuum, and one must make any assignment with one eye on the person's previous assignment and the other on the next step the person might take.

How long a view one can afford, of course, hinges on one's ability to predict and control changes. Two-stage sequences can always be planned by making Stage 2 contingent on responses to Stage 1. One typically tells an inmate, "When you get the equivalency diploma, you can take college courses," or "When you handle this setting, we can try you in population." Longer projections are riskier and iffier, and they become increasingly hypothetical the longer they extend. Long-term projections risk being overly optimistic (e.g., "After you finish the remedial education course, you go to high school, college, graduate school, and get a Ph.D. before you get out"), or they can be insufficiently dynamic ("After five or ten years as porter, you might try stamping license plates for a change of pace, and then . . .").

The object of the game must be to sequence prisoner assignments so that experiences dovetail and build on each other. We must ask, "How does this assignment enable the person to do more or better at something he or she values?" or "How does this prevent or retard incapacitation?" If possible, each step the inmate takes should yield improvement or escape from anticipated harm. We must recall that the dictionary defines a career as the "pursuit of consecutive progressive achievement." The fact that a career must be an institutional career should not deprive it of the potential for yielding increments of status and personal improvement (Chapter 6).

The deployment of contracting between inmates and staff is attractive, but contracts cannot be used to cover long prison terms. In thinking about long prison terms, one must expect to accommodate changes in the inmate's goals and perspective. Career moves occur among persons in the free world after thoughtful reviews. They can similarly occur in prison, and they can "dead-end" vocational or educational sequences in midsentence. Classification must be flexible at such junctures, and it must assist the inmate to evolve new sets of plans. Classification can in fact promote reassessments and can invite the inmate to review his life from time to time. It would make sense, for example, to trichotomize long prison sentences into opening games, mid games, and end games, and to try to schedule review-planning sessions at the inception of each segment.

Engineering the social environment

We must be concerned not only with what the inmate does but also with whom he does it, and with whom he lives while he does it. This has no counterpart in the free world, where we select cohabitants, and sometimes divorce them. But in the free world interventions (such as police action) may separate victims (e.g., spouses or children) from aggressors. Counseling is also used in the free world to address incompatibilities, and can be similarly used in prisons.

What makes prisons unique is that they assign people to live with each other and thereby engineer environments, including settings in which exploitation and conflicts arise. This assignment process confers the obligation on authorities to monitor the outcome of groupings, particularly for socially disadvantaged members of the community. Where social disadvantages change over time, monitoring must occur over time, and because one person's advantage is another's disadvantage, monitoring presupposes not only the classification of some inmates with respect to other inmates but also their reclassification over time.

The "old con," revisited

Institutionalization is a problem, but it typically arises where inmates' needs are ignored or squelched in institutions. If we retain older inmates in settings that do not match their needs, the inmates can be harmed in this way, or "institutionalized." Overstimulation is stressful, as is its opposite, understimulation, which is likely to become a problem for the inmates early in their terms. Both types of problems can be avoided, however, through the use of classification over time. With flexible programming we can adjust environments to evolving needs, and long sentences can be served with dignity. If this were to be achieved, we might encounter inmate biographies very different from those we customarily hear when we do prison research.

Part Four

Working with Disturbed Prisoners

PSYCHOLOGISTS, psychiatrists and nurses in the prison intersect with prisoners who are disturbed, or suffer from mental health problems. Their mission is that of reducing suffering and ameliorating symptoms of mental illness. This task may sound compartmentalized and unrelated to the management of prisons, but is not. Prisons are settings in which conformity is prized and lack of conformity punished. Disturbed prisoners can be persons who are also adjudged to be disruptive to the prison, so that ameliorating suffering and reducing incidents of disruption can become interconnected tasks. The same point holds in the community, where disturbed persons disproportionately end up under the jurisdiction of the criminal justice system, which must arrange for mental health and other services for offenders who have problems. Far from being separate compartments, mental health and corrections are overlapping enterprises.

16

Ruminations About Prison Mental Health Work*

IN THINKING about mental health work in prison, I often recall an incident that changed the direction of my concerns over the past forty years. At the time of this incident I had to spend time immersed in inmate records, and for weeks I did so at the California Medical Facility in Vacaville. For the sake of convenience I would take folders to the prison library, which was deserted, friendly and quiet.

During much of the day, the sole occupant of this facility was the inmate librarian, a small, middle-aged man who knew and loved every book in the room, and never seemed to be anywhere except at his desk. The man had been involved in one of the most publicized crimes of the century. He had served a good part of his term on death row, and most of the rest in segregation settings outliving his reputation as a hard-core anti-authoritarian militant. By the time I got to know this prisoner, he was a charming, self-educated eccentric—a voracious reader and self-styled agnostic socialist, dated, but erudite, original and homespun, serious but self-deprecating—a proletarian sage

---

*Originally presented at a Mental Health and Corrections Symposium (1993), Kansas City, Mo. Reprinted by permission from the *Journal of Offender Rehabilitation*, 1995, 22, 21-28.

Ruminations About Prison Mental Health Work

with a touch of pixy. One could sense residues of the tough time the man must have had—he talked of conquering isolation through self-induced lapses of consciousness, and he communicated with me with unnecessary secretiveness (insisting on intimate whispers and passing notes)—overkill, considering that we mostly had the prison library to ourselves. At the time of our acquaintance, the inmate's partner (the senior figure on his team) had been released, and his own parole hearing was impending. The man's prospects of freedom seemed assured.

At this point in the chronology I had to leave for another prison. Before my departure I noticed protracted visits by mental health staff to the library, mostly to engage the librarian in conversation. He wrote me at the time, "They come to watch you drown instead of throwing you a rope," but I did not know what he meant by this cryptic statement.

A week later, the small librarian was dead. He had stabbed himself after the parole board had turned him down for parole. The reason the board had turned him down is that he had earlier told his assistant that he would kill himself if he was not paroled. The assistant had included this tidbit in a letter to his wife, which was read by the prison censorship committee, who informed a psychiatrist. The psychiatrists told the parole board that the inmate was suicidal, and should not be released.

Needless to say, I felt devastated about having been unavailable to register my view, however impotently. And I resolved to spend part of my working life trying to highlight Catch 22 situations through which we compound the difficulties of troubled inmates in the system.

Pulling switches and pulling strings

I conceive of two types of mental health-related thinking in the prison: (1) administrative clinical and (2) clinical. The first provides a basis for pulling switches. The second is the sort of thinking which tries to reflect the messiness (or complexity, if you will) of the human condition. I think of it as a basis for pulling strings. Both modes of thought are necessary and must respect each other, because each reflects a reality of consequence.

Some years ago I met with classification analysts at a reception center to talk about prison environment-related classification (Chapter 14). However, the first question I was asked was, "Does the procedure you are discussing distinguish between mentally ill and non-mentally ill inmates?" I was tempted to trace overlapping circles on the board, or talk about how no one could draw that distinction with most people in that room. But I restrained myself because I knew what the classification analysts were *really* telling me. They had a job to do, and I could not help them. I compromised by saying that if they wanted to talk about the MMPI, I was the wrong man.

That may have been a flippant response, but there is nothing flippant about the need for ambidexterity. As an example, consider the fact that most patients committed to hospitals are diagnosed as suffering from some type of schizophrenia, and are discharged as schizophrenics in remission. That is as it should be, and the enterprise has integrity. But it is also true that while symptoms come and symptoms go, underlying process is more obdurate, and the word "remission" covers a great deal of ground. Mapping and somehow covering such ground means working with persons who are no longer sick but not completely well. It calls for a concern beyond discharge and beyond standard post-discharge recommendations such as for continued medication and follow-up interviews.

If this assertion is confusing, let me confuse it further by confessing that I am not sure what I mean by "clinical thinking" (as opposed to administrative clinical thinking) though I know it when I do it. The closest I can come is by recalling Adolf Meyer, who saw mental health work as a running inventory of a person's coping capacities in relation to the sort of environment in which the person lived and worked. Meyer thought of clinical work as including intervention in the environment where it taxes coping skills beyond what the person could handle. He very much thought of clinical work as keeping people from going under and helping them to adjust, and doing this flexibly over time.

My point is that once we have pulled a switch we can try to predict and affect the consequences for the inmate of what we have done, even though the inmate is on someone else's turf. I am advocating stretching one's job to accommodate one's vocation, which means pulling strings *after* pulling switches. Informal phone calls along person-to-person networks that circumvent bureaucracy do not cost much, and there is no explicit rule in most organizations against fraternizing with other staff in constructive conspiracies. It is very easy to take a correction officer aside and tell him that one would be concerned if Inmate Jones looks preoccupied, because chances are he is not worrying about car payments. One can at the same time suggest to the officer that he ask Jones a friendly question or two—and refer Jones for an early appointment if he takes time to answer, or if his answers are not completely responsive to the question(s). The point being, why wait until Jones arrives at his next switching point?

It is especially satisfying to clinicians to work with prison guards who are puzzled about and interested in inmate behavior, would like to constructively intervene, but feel a profound sense of inadequacy—usually about a lack of academic qualifications. Even if such guards put up a tough front, maintaining that they are only concerned about the custodial impact of disturbed inmates on other inmates, there is usually a great deal of concern under that front, and a desire to expand a custodial job that can be narrow and uninteresting, into a more meaningful, consequential role.

Real communication can take place around joint concerns for the personal difficulties and adjustment problems of individual inmates whom individual staff members—civilians and officers—have come to know, and about whom they care because they feel that the inmates are especially worthy, suffer more than the average inmate, or have reached a turning point where they can use help and benefit from it, and where this help *matters*.

Even an orthodox medical perspective suggests an obligation to cross borders. My cardiologist affects what I do outside his office—or tries to influence it. He dispenses prescriptions but also talks to me about exercise and discusses my diet. If I worked too hard (which I don't) he might suggest that I cut down. I have had others around me who tried to affect my environment to preserve my health; I have had a wife who hid the salt cellars and offspring who berated me for lighting a cigar.

With regard to interface problems between some prison staff and other prison staff I would argue that there are two opposing ways of mishandling the matter, one of which is more obvious than the other. The obvious mistake is to role-play one's assigned stereotypic role, which is for the officers to act tough and custodial and hard-bitten and practical and experienced and for the professionals to act academic, to wallow in jargon and to pretend to exclusively have the inmates' interests in mind and at heart.

The opposite mistake would be for civilian staff to act cynical and talk custodial, to swagger and regale fellow guests at cocktail parties with anecdotes about hard-bitten thugs they have known and other prison war stories, while officers take night college courses in Psychology 101. In such role reversals, it seems to me, one adapts the most dysfunctional and least flattering attributes of the other role, while underselling the humanity that is—or ought to be—the common denominator of *both*.

In this connection it is well to guard against a deeply felt concern which is endemic among staff in prisons. This concern has to do with not being conned, corrupted or used by individual inmates, with not getting close to an inmate because this invites being taken advantage of, on the assumption that it is a short distance from favoritism to breaches of security, given the wiliness of inmates and one's relative lack of sophistication with respect to the jungles of the offender underworld. This theme is *complex* because it refers to a delicate balance, an individualized judgment and a precarious line it is very hard to draw, and because it is based on truth or untruth depending on whose relationship with whom is at issue, and on the quality of that relationship.

Clinical classification

One reason for belaboring the subject is that forensic mental health workers are blessed—if that is the word—with clients who are uniquely prone to being categorized in strange ways. There are all sorts of taxonomic specimens, and the problem is that few categories make sense in the only way a mental health problem can make sense—as a description of a person in terms of the sort of service he or she could benefit from in the absence of bureaucratic constraints.

At the inception of this chapter, I mentioned an example of the disjuncture: The category "suicidal"—meaning a person someone has set aside because it is possible that the person might try to commit suicide. Clearly, that is *not* a description of a need for service.

A prescription would have something to do with the person being profoundly depressed and needing someone to talk with, which is not the same as being placed in an observation cell so that he or she can be observed. And it is certainly not the same as being refused parole.

A story appeared in the APA *Monitor* in 1984, about a group of Cubans in the federal system who had arrived in 1980 and were receiving mental health care under the threat of being involuntarily repatriated. According to this article:

Within the Cuban culture, clinicians learned, men may express frustration through self-injury. Some took sharp objects and cut themselves repeatedly on their arms, legs or stomachs. Emergency room personnel diagnosed them as mentally ill, but further evaluation didn't support that diagnosis.

I had lived in Cuba for six years, and never heard of the cultural prescription at issue. I have no doubt that the Cubans who mutilated themselves had earlier been over-diagnosed, but I also have no doubt that they were later underdiagnosed, though self-injury is the sort of language which carries no translation problems from Cuban Spanish to pigeon English. I suspect that what was involved was not a cultural tradition but an overwhelming sense of impotence and frustration. It may also be that at some level those who responded to the Cubans did not *want* to understand this last-ditch protest against what we in the system were doing when we could think of nothing else to do, and our impotence met the inmates'. The closest to a cultural theme in the inmates' behavior was probably the sort of plea for nurturance and assistance which we pejoratively call "attention getting" to undersell its seriousness.

The same point holds for Hispanic prisoners in general, who injure themselves more frequently than non-Latin whites, who in turn injure themselves more frequently than black inmates. I know of no white culture that says that "men may express frustration through self-injury." Pseudo-anthropology should have no place in prisons, and neither should the substitution of diagnoses for understanding.

I once perused the folder of a former prisoner that illustrates some of the risks we incur. The man had been hospitalized five times; on three occasions the shipping invoice described him as a psychotic and the receiving form classified him as a sociopath; on each occasion the invoice accompanying the shipment back to the prison diagnosed the prisoner as a malingerer. Three days after the first return shipment the man hung himself, but was cut down in time. And the inmate's behavior in the prison was sufficiently strange to have suggested to the most hard-hearted hospital staff member that here was a person with very serious problems.

Mental health staff in the prison expressed outrage and resentment through entries in the man's file. One psychiatrist noted that hospital diagnoses notwithstanding he thought that the patient was psychotic; he admitted that he could not elicit delusional thinking—assuming, of course, that the inmate really owned a hotel in the Bahamas! To illustrate the viability of the malingering label, someone pointed out that the inmate described his vocational plan to the parole board as proposing to run an international pornography ring. He had accumulated samples of merchandise, and tried to sell some during his pre-parole interview. Such stories could not be told if mental health workers saw their business as jointly making sense of inmate difficulties, and if they pooled observations and thinking to this end alone.

The fact remains that mental health is a continuum. If our interests gravitate toward extremes, and we wish to preclude people from obtaining assistance, we can become obsessed with tracing borders between people who *almost* qualify for attention and those who unqualifiedly *do*. With health this makes sense but with mental health it does not. There is no such thing as *almost* having the measles or being a borderline host to cancer, but many persons walk around being somewhat schizy or paranoid, or depressed beyond the call of situations, or compulsively exploitive, or moody or explosive. And while some individuals wear pathologies on sleeves, others strain to put up a front to keep off mental health caseloads.

Transcending the prison environment

Mental health workers in prisons are apt to suffer from what I have referred to as pluralistic ignorance (Chapter 12). I first encountered this phenomenon in a hospital, where clinicians bewailed the impossibility of working in the setting, the constraints posed by administration and other stultifying conditions and the ingratitude and unresponsiveness of patients. During more intimate moments, I heard about victories and successes, about the times when a humane or insightful intervention had made a difference, about ex-patients who kept in touch, and about things that one had learned on the job that one had not learned in graduate or medical school.

But pride and idealism were the subjects of almost secret confessionals, and alienation and cynicism were the public, advertised facade—the vociferous consensus. Of course, this situation meant that everyone assumed that everyone else was bitter and cynical and hard-bitten, and was just putting in time.

One cannot be sure why a majority of closet idealists can become convinced that they are surrounded by a hard-bitten majority of jaundiced cynics. I suspect there is something about not wanting to be mushy and humane and vulnerable in a world we know calls for realism and toughness and pessimism and a feeling of sadder-but-wiser impotence.

Postscript

One sometimes gets a feeling that prison mental health work is seen as a slightly disreputable, marginal enterprise—a bit grubby, perhaps—something that ought to be done but it is nice that somebody else is doing it—like garbage collecting.

I suspect the real point is twofold: (1) most mental health workers at some level feel they do not have the expertise to deal with offender clients, which makes them denigrate the expertise that is involved, and (2) most mental health workers are afraid of criminal justice clients and fearful they might get assaulted the first time they walked into a room with an inmate, besides not knowing what to say to the prisoner. Some professionals feel similarly about the experience of walking through the gates of a prison into an incipient riot. Again, an inviting way of handling these feelings (beside denying them) is to downgrade the work that is performed by people who successfully cope with what respectable persons like ourselves could never face.

17

Mainlining Disturbed Offenders*

IN A LEGISLATIVE hearing a few years ago, the official in charge of New York State prisons expressed reservations about the number of disturbed and retarded offenders who seemed to be routinely sentenced to prison despite obvious handicaps.[1] The Commissioner said in part:

> A number of mentally retarded inmates with abysmal coping skills have been tried, pled or convicted and sentenced to DOCS (the prison system's) custody. In some instances, these individuals were in noncorrectional custodial care when the crime of conviction was committed ....
>
> Although the most severe cases are few in number, they account for a disproportionate amount of staff intervention. Their presence in correctional facilities is highly disruptive to both staff and other inmates.
>
> Although these offenders have been adjudicated as being legally responsible for their actions, they function at an intellectual and social level well below that of the general inmate population (Coughlin, 1987).[2]

---

* With Kenneth Adams. I am grateful for permission to reproduce this paper, which appeared in the *Journal of Psychiatry and Law*, Winter, 1987.

Mainlining disturbed offenders

The problem of deadpan sentencing

Questions about the appropriateness of a prison sentence for many disturbed offenders can be easily raised. Such questions particularly arise in situations where (1) the offender is clearly not a menace to the public (2) his or her offense appears to be irrationally motivated and/or to reflect the influence of serious disabilities (3) the offender remains disturbed in the period following arrest and preceding trial, and (4) he or she continues to be disturbed at the time of entry into prison.

Examples of cases that meet these four criteria are not hard to locate, although the number of inmates involved is impossible to determine, given that delicate judgments must be exercised and that information is often sparse.[3] However, it is the nature of the problem rather than its magnitude that must be our first concern.

What is the nature of the problem? It is that some inmates are *primarily* disturbed and *secondarily* offenders but have been disposed of as if they were *primarily* offenders and *secondarily* (if at all) disturbed. Such actions do not deprive mentally ill persons of treatment, given that mental health services are available in prisons. Rather, the consequence of these actions is that fragile individuals must receive services in a setting that strongly challenges the limited coping capacities of nonresilient personalities. This fact holds even where inmates must be hospitalized on one or more occasions, because hospitalization usually provides only a brief respite from prison life, and the commitment process can involve abrupt discontinuities in service levels and environmental demands. Moreover, prison staff must often respond to the disruptive behavior of disturbed prisoners with punitive sanctions that exacerbate their difficulties (Chapter 18).

Among the disturbed offenders who are sent to prison, we encounter both variety and consistency of backgrounds. Examples of career vignettes illustrate this fact, and may help students of the problem understand the dilemma that faces the system and its clients in concrete and specific instances:

> An offender has broken into his neighbor's house. The police discover that he has stolen a plate of chicken wings, a bottle of wine and a yellow garbage can. The man is hospitalized because he is "grossly psychotic," and is diagnosed as suffering from paranoid schizophrenia. He is released from the hospital, found competent and sentenced to prison.

***

> The man commits a burglary and is surprised in the act but does not flee, although he could have done so. He is declared incompetent and hospitalized. He is subsequently released with the diagnosis "brief reactive psychosis in remission, adjustment disorder with emotional features, borderline intellectual functioning, possible mild organic brain syndrome, mixed personality disorder with histrionic and borderline features, history of head trauma," and is sent to prison.

***

> The offender (who has spent most of his life in institutions) snatches the purse of a woman in a subway station. He is hospitalized for two years after his arrest, and diagnosed as suffering from schizophrenia (undifferentiated type, chronic). He is finally found competent to be tried, pleads guilty to attempted robbery and is sentenced to prison. In the prison reception center, staff observe that the man "became increasingly withdrawn . . . sat sideways in a chair and barely talked."

Later, they record that "continued deterioration required transfer to (the hospital)."

Some cases involve more serious offenses, with at least the potential for violence at the time they take place. Nonetheless, these offenses raise the issue of prison's appropriateness because the offender's motives appear to be clear products of his pathology:

> The offender, a mentally disturbed alcoholic, has no history of violence, but throws a bottle at a parked police car which injures a police officer. He cannot account for his offense. While awaiting trial, the man spends three months in hospitals, where he is maintained on thorazine. Prison staff find him "lethargic, monosyllabic . . . preoccupied," and refer him for mental health assistance.
>
> ***
>
> The offender has been a resident of several hospitals. He has been diagnosed as suffering from paranoid schizophrenia and as having drug and alcohol problems. He also has shown a propensity to carry weapons. The offense for which he is imprisoned is one in which the police find him sitting on a curb stuffing a machete down a sewer. The man has a bag with drugs, ammunition and a handgun, and he warns the police, "Don't you put any bullets in the gun." Despite the man's strange obsession, he is found competent and convicted, though diagnosed as "probable mixed personality disorder with schizotype features."
>
> ***
>
> The offender walks into a store in which his nephew works, carrying two knives and demanding money. In disarming him, the nephew is wounded. The offender is angry at his nephew, who had gone to the police to inform them that his uncle was convinced that his family was trying to poison him. Unsurprisingly the man is diagnosed as suffering from paranoid schizophrenia and is hospitalized for nine months before he is declared competent and convicted. The man arrives in prison "barely functional but taking his medication," and has to be transferred to the hospital.

The issue that is raised by such cases is not whether the prison sentences can be legally justified. The offenders can be convicted and punished, since their culpability is not at issue[4] and they have been found competent. The question, rather, relates to the nature of the constraints that impel judges to consider imprisonment as an option, even though the record suggests that the offender being sentenced has obvious mental health problems. In this connection, it is necessary to consider that (1) the dispositional options that are available to the judge are often nonexistent (as with offenders who are subject to mandatory sentencing provisions), and (2) community-based alternatives may be sparse, because agencies select their clients under restrictive definitions of eligibility.

Such considerations, however, do not account for the routine use of prison sentences for inmates who are disturbed, which suggests that sentencing rationales or other affirmative considerations must be at work. Closer scrutiny reveals at least two reasons that may inspire judges to consider prison as the milieu of choice for some disturbed persons.

I. THE PRISON AS BACKUP STRUCTURE

Prison sentences are sometimes invoked for persons whose distinguishing attribute is their demonstrated incapacity to negotiate life. This observation raises the possibility that prisons may be selected on humanitarian grounds because they furnish sustenance, shelter and supervision.[5] The third attribute (supervision) may be particularly prized because it ensures the availability of supportive assistance around the clock. This fact may become a prime consideration where the person who is being sentenced looks particularly helpless or lost:

> The offender has held up a gas station, has "a blank stare on his face" and is incoherent. He is found incompetent to stand trial, and he shuttles between jail and hospital for three years before he is convicted. He has been raped by fellow inmates, both in the jail and in the hospital. While interviewed in the prison "he felt there was an umbrella with falling rain over his head." The interviewer's impression is that "schizophrenia is draining all of (the man's) energy" and concludes that he "needs protection or state hospitalization."

***

> The offender mugs a used car salesman and is arrested. The victim describes him as a bum "who was not all there." (The offender's history is that of a chronic hospital patient, who otherwise "leads a nomadic existence.") The man is twice declared incompetent to stand trial. After years of hospitalization he is convicted and sent to prison, where he must be committed. Prison staff point out that the man "doesn't know why he is in prison . . . . lies in his cell a lot. Finds it hard to get up or get started . . . . Impresses (them) as a man who is content with his psychological condition and has no interest in . . . participating actively in life."

The use of prisons as a supervised multiservice environment may become attractive where less structured interventions have failed to mobilize the offender, who appears to require more supervision, guidance or support:

> The offender has attempted to commit a burglary. He has been resentenced as a probation violator because he is not employed and refuses to submit to vocational training. After he arrives in prison, he is referred to mental health staff during classification "due to depression with suicidal ideation."
>
> The probation officer describes the offender as "a young man whose emotional problems have played a role in preventing him from complying with the terms and conditions of probation .... Curiously, he cooperated with his obligations such that he never missed a probation appointment and basically kept most of his mental health appointments as well .... This officer tried repeatedly to discover the source of the defendant's inhibition to look for work or accept vocational training. I can only conclude that the defendant lacks the motivation but also seems to have a genuine fear of academic/training situations which may be difficult for him to overcome . . . He was told that probation did not exist to allow him to remain at home and do nothing with his life. The crux of the matter is that the defendant has been unwilling or unable to accept this basic premise of probation supervision."
>
> The offender has been diagnosed as suffering from schizophrenia (chronic, undifferentiated) with mental retardation (his IQ is 67). His offense consists of a "tug of war" in which he tries to separate a lady from her handbag, but fails. The offender has been paroled from prison (where he has spent most of his time hospitalized) to a civil hospital, from which he absconds. He is consequently resentenced to prison, where intake analysts point out that he "has a history of being unable to function in the community" and "has requested that the police arrest him

simply so he will have somewhere to be cared for." At prison intake the man refuses to take medication, requiring an emergency commitment (the man is "eager" to be transferred to the forensic hospital) with the recommendation that "long-term psychiatric residence be provided for him in the facility and upon discharge to the community."

A more direct incentive to imprisoning the offender may exist where he has evaded or rejected community services whose staff cannot enforce their prescriptions. The prison serves as an inviting backup, particularly where backsliding by the offender makes him a nuisance or raises the presumption (at times remote) that he may reoffend. In such instances the prison is seen as not only having the virtue of being escape-proof but also as serving to interdict trouble for which the offender seems headed if left at large:

> The man has grown up in foster homes and has graduated to psychiatric settings. He is arrested for a burglary and placed on probation. Within three months he has violated probation by absconding from a halfway house and not responding to treatment. He has also been dismissed from an alcohol program for showing up drunk and not attending group therapy sessions.

***

> As a child, the offender has been taken to a mental health clinic for punching a teacher in the mouth. He is later convicted of stealing a motorcycle running away from his seventh foster home placement. He is put on probation and referred to a youth corrections program, from which he also absconds. He is placed in a residential substance abuse program, from which he again absconds, and is sentenced to prison.

***

> Six years before, the man committed a violent sex offense and was declared not guilty by reason of insanity. He has been committed to a hospital, from which he is released subject to conditions that include therapeutic involvements. The man's probation is revoked because he "is said to have not taken his medication on several occasions, to have missed two-thirds of his rehabilitation classes and about one-third of his therapy appointments." Prison officials find the man "distant, removed, unkempt" and "not always in touch with reality." They commit him to the forensic hospital.

***

> The man first arrives in prison ten years after committing his offense, an assault. The man had been involved in a family fight and was ordered (by the police) to sleep in a hallway. He knifed a neighbor who objected to his presence and was placed on probation, but later hospitalized. He is imprisoned again after he rejects the hospital's discharge plan, indicating he would prefer living in men's shelters. He arrives in prison actively psychotic and is transferred to the forensic hospital.

II. Prison as a Secure Hospital

Some disturbed persons evoke worry about risks that relate to their self-care, including being a danger to themselves; others spark concerns about the milieus in which they must function, which they can disrupt with noisy, unseemly or destructive behavior. Such concerns are particularly inspired by offenders whose symptoms

Mainlining disturbed offenders

include a history of acting out, both in institutions and in the community:

> The offender is a patient who is given to episodes of bizarre explosive outbursts. He has been hospitalized for behavior such as running through the street nude proclaiming that he is Jesus Christ. He has also been arrested for unprovoked assaults. Jail staff note that "he goes nuts and throws things, sets fires and talks constantly ... he said he was a voodoo doctor and stood naked in his cell."

***

> The offense for which the man is convicted is one in which he wakes up residents of a house, shouting at their windows that he needs money for drugs. The victims instruct the man to come to their front door, where the police arrest him. After the man arrives in prison, prison staff complain that he is "hostile, verbally aggressive and emotionally unstable."

***

> The man has been convicted for an incident that took place two years before in which he set his apartment on fire. He had spent much of the intervening time in a hospital, from which he is gratefully discharged with the diagnosis schizophrenia (chronic, in remission). As soon as he enters prison, the man proves disruptive, "disturbing the entire block and staff." He cannot be processed because he "shouted throughout the (intake) interview" and refused medication. He had to be transferred to the hospital.

***

> The offender has committed a mugging during which he "made stabbing motions to the shoulder of a female victim." The victim describes the offender as "somewhat off." The man has a history of assaulting his mother, which led to multiple hospital commitments. The diagnosis accorded him is schizophrenia (paranoid type, chronic) with acute exacerbation. In the hospital he engages in disruptive behavior, such as burning holes in sheets and setting his mattress on fire.

***

> After the man arrives in the prison, staff write that "his adjustment is marked by continuous hallucinations with which he dialogues while in his cell, and extreme mood swings." The man sings, sometimes loudly, in his cell. Staff write (half facetiously) that "a significant feature of a positive nature is that he has a beautiful singing voice which impresses all who hear him."

The notion that prisons may be envisioned as secure hospitals, or hospital-equivalents, is in the abstract implausible. Without considering this possibility, however, it becomes hard to explain why hospital offenses with clear psychotic overtones result in imprisonment, instead of in the upgrading of security arrangements within the hospital. The same point holds for disturbed persons who prove troublesome in community settings and are imprisoned rather than institutionalized in more treatment-relevant settings:

> The man is convicted of a robbery after he is declared incompetent on five occasions, but later found competent. He serves six years, mostly in prison hospital settings. After leaving prison, the man is sent to a civil hospital for a fifteen-day evaluation. He becomes disgruntled when his release is delayed and assaults a fellow patient who "said the wrong thing at the wrong time." He explains that "something snapped." The man is sent back to prison, where staff conclude that "he

will need ongoing psychiatric care."

***

The offender is a badly retarded young man who set his bed on fire because he is "angry at his brother." He is charged with committing arson, but is hospitalized. While he is in the hospital, the man fondles a female fellow patient and is again arrested. He is found fit to proceed and is convicted of his sex offense.

***

The offender is a retarded schizophrenic. He has a long history of hospitalizations and brushes with the law. He has attempted suicide by choking himself and jumping out of a second story window. In the hospital he enters the rooms of fellow patients looking for money, takes a wallet and is caught. He is declared incompetent but is later sent to prison on a guilty plea for attempted burglary. The prison staff finds that "obviously, he is a disturbed psychiatric patient" and commits him to the forensic hospital. There, staff note that "he prefers the role of patient and is a difficult client whose prognosis is bleak."

***

The offender is a mentally retarded man who has been convicted of rape after engaging in intercourse with a fourteen year-old agency client who "apparently (was) a willing participant." The man had sustained brain damage as the result of an accident in which he was involved as a child. He subsequently experienced "nervous breakdowns," attempted suicide and was diagnosed as suffering from a schizoid personality disorder.

A final category of imprisoned offenders enhances the plausibility of the "secure hospital" image of the prison because the offenders at issue are persons who are imprisoned after becoming destructively refractory in other settings. These offenders are not only difficult to manage, but react violently to efforts to manage them. The other side of the coin is that these persons are not premeditatedly violent, and are clearly disturbed at the time that they pose a danger to their treaters. This second fact, however, recedes in relevance to sentencing authorities, given the safety concerns of treatment staff, which seem to underlie community demands for prison sentences:

> The offender is a severely retarded man who has become convinced that the staff members of a mental health program are laughing at him. He sets fire to the agency's building and tries to burn its van. He throws bottles at agency staff, and arrives at its building with a knife in his pocket, announcing that he intends to stab someone. He also threatens to rape a social worker who works for the agency. The man is sent to jail, where he is repeatedly raped. He is declared competent, pleads guilty to Arson 2, and is sent to prison with a long sentence.

***

The man is a former hospital patient who is imprisoned for arson after he sets fire to a group therapy room in an outpatient clinic where he is treated. While he is being arrested the man is described as "rambling continuously." He makes statements such as "it was a political arrest, there is a question of constitutionality involved here; I didn't want to gain any more weight, it was all after the fact and there is defamation involved. I got lonely and I wanted to be with my people at the clinic, and I never got over the first hump." The man is subjected to competency examinations, but he is declared competent, convicted and imprisoned. In prison, according to staff, he "suddenly experienced a full psychotic breakdown."

***

The offender has been sentenced to probation for assaulting his girlfriend. At the time he is diagnosed as experiencing a "depressive reaction with paranoid features." Six years later the man has a psychotic breakdown after he is both fired from his job and evicted from his room for "bizarre" behavior. While disturbed he enters his probation office, refusing to leave. He ransacks the office, traps the staff behind desks, and threatens to assault them. He is restrained and removed from the premises. His probation is revoked and he is resentenced to prison, where he arrives medicated, and is adjudged "friendly and cooperative."

***

The man has a long career as a hospital patient. His offense takes place in the hospital in which he is confined. There he assaults a psychiatrist, breaking a chair over his head. He also destroys windows at the nurses' station before he is subdued. In the past he has assaulted a social worker and tried to choke an attendant. In jail the man attacks a corrections supervisor, who loses two teeth. In prison, he threatens to "deck" correction officers at the reception center. Staff write that he "impressed (them) as having limited intellect, horizons and mental sophistication."

What is to be done?

The illustrations document one's impression that disturbed persons are sometimes adjudicated in surprisingly routine fashion as they are sentenced to imprisonment. The probability of such prison sentences appears to be enhanced where (1) offenders have failed to respond to community programs, or (2) have proved disruptive to community settings. In neither case can the concern of sentencing authorities be deemed misplaced, but it is also not obvious that prison is the most appropriate solution to meet these concerns.

The difficulty lies in the fact that the hypothetical type of setting that does address concerns about the need for support and structure for disturbed persons does not at present exist, nor are public pressures being exerted to create such a setting. This indifference is understandable because (1) the types of persons we have described are rejected individuals who have no constituency (2) they do not fit neatly into service-related classifications[6] (3) once they are in prison, these offenders are invisible to the public, as are the problems they experience, and (4) prisons are institutions of last resort; they have the obligation to deal with persons sent to prison even if they have proven to be inhospitable and thankless clients elsewhere. The dilemma is further compounded by the fact that problem persons can become correctional clients for life, because once they have been in prison their chances of being recycled into prison are enhanced.

Admittedly it is easier to delineate the current situation than it is to envisage its resolution. The best for which we can hope is that in the future programs will be created into which offenders can be diverted after they are sentenced. We can also hope for interagency arrangements and hybrid systems in the community that will willingly accommodate persons who now fall between cracks, most notably those impaired, disabled and disturbed individuals who become correctional clients because we don't know what else we can do with them.

Notes

1. Throughout this paper we refer to "disturbed" offenders. Attention to our illustrations will make it obvious, however, that many of the inmates we discuss have multiple problems, combining to varying degrees serious retardation, learning deficits and manifestations of mental illness.
2. Commissioner Coughlin advocates expansion of supportive services in the prison but recognizes that " in the short term, pressure (must) be put at the front end of the system, the courts, the prosecutors and the defense bar. Chronic schizophrenics with IQs of 67 should not be allowed to plead guilty and be sent to prison" (Commisoner Thomas Coughlin, personal communication).The timeliness of Commission Coughlin's testimony is illustrated by the fact that on the same date on which his remarks were publicized, a newspaper story appeared in which a county judge was quoted as objecting to provisions in the courts that allow "incapacitated persons to avoid criminal proceedings, (creating) a class of persons immune from the criminal justice system and given carte blanch (sic) to commit crime" (Cather, 1987).
3. The case material summarized in this paper derives from New York Department of Correctional Services central office folders for inmates entering the system in the calendar year, 1985. Access to the data was provided through the courtesy of Dr. Raymond Broaddus, then Deputy Commissioner for Health Services, DOCS, and of Frank Tracey, DOCS Director of Research.
4. The insanity defense does not come into play for the types of offenses with which we are concerned, since the defense is in practice invoked only where serious crimes have been committed and the offender faces very heavy penalties. Seymour Halleck, a forensic psychiatrist, writes that "in our current political climate, pressure is actually growing to avoid examining psychological issues related to culpability by narrowing the insanity defense or doing away with practices associated with the diminished capacity doctrine . . . By providing a loophole for dealing with the worst possible cases, the insanity defense allows society to acknowledge that at least some offenders are different. This enables society to avoid the formidable problems that would arise if it were to adopt a more flexible approach in assessing the relationship of psychological disability to liability in the case of all offenders."
5. The same issue arises for the parole board when it comes to releasing multiple disadvantaged offenders from prison. William McMahon, Chairman of the New York State Commission of Correction, testified, for example, that developmentally disabled inmates are "less likely to receive parole, and are more likely to serve longer (prison) terms." He pointed out that the inmates "are perceived as poor candidates, largely because the combination of community-based services considered essential for the success of these individuals are not available in most localities. Thus, the parole board believes that it is protecting the inmate and the community." (McMahon, 1987).
6. Commissioner Coughlin notes, for example, that "it is abundantly clear that a person suffering from mental retardation and some form of mental illness is the bane of everyone's existence. The retardation people point to the mental illness and throw their hands up. The mental health people point to the retardation and do the same . . . . The current practice of labeling everything just reinforces this process. I once proposed a State Department of Dual Diagnosis, so that no one could hide behind a label" (Commissioner Thomas Coughlin, personal communication). Chairman McMahon (note 5,*supra*)concurs. He testified that "in the case of the dual diagnosed, it is difficult to access services because (agencies) have difficulty agreeing upon primary responsibility." He cites as an added problem the fact that "residential and treatment programs, in general, avoid persons with a criminal record."

18

Coping with Noncoping Convicts*

NED NOLAN (not his real name) had been sentenced to prison for an attempted robbery. At the time of his arrest, Mr. Nolan reported that he had been sleeping in an abandoned building and had been hungry much of the time. He also explained at the time that he was unemployed because work made him dizzy. His probation officer wrote that:

> The defendant . . . claims a physical disability and showed the probation officer what appeared to be a malformed large toe. He indicated he has a metal plate in his head. He describes severe pain in his feet, headaches, and general aches throughout his body as well as dizziness. He seems to be of limited intellectual ability.

After Mr. Nolan arrived in prison he signed himself into protective segregation, claiming to be "in fear of his life." He then announced that he did not want to be released into any part of the population. The prison was fortunately able to place Mr. Nolan in a program for victim-prone prisoners,[1] but the staff of this unit soon lodged objections to his presence. They wrote:

---

*With J. Douglas Grant. This chapter is excerpted from *The American Prison: Issues in Research and Policy,* edited by Lynne Goodstein and Doris Layton MacKenzie (New York: Plenum Press, 1989). Reprinted by permission.

He first impressed [us] of limited intelligence, paranoid, lacking social skills and a malingerer who is unable to accept responsibility for his actions. His actions over the past several months have reinforced this impression. His disciplinary record is terrible. He has numerous misbehavior reports of a serious nature (fights, possession of a weapon); he has mutilated himself to obtain attention; his ability to get along with inmates is nil. He can best be described as infantile in his dealings with staff. . . It is easy to discuss the resident's strengths, he doesn't have any . . . . He is not prepared to function in any program where responsibility is required, mainly because he does not know what the word means.

A year later, the same staff wrote about Mr. Nolan that "his program participation has been nil, and he has been a distinct disciplinary problem." Mr. Nolan was therefore gratefully released from prison, but was returned for absconding from parole. Soon after reentering the prison, he again requested protective custody, surrendering a homemade weapon and offering detailed information about illegal activities of other inmates. Shortly thereafter, he threw a tantrum because he objected to a cereal that was served to him for breakfast.

A contemporaneous observer could have written that Mr. Nolan is an exemplar of the frustration aggression theory in action, has a penchant for feeling persecuted and attacks those of his peers whom he fears. He also throws tantrums in which staff members are targets. These assaults paradoxically occur despite the fact that Mr. Nolan regards prison staff as parental figures who reliably protect him after he has surrounded himself with enemies.

The multi-problem inmate

Though it is true that a person must be sentenced for a crime to be committed to prison, this requisite for confinement is often not very informative, in the sense that the person usually has more salient attributes than the fact that he is an offender. This point holds for a great many more offenders than one would suspect because most crimes are casually committed and involve limited skills. In dealing with inmates, therefore, we must realize that we can be distracted from assessing all sorts of liabilities they have by centering on their criminal histories.

Ned Nolan illustrates the need for an uncontaminated perspective. Nolan is technically a robber, but he is more prominently a man relegated to a life of vagrancy by a combination of real and perceived handicaps, which continue to manifest themselves in the prison, making Nolan an irrepressible and annoying inmate. Neither the causation nor the consequences of Nolan's difficulties are easy to describe: Nolan can be labeled as a multiproblem individual, meaning that an extended list of his personal deficits, liabilities, and handicaps can be presented. Such a list would include the fact that Nolan has been reliably diagnosed as brain damaged and that his measured intelligence is low. The list might also include depressed self-esteem and limited aspirations, and it could describe traits such as high impulsivity and low frustration tolerance and clinical states such as bouts of depression.

A list of measurable deficits, however, at best provides clues to problems and offers reasons why problems might arise if they arise. This sequence is suspect, in that postdiction is easier than prediction. The fact that an offender is diagnosed as brain damaged does not portend prison misbehavior nor foreordain difficulties for the offender in the community. A diagnosis for a recalcitrant person, however, beckons as an explanatory formula because the label becomes a substitute for the question "Why does this person do what he or she does?" which is invariably difficult to answer. The formula may also allow for simple remedies, such as medication that suppresses misbehavior by lowering energy levels or inducing depression.

But explaining means not only answering the question "what?" but also responding to "how?" and "why?" questions. This enterprise would entail specifying the role Nolan's brain lesions play in producing his misbehavior, a task that no one can undertake. Deficits, moreover, are ingredients that must be combined, with different combinations yielding different, frequently contrasting, products. There are persons with IQ scores comparable to Nolan's, for instance, who have gentle, sweet, and angelic dispositions and are congenial as clients. Even impulsivity (which looks like a behavior propensity) can lead to divergent outcomes, depending on the forms that impulse release takes, the efforts a person makes to use supports to supplement poor controls, and the effects of anticipated and/or experienced reactions from others.

Impulsivity-related prison misbehavior such as Nolan's thus ranges from serious to nonserious and from lighthearted to grim. Some "impulsive" inmates pose danger to other inmates, in that they regard others as objects of need satisfaction and use violence to intimidate, extort, expropriate, or strong-arm those susceptible to intimidation. Other high impulsivity prisoners are amusingly minor league and inconsequential miscreants. They may play "Russian roulette" with prison rules, taking risks in the casual pursuit of short-term goals, seemingly oblivious to predictable repercussions. Other such inmates have a propensity to "jail" (Irwin, 1970). In operationalizing their personal definition of the "good life" — which consists of accumulating illicit amenities — such inmates engage in *sub rosa* activities (including hustling), viewing the "official" prison as an irrelevant sideline.

Impulse management issues can also pose more serious problems for the offender than they do for others. Stress-aggression and frustration-aggression patterns sometimes have this attribute, in that the stimulus experiences (frustration or stress) can be incredibly painful. Where a frustration-aggression pattern obtains, the inmates, whenever they are disappointed or obstructed in the pursuit of goals (which may be a frequent experience), become disgruntled and react with bursts of blind and irrational rage. In stress-aggression patterns, the inmates tend to feel that situations close in on them, whereupon they experience panic and anxiety and blow up under pressure with tantrums that express a sense of helplessness. Impulsivity-related games also often turn sour: In examining chronic misbehavior in prison, we encounter inmates who engage in nonreflective, childlike, self-serving, and short-sighted behavior that elicits boomerang effects, leaving the inmate despondent and suffused with self-pity.

Mr. Nolan's outlook makes him operate at a level of infancy, satisfying his needs in a direct and primitive fashion. Prison officials would say that Nolan is a chronic, serious management problem. Statistically, they can make a strong case. The average inmate records two to four disciplinary violations per year, and many inmates are never (or hardly ever) charged with misbehavior, whereas Nolan has continuous disciplinary charges pending. This means that authorities must subject Nolan to many sanctions, which have no deterrent consequences. As a result, both Nolan and the system have insoluble problems, a point that also holds for other inmates who engage in considerable misbehavior.

Responding to the noncoping inmate

Like most maladaptive inmates, Nolan represents a checkered problem. He at times acts out, subjecting other persons (both inmates and staff) to assaults; but Nolan is also a redundant victim, who must often seek protection. Nolan's motives are hardly standard motives. We may notice, for example, that at times Nolan appears lost, aimlessly perambulating about, whereas at other times he can be rigid, and at such times he seems unable to tolerate deviations from private rituals. Is Nolan a disturbed or disordered inmate? Mental health staff have seen Nolan after suicide gestures and have certified that he is not disturbed. But what this means is that Nolan does not reach the threshold of "disturbedness" that qualifies him for mental health services, and this threshold is relatively stringent because prison mental health resources are scarce (as they are in the community) and must be rationed.

As it happens, Nolan had been sentenced to a prison system that has settings for unusual inmates. Nolan is assigned to such a setting, but he strains its hospitality, contaminates its climate, and is only retained, against staff advice, because no place can be found that more appropriately fits Nolan's needs.

This type of dilemma is not accidental. Persons who fail in the community also fail in prison because prisons, like other settings, test personal coping skills and adaptive resources. Of course, in some ways prisons are more protective than the community, so that Nolan's capacity to earn his keep — which is minimal or nonexistent — is not tested. But prisons have accentuated stressful features, such as ever-present guards who demand compliance with rules, and peers who feel that fear calls for exploitation (Chapter 22), and these are features that produce disproportionate difficulties for some imprisoned persons. Adolescents who have unresolved resentments against parental figures, for example, may feel unable to cope, or at least cope dispassionately, with the authority of prison guards.[2] Such chips-on-the-shoulder patterns can produce inmates who alternate between dependent and rebellious behavior, depending on whether they feel their needs are met or frustrated. Other such prisoners may expect rejection from guards, and invite it, by behaving in obnoxious, challenging ways. Still others can take a straightforward rebellious, defiant, and challenging stance or feel that no one has a right to tell them what to do, and react angrily to perceived infringements of their autonomy. Disciplinary sanctions can make such situations worse, in that some inmates cannot gracefully accept sanctions, which conflict with their versions of adulthood.

In sum, prisons offer tests of resilience that nonresilient persons, of the kind who disproportionately inhabit prisons, cannot pass, and the disciplinary process thus becomes overloaded with the results of coping failures. Not surprisingly, inmates who appear on mental health case loads have higher disciplinary violation rates than do other inmates (Toch and Adams, 1989), and disturbed inmates figure disproportionately among chronic disciplinary violators; the same point holds for inmates who have low measured intelligence, such as Nolan. If accurate information were available on more diverse predictors of poor coping competence — such as data about learning disabilities or language deficits — these measures would no doubt be equally predictive of high disciplinary violation rates and of chronicity of violations (Finn, 1989).[3]

Disciplinary sanctions, by default, become standard responses to maladaptive behavior, though formal sanctions are supplemented at times with more constructive responses, such as Nolan's placement in the special (protective) setting. Such responses, however, can be deployed for only a small number of inmates, and they are often — as in Nolan's case — compromise resolutions. These options also are — with rare exception — exercised independently of disciplinary proceedings, and address different aspects of the same behavior.

Dramatic examples are the careers of psychotic inmates who are alternately hospitalized and penalized (Chapter 19). Such inmates often disrupt prison routine because they withdraw from their surroundings, living seclusively in private worlds, neglecting self-care and hygiene to the discomfort of other inmates. Disturbed inmates can also engage in seemingly unmotivated attacks on others, or against themselves, in response to hallucinations, delusions, cumulating anxiety or tension and self-hate. Such inmates may also feel extremely persecuted and explode at persons they imagine wish them ill or want to harm them. They can lastly manifest mixed disruptive patterns in which they alternately withdraw and explode.

Disciplinary responses to eccentric violations

The responses of prison staff to behavior that violates prison rules range from informal to legalistic and very formal. When behavior that comes to the attention of authorities is marginally disruptive, particularly when it consists of nonpublic, one-time offenses, the response the behavior receives is often limited to rebukes or sermons, which are called "counseling" by guards (Lombardo, 1981). More serious or more patterned misbehavior invites formal dispositions and sanctions, and serious violations, such as acts of violence and destruction of property, lead to major disciplinary hearings and heavy penalties.

Though there are observers (e.g., Fox, 1958; Glaser, 1964, 1977) who argue for flexible and individualized discipline, most correctionists favor a system that allots standard dispositions to equivalent offenses. Such a system is advocated on the grounds that it provides equity and fairness (Fogel, 1975), but it is also sometimes defended as a way of instilling a sense of responsibility in miscreants for their reprehensible acts.

Where the impact of dispositions on the inmate has to be considered, because the inmate is in very poor shape, an unmodified legalistic stance becomes hard to sustain, even for those who favor mainstreaming (the emphasizing of normalcy) as a goal. A New York survey report notes that an inmate who breaks down with a psychotic episode in a disciplinary confinement setting may be removed "for crisis intervention" but is later usually returned to serve the rest of his time, with predictably adverse results (Steelman, 1987: 39). The problem is one of inflexibility of a system which sees no alternative to the option of the prisoner serving a full segregation term, no matter what the costs may be in terms of his mental and physical well-being, or the financial burden born by the state for his frequent terms of psychiatric treatment (pp. 41-42).

The sponsors of the New York prison survey suggest that "any inmate who has received [mental health] services be screened [by mental health staff] prior to being placed in punitive segregation" and argue that "alternative housing arrangements" ought to be provided for inmates for whom segregation is deemed "seriously detrimental" (p. 86). This solution is based on the supposition that the inmates' level of suffering and their reaction to stresses of confinement can be predicted by the staff, which is not the case. Moreover, such a system would give mental health staff the *de facto* power to administer or withhold punishment, a responsibility that has elsewhere provided heart-wrenching ethical dilemmas to prison medical personnel (Smith, 1984).

There are other issues in the disciplining of disturbed inmates that raise fundamental questions. In the New York survey report, a retarded inmate is described as one who was frustrated by an officer, set his cell on fire, was locked up, and ended up weeping inconsolably. In connection with another case, staff learned of "instances where inmates had been sentenced to time in punitive segregation *as punishment for having attempted to kill themselves*" (Steelman, 1987, p.41; emphasis in the original). In one such case, the hearing officer advised the inmate that he would simply have to learn to "face his problems."

Given the system in which the hearing officer exercises his function, this statement represents the most humane position he can take, recognizing the irrationality of the inmate's motives. What the officer does is to restate the premise of the disciplinary process, which is designed for punishment and deterrence. Penalties are meant to discourage disruptive acts, which include suicide attempts, presupposing that inmates possess sufficient rationality of motive to make punishment plausible and deterrence possible. In his capacity as client of the mental health system, the inmate may be a panic-stricken youth who embarks on an ambivalent gesture of self-destruction; in his capacity as target of discipline, the inmate becomes sturdier; we assume he can learn to "face his problem" after a protracted term of enforced solitude. In his capacity as disciplinary client, the inmate also serves as object lesson to those who (unlike himself) premeditatedly contemplate jailbreaks or suicide attempts.

The point is not that such an inmate is inappropriately disciplined but that the inmate looks different from the stereotypic offender for whom the system is intended. It is to the latter sort of inmate that the hearing officer's admonitions are addressed.

The problem is that the system contains an insufficient number of options (essentially two: disciplinary and mental health), and has no easy way of combining these options.[4] Standard responses must thus address nonstandard problems, and the outcome is often strained and ill-fitting.

Supplementing disciplinary responses

Under the current system, priceless opportunities may be missed because disciplinary hearing officers make ideal referral agents. This is so because they have data about inmate behavior that enables them to identify problem inmates. Most importantly, they have data about past transgressions that permit them to think about patterned chronicity. Incident descriptions in disciplinary dossiers provide clues as to whether the motivational pattern of the inmate is nonroutine, in the sense that his or her behavior reflects low maturity level, emotional problems, intellectual limitations, or social ineptness. The hearing officer obviously knows about any sanctions that have been tried in the past without success, in efforts to break cycles of misbehavior. Finally, the officer is in a position to decide whether sanctioning the inmate makes sense, not only in terms of what sanctions have accomplished but in terms of whether the personality and behavior pattern of the offender corresponds to the offender stereotype (volitional, deliberate, and malevolent) for which the sanctioning process is designed (Fox, 1958).

If, in the disciplinary officer's mind, standard punitive dispositions sit uneasily when applied to an inmate, the prison system could in theory provide the officer with tools that have rehabilitative potential as an adjunct to disciplinary sanctions. Such tools could be elected by the inmate in that the inmate must ultimately decide whether he prefers to see himself as *being* a problem and/or as *having* a problem, provided he does not contest his culpability. One would hope that some inmates might consider the appropriateness of self-appraisal, particularly at a career juncture — such as having been caught with the goods for the umpteenth time — that links their conduct with an impending undesired fate. Even more tangible incentives could be provided, of course, such as the hearing officer suspending his disposition to permit the inmate to try a new or different program.

Resocialization options one can consider vary, and though we shall delineate an option to show how it would work, many others come to mind. One model, that of the Just Community (Hickey and Scharf, 1980), offers moral education as its modality and looks particularly germane for relatively bright prisoners. Expanded mental health services could cover adjustment and coping problems, provided mental health staff decided they were willing to deal with mental health, as opposed to mental illness, concerns. Cognitive, behavioral and social learning approaches also have relevance to maladaptive behavior (Chapter 12).

No matter what referral or program options are considered, one must face the basic question of whether a socialization or rehabilitative effort can be grafted or appended onto the disciplinary process. The latter, after all, serves the prison's interest, whereas the former's goal is usually defined as assisting people to lead happier, fuller, and more productive lives.

Improving coping skills: the ethical dilemma

One cannot treat an individual as a "noncoper" should the demands that are made on him be inhumane, unreasonable, or unfair. If a person fails to conform to conditions to which no one should be expected to conform — or if he stands out because he is "sane in insane places" (Rosenhan, 1973) — his conduct may indeed be descriptively maladaptive, but the cause of his problem — and the solution to his problem — lies in reforms of the environment. In most settings, however, the environment and the person are both imperfect; the maladaptive behavior may be sparked by constraints and pressures, but it is disproportionate, destructive, or self-destructive and/or harms both the person and the environment. There may be no excuse for stultifying educational settings, for instance, but one can legitimately center attention on students who engage in vandalism, predation, or disruptiveness in such settings on the grounds that their behavior:

1. Is not really a corollary or consequence of imperfections of the setting; and
2. Makes the perpetrators a liability to their environment, themselves, and to others; and
3. Worsens the quality of the environment even further, both for the noncopers' contemporaries and those whose follow in their wake.

These considerations only make it doubly necessary that any interventionist's goals be uncompromisingly clear and that such goals unambiguously translate into details of program design. The demise of behavior modification in 1974 after its short-lived introduction into adult prisons is a lesson in point. As noted in an authoritative overview sponsored by NIMH (Brown, Wienckowski, and Stolz, 1975):

> Persons using behavior modification procedures have been particularly criticized for their attempts to deal with rebellious and nonconformist behavior of inmates in penal institutions. Because the behavioral professional is often in the position of assisting in the management of prisoners whose antagonism to authority and rebelliousness have been the catalyst for conflict within the institution, the distinctions among his multiple functions of therapy, management, and rehabilitation can become blurred, and his allegiance confused (p. 16).

The NIMH authors conclude that:

> Behavior modification should not be used in an attempt to facilitate institutionalization of the inmate or to make him adjust to inhumane living conditions. Further, no therapist should accept requests for treatment that take the form "make him 'behave,'" when the intent of the request is to make the person conform to oppressive conditions (p. 17).

Where maladaptive inmates are the targets of intervention, the issue for the inmates would be different than that for staff, whose concern revolves around the bankruptcy of custodial alternatives that leaves the system no recourse but to place prisoners in perpetual lockup. But the inmates, as it happens, have ended up equally resourceless, as reflected in the impotence of the blind rage with which they express their helplessness and their inability to extricate themselves from escalating confrontations.

This means that interventions could solve the prison's problem while solving that of the inmates. One at least could solve the problem of inmates who might consider having a problem after mature deliberation, under circumstances that show respect for them as responsible, self-determining adults. Given the exercise of such options — followed by program participation providing opportunities for self-examination — the inmates could preserve their dignity and the prison could also benefit, without need for the interventionist to wallow in the question "Which master do I serve, and who is my client?"

A regenerative approach to the chronic offender

Langer (1983) has described a sense of power that comes from participating in decisions that contribute to mastering one's internal and external environment. Her work suggests that if a person can evolve a formula that extricates him from a dilemma he poses to himself or others, such regenerative problem solving can increase the person's feelings of self-esteem and his feelings of mastery in addressing problems of social living. I have also noted (Chapter 12) that through self-inquiry in group settings, a person can move through cognitive problem solving, to what Maxwell Jones (1953) called "emotional social learning." In this modality, a great many feelings can be explored and experienced beyond whatever insight is derived from engagement in creative thinking.

Social learning of the sort discussed by Jones centers on feedback about a person's maladaptive behavior, particularly, maladaptive behavior that causes problems, which provides "live" learning content for social learning (therapeutic) groups. It is a short step from this view to envisage a group that centers on each member's pattern of maladaptive behavior, which can be deduced from a series of incidents in which the person has encountered difficulties and produced problems for others. This approach has not yet been attempted with prison disciplinary incidents but has been deployed in the peer review panels that I have discussed (Chapter 8) that centered on arrest reports filed by problem police officers. The review panel process consisted of the following stages:

(1) The necessity for the panel is documented. Typically, the process would be initiated when an officer reached a threshold number of incidents on an up-to-date inventory of violent involvements.

Other ways of mobilizing the review panel would include requests by supervisors or by the subjects themselves. In such cases, however, the record would have to bear out the officer's eligibility by showing a substantial number of recent involvements.

(2) A preparatory investigation for the interview is conducted. Data relating to the subject's performance on the street is obtained from available secondary sources. This includes interviews with supervisors, reports by peers, and all information on record. The investigation culminates in a planning session in which panelists formulate hypotheses and draft questions that streamline the panel session.

(3) Then comes the interview itself, which can be divided into three stages:

    a. Key incidents are chronologically explored, including not only actions taken by all persons involved in the incident, but also their perceptions, assumptions, feelings and motives.

    b. The summation of these data in the form of common denominators and patterns is undertaken primarily by the subject, with participation by the panelists. An effort is made to test the plausibility and relevance of the hypothesized patterns by extrapolating them into other involvements.

    c. The discussion of the pattern occurs last, and includes tracing its contribution to maladaptive reactions. This stage features the exploration of alternative approaches that might be conducive to more constructive solutions (Toch, Grant and Galvin, 1975, pp. 246-247).

In transposing this model into a prison context, one could assume for simplicity's sake that the program can be developed as a component of an ongoing therapeutic community. The administrative entities involved would then be the disciplinary panel of the prison and the therapeutic community's participants, and the inmate who is nominated would have the choice of volunteering or not for participation. The therapeutic community staff could have the final say about whether they would accept the volunteer. For at least the initial effort, it would seem reasonable that if the therapeutic community staff would not want to accept an inmate because they felt that he posed a disruptive potential for the rest of the community, it should be up to the disciplinary staff to make another decision as to appropriate action. A disciplinary pattern, however, should not be grounds for rejection from the program because the nominated inmate would have to be a chronic disciplinary offender facing the disciplinary board's action following a specific formal incident charge.

Though intake screening poses a risk of creating interface problems (through accusations of "dumping" countered by charges of excessive intake selectivity), there are countervailing advantages. For one, the step provides staff with the opportunity to study the inmate's folder, to formulate hypotheses, and to plan social management approaches; for another, staff (and possibly inmates involved in screening) would have a chance to make a public commitment to take risks of their own devising, which is a powerful means of reducing resistance in planned change experiments (Lewin, 1947).

The core of an inmate-centered intervention could consist of a group comprised of four or five review candidates, and a staff team including a mental health and a custodial staff member and an inmate peer counselor. The latter role could evolve as the program matures, in that the peer staff member could then be selected from a pool of successful program graduates, and could be picked for having charisma and demonstrated problem-solving competence.

Sequences of events in the group's operation could vary, but a plausible sequence could consist of four stages or phases. Phases 1, 2, and 3 could be scheduled for two hours a day over five consecutive days each week. In the first part of Phase 1, the group would review with each of its members his recorded formal incidents over his entire career thus far, as they appear in his record. Following an analysis in which themes and patterns are hypothesized, the inmate could be allowed to add additional information to expand and/or modify the initial formulation. All members of the group would be expected to participate in sharing ideas and questions in an effort at mutual problem solving, the goal being to reach a consensus as to patterns that describe each individual's incident sequence and account for his repetitive nonadaptive behavior.

Phase 2 could consist of role playing and reverse role playing by participants for pattern clarification and understanding. In such role playing, the inmate would play himself and assorted opponents (fellow inmates or staff) in characteristic personal encounters. Other means could also be used to ensure that the inmate internalizes the results of his pattern analyses. This task, moreover, need not be confined to pattern definition, in that once the pattern is defined, cues must be identified that set off incidents. These cues could be a suspected put down, a guilt feeling, a sense of crowding, anger, pangs of loneliness, and direct and/or imagined threats from others.

Once incident cues have been surfaced, the strategy calls for self control routines, actions that the person derives from the role playing and shared thinking of the group about just what sets him off. These self-management responses to incident cues could be breathing and muscle-flexing routines, a "time-out" session, a memorized talk to oneself (counting to ten or its equivalent), contacting a previously identified supportive other, working out, counseling, sharing with peer inmate counselors, involvement in program development or conflict negotiation or mediation, AA-type procedures such as apology and seeking a fresh start in one or more relationships, scheduled and/or emergency group meetings. Such techniques would make up Phase 3 of the process, which would consist of the development of a change strategy for each of the offenders, with the crucial requisite being the participation of the person in developing his own strategy for self management.

Phase 4 would consist of quality control reviews. At some point following the termination of Phase 3 (possibly after several months), the panel could meet to check on the progress of each offender, reviewing critical benchmarks that would be included in the inmate's plan of action. This review would be followed by a discussion of possible strategy modifications. Additional progress reviews could occur after reasonable intervals, leading to further modifications of coping strategies for the inmate.

Obstacles and resources

Some major concerns must be addressed in proposing a program such as that outlined above. For openers, how much staff, inmate, and organizational resistance must we anticipate? Beside the initial resistance to letting any new program be established, what are the probabilities that an effort such as this would become an "innovation ghetto," with its operation seen as a competing not-part-of-the-regular-program irritant? After top-level legitimating, it would seem in order to spend considerable time addressing the concerns of key prisoners and groups in the organization — very much including employee unions. Custody, mental health, and disciplinary staff would have to be represented in organizational meetings in which the program is discussed.

A second consideration is how the target group of chronic offenders would be perceived by their significant and general others as a result of their participation. Would they be flooded with problems of being seen as "snitches," "crazies," or "manipulators," as opposed to people with a real problem who are engaging in a legitimate effort at problem solving? Having the inmate participate in lieu of a suspended sentence is a possible motivator, but this context raises the specter of blackmail. On the other hand, it might help the offender to justify his program participation and help him to provide a rationale to others as to why he is participating.

Putting aside the possibility of participation as an alternative to a suspended sentence or to punitive custody, what might be "in it" for the participating chronic offender? Most critical, it would seem, is the opportunity provided for the inmate to gain support and recognition of his or her ability to change, a rare commodity within the prison culture in general and for chronic offenders in particular. Another major benefit to the participant would be the chance of solving a difficult problem. Although it is certain that any self-respecting chronic offender will experience a sense of injustice during and following repeated disciplinary encounters, he or she will also perhaps have experienced moments of doubt. We have already suggested that no one — including the chronic problem inmate — is bad, mad, or deviate all of the time. The appeal one could offer such a person, therefore, is one of redemption and escape from a seemingly insoluble dilemma at a time of personal crisis.

Notes

1. The New York prison system had pioneered the use of settings for inmates who were deemed lacking in resilience or adjudged to have "victim attributes." Such settings provide low-pressure social environments but encourage participation in educational and vocational activities.
2. Glaser (1977) thus points out that "those familiar with correctional institutions soon learn that punishment of disobedient inmates tends to be much more extreme in juvenile and youth facilities than in prisons for adults. . . . This attitude develops because stubborn rebelliousness, as an assertion of autonomy and of what is perceived by them as their manly or womanly strength of character, is more common among younger offenders than it is among older ones . . . . Hostility between offenders and criminal justice personnel reaches passionate levels whenever the most actively and compulsively alienated offenders enter into escalating exchanges of hostile gestures with the most actively and compulsively conformist members of the staff" (p. 312).
3. In a New York prison cohort, 3.7 per cent of inmates could be described as "chronic violators," defined as sustaining a rate of eight or more violations over 75 per cent (or more) of their prison careers. The proportion of chronics becomes 5.7 per cent for inmates who have low measured intelligence, 6.3 per cent for prison mental health outpatients, and 7.3 per cent for outpatients with low intelligence. Chronicity translates into a serious management problem in that the 3.7 per cent chronics (who overrepresent short-termers and whose "time at risk" is thus understated), account for 15 per cent of prison violations and 18 per cent of violent infractions committed by the cohort.
4. Glaser (1977) is one of few observers who argues against a pristine conception of discipline. He writes that "a deliberate effort to integrate discipline with counseling is appropriate...discipline rehabilitates inmates providing that the rules become internalized as their personal opinions. Also, habits are best extinguished if they are not merely punished, but if alternative behavior is reinforced by reward" (p. 308). Fox (1958) suggests that "within the system of rewards and punishments, the prison administrator must maintain a treatment center or adjustment center, which is a 'therapeutic community' without the sanctions of reward and punishment which the incorrigible offenders have already demonstrated by their incorrigibility that they are not prepared to take....The custodial personnel who attempt to maintain discipline in a prison must be prepared to understand human behavior, rather than trying to judge the amount of pressure necessary to keep a man in line" (p. 326).

19

The Disturbed Disruptive Inmate*

IF PRISONS had yearbooks, there are inmates who would unquestionably be voted "least likely to succeed." Among convicts who would qualify for this honor is a long-term New York prisoner who had served 13 peripatetic years of a 20-year sentence. By "peripatetic," I mean that the inmate had been frequently transferred or "shuttled." Ed (as we shall call the prisoner) had experienced 30 institutional moves, a career which, in a prison system, is an index of continued unpopularity.

One reason for Ed's singular status becomes clear when one reviews his folder. Ed's disciplinary dossier is horrendously long and variegated. Some of the recorded infractions suggest that Ed may occasionally be disoriented ("out of place," "loitering"), and that he has difficulties adjusting to prison routine. Some of the difficulties may appear simple (Ed is repeatedly late for mess), but others are more obviously complex ("had dirty cell and had burned his blanket and pillow cases"). Ed is responsible for strings of personal attacks against fellow-inmates and sometimes

---

*Reprinted, with permission, from *The Journal of Psychiatry & Law*, Fall 1982. A modified version of this article was presented at the 1982 Conference on Correctional and Forensic Issues at Sam Houston State University.

against guards. Some of these incidents are serious (e.g., "attempted to strangle inmate X"). Similarly serious is a series of suicide attempts and self-mutilation efforts, including an episode in which Ed had cut his own throat.

Twelve of Ed's transfers — approximately one each year — placed him in a residential mental health setting. The first such transfer occurred straight out of prison reception. At the time, Ed was experiencing what was diagnosed as an "acute depressive reaction." In Ed's case, difficulties arose from the bizarre form his so-called "depressive reactions" tended to take. As an example, Ed's disappointment with a Christmas turkey shipment not only included manifestations of despondency, but (according to an officer's report) "he [Ed] put an edible portion of turkey in the garbage can, poured water over his head at 12:00 midnight and swallowed a cigarette butt instead of a pill." Private rituals such as these create disciplinary incidents; tardiness occurs, for example, because "I have to wash up and kiss [his family's photograph] . . . because I respect God and my family." Violence has mystifying origins. An officer is assaulted "because he called me wise guy and cocky;" a fight breaks out when Ed insults a group of black inmates whom he has never met, the day after arriving at a new institution for a predictably short stay.

Other incidents are clear psychotic episodes. A report describes Ed "eating feces from the mess hall toilet;" it notes that he has "burned his hands under boiling water from the faucet" the previous day. Another report describes Ed:

> Screaming without any reason, laughing inappropriately looking at his family pictures and stating that he will kill them, pouring hot water over his body, talking to himself and picking up and moving things back and forth constantly.

Crises arise where such incidents take (as they often do) blatantly destructive or self-destructive turns. The same report continues:

> His condition has become quite critical today, when he started putting his hand in an electric fan, putting his hand in the cigarette lighter socket, burning his hands and arms with cigarettes . . . . threatened to stick his finger in an electric socket while having his foot in a pail of water in his cell.

Outbursts oscillate between attacks on others, such as sleeping fellow-inmates, and attacks on self. The rationale is invariably delusional — for instance, "a voice told me;" "I had the urge to get rid of myself because I had the devil in me;" "the officer [whom Ed assaulted] tried to kill my son — tried to nail me to a cross;" or "I hear voices that [tell me that] my wife and children are dead."

Ed's dilemma, and that of the system, are eloquently described (under the evaluation heading "adjustment in prison") by a prison-employed psychiatrist. The psychiatrist writes:

> Instead of discussing this as Ed's adjustment to prison, one might more appropriately consider this as the Department of Correction's (and Mental Health's) adjustment to Ed. The psychotic episodes were successfully handled by providing hospitalization and/or medication and counseling. Long-term rehabilitation has taken a second place with day-to-day handling being the main consideration. Ed has neither the ability nor the inclination to analyze his own problems and has requested transfers when he could not cope with the pressures of prison life. The transfers were effected

The Disturbed Disruptive Inmate

without any fuss because Ed's desire to move was equaled, if not exceeded by, the institution's desire to get rid of the problem.

No one, however — least of all, Ed — has "gotten rid" of the problem, which we sense may climax in a completed suicide attempt. Ed is not served because he falls between the cracks of management options and because he is a notorious hot potato. More seriously, Ed defies our capacity to understand who and what he is. He is a conceptual Humpty Dumpty separated into two watertight and irreconcilable components: Ed the "mad" component and Ed the "bad" component.

It is paradigmatic that there is increased concern in the prison field about the prevalence of inmate mental health problems (Chapter 14). One hears the topic broached in prison staff interactions ranging from superintendents' meetings to conversations with guards. A federal agency (the National Institute of Corrections, 1982) reports that "during recent . . . Advisory Board hearings, the increase in the number of mentally ill and retarded inmates was identified as a major concern of practitioners." Similar alarm revolves around perceived dramatic increments in prison violence. The impression is that many more inmates have serious adjustment difficulties, and that a "new violence-prone breed" of offender is abroad in the land.

But such difficulties are at least familiar in kind, and in theory at least can be responded to by improving and expanding on what we now do. Such is not the case with composite syndromes such as Ed's — syndromes that combine mental health and adjustment difficulties. Such syndromes of necessity are inappropriately and ineffectively responded to through existing modalities. The composite (disturbed and disruptive) inmate falls between available chairs. He does so because standard responses separately address (mental health or management) problems that are obviously linked. Unsurprisingly, inmates who have disciplinary and mental health problems are notoriously refractory to treatment and their careers through the system are biographies of escalating conflict and suffering. Inmates such as Ed are also at present uncharted and not understood. They mystify peers and staff, inspire fear and aversion, and feelings of impotence based on a sense of our ignorance. Presumptively, the impotence extends to community settings faced with such persons, including criminal justice and mental health settings, neighborhood groups, schools, and families.

Zero-sum diagnoses

As a category, disturbed disruptive inmates (DDIs) have no theoretical standing, and one reason why the combination "disturbed-disruptive" (DD) is a non-concept is because we are often placed in a "forced choice" situation where what someone does must be interpreted as symptomatic of an underlying disturbance or where we must react to it as a responsible exercise of unfettered malevolence. This occurs because symptomatic behavior and premeditated recalcitrance have mutually exclusive implications as to consequence and culpability. Even where the presence of both manifestations is obvious in the same individual, at any given point we may have to categorize one manifestation as relevant and the other as not.

In practice, the disturbed disruptive person tends to be conceptually segmented over time into a "disruptive" person and a "disturbed" person. At one juncture (for instance, when prison staff review the inmate's latest assault on an officer) they must unambiguously class him as disruptive; at a subsequent juncture (such as after the inmate's "voices" have instructed him to hang himself in the disciplinary segregation cell to which his disruptiveness has taken him) they must adjudge him psychotic. To be sure, the segmentation becomes increasingly unstable with chronicity of disturbance and disruptiveness patterns. Such chronicity makes the DDI combination obvious, but invites a second "forced choice" involving selection of the pattern to be regarded as primary in classifying the person. With regard to this choice, the uninviting nature of the person's disruptive behavior reliably overwhelms decisions, and inspires caretakers to classify the person so as to make him primarily the client of other caretakers. This tendency is reinforced by the fact that symptoms of disturbance tend to wax and wane over time.

The competition of rival diagnostic efforts (sometimes referred to as "ping ponging") results in a tendency to shuttle the disruptive disturbed person to mental health settings (invoked by caretakers of disruptive inmates) from which he is returned to mainline disciplinary or custodial settings (by caretakers of the disturbed). This procedure is called "bus therapy," and it reveals pressure to make the "bus stops" as brief as decency permits. In *Corrections* magazine, reporter Wilson noted that:

> Administrators from mental health and corrections agencies will each maintain in theory that they are best qualified to handle the "mad and bad." But in practice, neither wants to deal with him. The frequent result is a brutalizing series of transfers. . . . There are, says Rowen [of the AMA] "problems in both camps. Correctional administrators, wanting to get rid of their bad apples, will ship them off to mental health. And the mental health administrators don't want to monkey around with acting-out clients, so they send them back" (Wilson, 1980, p. 8).

Three prison experts, Freeman, Dinitz, and Conrad (1977), concluded that:

> Neither mental hospitals nor prisons welcome the disturbed and dangerous inmate . . . . The resulting "bus therapy" expresses the reluctance which both kinds of institution feel in contemplation of the burden of this kind of inmate. Until courts and administrators can establish rules to govern the disposition of such inmates their programming will be punctuated by bus movements which are clearly not intended for their benefit (p. 30).

Bus therapy obfuscates the disruptive-disturbed syndrome because the inmate who gets on the bus is labeled disturbed and the one who exits (presumptively after "therapy") is adjudicated disruptive. Such judgments are even made before the person gets on the bus. Recently, an APA *Monitor* reporter claimed that he had been told by a forensic mental health administrator that "corrections officials have sought to use psychologists to control — not necessarily help — prisoners. Prison staff have been known to ask mental health care personnel to get troublemakers committed or given medication . . . . And psychologists have been 'obliged' to honor such requests . . . in order to keep their jobs" (Reveron, 1982, pp. 10-11). The administrator later pointed out that he had been misquoted, but *Corrections* magazine also tells us that "a common criticism by psychiatrists of prison administrators is that they want the doctors to handle the problem cases, which are not always psychiatric problems"

The Disturbed Disruptive Inmate

(Wilson, 1980, p. 14). A prominent clinician (Vicky Agee, 1981), by contrast, recalls that:

> We discovered that Mental Health institutions are for Mentally Healthy patients — not rotten patients, who obviously were not psychotic — but had behavior problems. We drove our disturbed delinquents there — they beat us back — with the diagnosis of "manipulation".... [We] tried to outplay Mental Health at the "Name Game." They won, of course — you can't help but win when you hold all the cards.... Most of the game revolves around the Psychotic versus Character Disorder names.... Character disorders (which I think means anybody who intimidates, messes over, or hurts people) particularly do not belong in hospitals, because they are untreatable.

Such charges are clearly not made out of whole cloth, because "games" such as those referred to by Agee are played on the record. Illustrative is a case I have reviewed of a disruptive and disturbed prisoner who was finally committed after having (1) attempted to hang himself twice in one week, and (2) set fire to his mattress and pajamas (while occupying them). This inmate was returned with the diagnosis "Explosive personality disorder-antisocial personality disorder." Later the same inmate was again committed. The report noted that "he hanged himself last night and was unconscious when he was found." The resulting "trip" was short and unproductive. However, the prison superintendent almost immediately returned the inmate, certifying that "it has been reported to me that this . . . resident's emotional condition is deteriorating. He has remained depressed, despondent and has smeared feces on his body and all over the room. He is reportedly reacting to auditory hallucinations and has had a serious attempt at suicide, by hanging, one hour after his return to prison." Only one week later, the same inmate reappeared with the discharge diagnosis "Antisocial personality disorder 301.70." The following year, he was again institutionalized. This time, the referring staff noted that the inmate was "hearing voices telling him to kill himself — got 'rope' last night but didn't use it. Harassed by other inmates to 'bug out.' " They also reported that:

> In the last two days he has made two suicidal attempts by hanging and set his mattress on fire. He says he is responding to voices telling him to kill himself.... On examination this morning he was smeared with feces, says that he did this to baptize himself since the water in his toilet was turned off.... He has been having difficulty adjusting to the open prison population and has manifested paranoid ideation.

The prison psychiatrist diagnosed the case as one of "paranoid schizophrenia." The hospital psychiatrist (six weeks later) entered "No diagnosis or condition on Axis 1; Antisocial personality disorder."

For most inmates the game is played more honestly and with more integrity, without callousness and risk as embodied in the example. The issue often revolves around remission, or the onset and termination of acute psychotic episodes. Discharges certifying "full remission" are often followed within weeks, days, or hours by renewed manifestations of symptoms. The fact is demonstrable, but it need not reflect on the validity of diagnoses. Among other things, as was pointed out somewhat bluntly to Wilson by an informant, "the mental health system drugs them up . . . gets them sufficiently passive, and sends them back to prison, where they don't give them their medication. Then they decide they have 'regressed,' and they send them back to mental health" (Wilson, 1980, p. 8).

The precise proportion of inmates who experience "bus therapy" is unknown. Equally to-be-established is the assumption that disturbed disruptive inmates are disproportionately subject to expeditious rejection. A disproportion of expedited transfers would be predicted based on (1) the availability to mental health staff of their patient's disciplinary record, which is calculated to inspire caution in any reasonable person; and (2) the tendency, of some DDIs at least, to resist therapeutic ministrations. Less sanguine predictions could be based on the assumption that psychotropic medication levels can be more or less adjusted to neutralize disruptive tendencies. Of course, if medication regimens are deployed as "therapy," it is improbable that lasting change will occur, and shuttling is therefore likely to continue.

Permeable conceptual borders

Failure to recognize the integrity of the DD cluster not only contaminates the understanding and treatment of DDIs, but also affects our view of disruptive nondisturbed and disturbed nondisruptive inmates. Where such inmates are conceptually merged with DDIs the result contains heterogeneous melanges whose attributes are understandably mystifying. For instance, the Mecklenberg Correctional Center (1981), the maxi-maxi-institution of the Virginia Department of Corrections which contains inmates deemed seriously disruptive, records that "twenty-seven per cent of disruptive inmates have been previously committed to a mental health facility for treatment. Of these with prior psychiatric commitments, the average inmate has been committed on 2.12 occasions." Another case in point is provided in an Ohio study of intractable inmates by Myers and Levy (1973), in which intractability is defined as "a chronic disciplinary and adjustment problem within the prison" (p.ii). Myers and Levy discovered, among other things, that "the intractable group had a higher frequency of sick calls (about twice as high), with tension as the primary complaint (22 per cent), and tranquilizers as the primary prescribed medication (44 per cent)" (p. 15). They also noted that "the Psychometric Test results show that the intractable group scored lower on all IQ, grade level, and psychometric aptitude tests," and that "the intractable group had higher scores on the MMPI (Depression) Scale" (p. 16). The psychometric data are particularly revealing. In the distribution of composite IQ scores (Optic and WAIS) the range of scores for the intractable group extended to a bottom score of 52 (compared to low scores of 72 and 77 for the "tractable" group), and the range for revised Beta scores was 47 to 112 for "intractable" inmates and 79 to 121 for the "tractable" group. Such statistics matter a great deal because prison syndromes in which extremely limited intelligence is a prominent feature seem to be disproportionately represented among DDIs.

The admixture of DDIs and disturbed nondisruptive inmates produces problems of similar complexity. One such problem is that diagnoses that (illegitimately) consider disruptiveness as a criterion highlight antisocial (psychopathic, sociopathic) features, which can be discounted as untreatable, and hence as nonpathological. The noninclusion of antisocial personality disturbances helps students such as Monahan

The Disturbed Disruptive Inmate

and Steadman (1983) to arrive at the "cautious conclusion" that "there is no consistent evidence that the true prevalence rate of nonpsychotic mental disorder is higher among inmate populations than among class-matched community populations" (p. 168). Presumptively different exclusion and inclusion criteria permit authorities such as the President's Commission on Mental Health to contrarily infer that "a high percentage of jail and prison inmates (markedly higher than in the nonprison population) are mentally handicapped" (Wilson, 1980, p. 6). This question is among issues that are unlikely to be resolved unless defensible lines are drawn between DDIs and disturbed nondisruptive inmates.

If DDIs are reliably differentiated from other inmates, some but not all of whose attributes they share, patterned differences within behavior dimensions — differences in disciplinary careers and mental health histories — not only can emerge, but are likely to do so. We expect different DD cross-fertilizations, such that a given act (like sleeping under the bed) can be disruptive (it interferes with the mandatory custodial body count) but can be pathologically tinged (it can be designed to ward off delusional danger), nonpathologically motivated (designed to resist surveillance), or ambiguously framed (aimed at ameliorating a psychosomatic backache). The disruptive act that is pathologically motivated (for instance, tearing a bedsheet to produce a rope with which to commit suicide) is as unambiguously disruptive (by destroying "state property") as the same act designed for gain (for pulling contraband from a neighbor's cell), but the quality of the disturbed disruptive act held up to scrutiny will meaningfully differ from that of its nondisturbed counterpart.

Some disruptive behavior patterns, such as cycles of extrapunitive and intrapunitive behavior, are probably most unique to DDI syndromes. Burtch and Ericson (1977) note that "a classic statement of the commingling of homicidal and suicidal impulses was propounded by Sigmund Freud in *Mourning and Melancholia*" (p. 45). The "commingling" may be less than universal, but may aptly characterize a subgroup of syndromes in the DDI population, such as inmate Ed.

Studies of disruptiveness in mental hospitals consistently show that chronic misbehavior is confined to a minority of patients. One study cited by Smith (1979) found that "two per cent of patients accounted for 55 per cent of all violent incidents" (p. 529). A Canadian team surveyed 198 patient assaults, and discovered that "13 per cent (N = 18) of the patients committed 61 per cent of the assaults" (Quinsey, 1977, p. 23). Clearly, disturbed disruptive patients exist in hospitals as in prisons. They exist, however, in small proportions that can be further reduced by chemical straightjacketing to the negligible levels reported in some of the studies (Kalogerakis, 1971).

What is a "syndrome"?

The most critical questions obviously revolve around the psychological link between disturbed and disruptive behavior. Where patterns of disturbance and recalcitrance coexist in the same person, the interconnection is an empirically to-be-investigated issue. Continuity of personality presupposes a connection. Common sense warns against assuming a connection. I have noted elsewhere that:

A schizophrenic who assaults people is a psychotic and is violence-prone. Both facts may diminish the person's popularity, but the combination does not make him a violent psychotic. If the patient obeys voices that tell him to kill, our understanding increases by considering this fact, but in most cases the link between behavior and emotional and cognitive problems is more remote (p. 649).

The point of the comment is not that psychopathology and disruptiveness are unrelated, but that we cannot explain one by referring to the other. A diagnosis is a shorthand label for the person's disturbed behavior; it is not a summary of his disruptive behavior; this makes it unsurprising, for example, that, as Kozol, Boucher, and Garofalo (1973) note, "the terms used in standard psychiatric diagnosis are almost totally irrelevant to the determination of dangerousness" (p.383).[1] The same caution applies in reverse. Disruptiveness — which invites disapproval and provokes anxiety — can obscure a diagnosis of pathology rather than illuminating it.

In exploring DD syndromes, the validity of findings is enhanced by approaching pathology and disruptiveness separately, and then determining what links (if any) can be surfaced where (if) patterns intersect. This calls for reliable criteria for independently diagnosing pathology and disruptiveness, inquiry into differences between DD patterns and non-DD patterns of pathology and disruptiveness, subcategorization of disruptiveness patterns in the DD group, and a search for DD patterns linking disturbance patterns to patterns of disruptiveness.

These links matter. If we are to address the problems and behavior of a disturbed disruptive inmate, it matters whether the inmate's disruptiveness is behavior that is premised on a delusional view of social reality; is a reaction to pressures that are routine for the average inmate but become overwhelming for the handicapped inmate; results from aversive peer reactions to the person's obnoxious symptoms; represents a last-ditch gesture deployed to secure needed support; is a pathetic form of protest against intolerable dependence or represents a failure of precarious self-controls. Surfacing and categorizing such links — and drawing out possible implications they may have for action — should be a high-priority enterprise. And it is not as difficult a challenge as the resistance to it may imply. A few summary examples follow to show that the task of surfacing pathology-disruptiveness links can often be met simply by carefully reviewing the folder.

Four examples

Take the case of George (again, not his real name). George is a large inmate (he weighs over 200 pounds) who is serving a 25-year term. His disciplinary record features a multitude of minor violations (mostly refusals to participate in activities or to obey orders), but there are also more serious incidents. Many of these incidents involve assorted acts of ponderous destructiveness: there is a profusion of notations such as "put his hand through window," "threw a pail of hot water at reporting officer," "threw a lightbulb and books on gallery, banged on the wall with his fists," "cut a square piece of material out of his state blanket," "destroying state sink," "flooded his section with water . . . tore a bible into pieces," "damaged cell door," "broke a glass jar against wall." There are also recorded fights and attacks on fellow-inmates, some pretty ineffectual. (Once, for example, George approached an officer "demanding to have another inmate's cell open so he could get him because he was a rat.'') There are a number of suicide attempts, and several self-protective requests.

Relatively early in his sentence George drank a large quantity of acid; in explaining his motives, George reported that he was being harassed by fellow-inmates, who made reference to "his crime and time to serve." The incident was classed as a psychotic depressive reaction. In another incident George cut his wrist and requested transfer because "he claims some inmates called him a 'rat.'" He later attempted suicide after he was (completely predictably) passed over by the parole board.

There is general agreement in prison about George being "a person of marginal intelligence who has emotional problems," and staff have also discovered that many of George's emotional problems have to do with his inability to digest or handle stress experiences or routine demands. George always withdraws — if he can — from situations that tax him because of their challenge or complexity. If he cannot withdraw, he explodes. He manages simple demands. For example, he likes a "dining hall assignment with strict supervision."

George has been assigned to a special program — a decent therapeutic community — where he remains after two years, generally under medication. Program staff have observed that George is "unable to learn anything except the most concrete concepts, is further unable to synthesize and learn from his experiences and further is generally unable to process logical thinking and subsequently reach productive conclusions." Among other things, George "doesn't really understand how to get along with other people on any more than a basic concrete level, involving exchange of goods and services." As a result, George:

> Has been observed on numerous occasions to involve himself in the trade or transfer of material goods with other inmates.... with the same predictable results. Usually, he very quickly over-extends himself financially, and when he is unable to withstand the pressure of repaying his financial debt or when he is unable to withstand the pressure of the person to whom he is indebted, he ordinarily acts out in some way, [though as] the only significant progress that can be credited to George, [he sometimes] brings his dilemma to the community or to his therapist in place of acting out.

Once George is bailed out—or once he has survived the consequences of ill-advised chronic trading and gambling—he invariably renews his self-defeating financial career, alternating between contriteness, emotional breakdowns, and dramatic explosions of impotent rage. Given no evidence of change, therapeutic staff understandably feel that their program, which is designed to achieve personal impact, is wasted on George. They consequently demand his transfer as often as they can. Unfortunately, no alternative plausible placement comes to anyone's mind.

****

Ben has recently left the state prison system after serving four years of a seven-year sentence. His disciplinary record is studded with preemptive fights and threats against staff. Three months into Ben's term, for example, an entry charges him as follows:

> You were seen with a "large push broom" and you were holding it over your head. You were expounding loud sounds and directed your anger to the employees. You were attempting to incite other inmates to riot and hurt the officers. But before you were able to assault employees, another inmate disarmed you of the broom.

You were ordered to return to your room but refused. Only after additional officers arrived on the scene did you return to your room.... You resisted being pat frisked and handcuffed....

Between such emotionally charged disturbances, other incidents are recorded that have a different quality. Some are self-destructive (entries such as "threatened to cut up — counseled and released," "fire in cell"), but most are self-insulating incidents — they reflect Ben's reluctance to leave his cell for program involvement (notations such as "did not go to gym," "refused to work," "skipped school").

A few weeks prior to the push-broom incident — two months after Ben's entry into the system — he is seen by a psychiatrist, who observes that Ben is "mildly depressed with vague reference to auditory hallucinations." In the interview transcript, Ben is reported as saying that "he could not take the pressure of population in the block [and] expressed fear of the inmates and correction officers around him." But also (insightfully, as it happens) Ben "expressed the desire to be in a set up where there are not too many people around him." Within days, Ben is again observed "depressed, nervous and crying," and on the day prior to the pushbroom incident he is referred:

> Because of an episode of depression during which time he made threats to "kill himself before others do it." Inquiry .... *revealed that he was approached by other inmates in homosexual relationships and felt depressed and anxious about this.* [Emphasis added.]

One week later, Ben's disciplinary record is reviewed with him, and he observes (again, insightfully) "that he [always] felt depressed prior to getting into trouble." The sequence—feeling of pressure and depression leading to explosions—is to repeat itself time after time during Ben's prison stay, including in several self-destructive episodes: the first of these occurs after all of Ben's belongings are stolen by fellow-inmates; in the second, officers "confirmed the staff's opinion that Ben was being pressured ... and that as a result of this pressure he decompensated to the point where he became extremely paranoid and eventually suicidal."

Like George, Ben is kept afloat in prison through placement in a special ameliorative program, with the evidence suggesting (as staff put it) "that if Ben were to be transferred to general population at this time, he would be unable to cope with the pressures of prison life and as a result he would decompensate to the point where he could no longer function." Unfortunately, even special programs have their pressures. Ben therefore indulges in numerous "sudden violent attacks against individuals who he 'thought' were going to hurt him ... though investigation of the incidents failed to reveal any basis in fact to Ben's assumptions that he was being threatened by the man he attacked." Only in complete isolation (keeplock) does Ben's behavior prove exemplary.

In Ben's case, the relationship between his disturbance and disruptiveness is direct; under stress, Ben's tenuous controls give way. As observed by an interviewing psychiatrist, "when Ben is sick, he becomes paranoid and does not get along with people and causes fights."

****

Dave has served eight years of a life sentence, and he has accumulated a long, variegated, and serious disciplinary record. Dave has on numerous occasions been

The Disturbed Disruptive Inmate

seen by prison psychiatrists, who have maintained him — very much at his own request — on psychotropic medication, tranquilizers, and sleeping pills. Dave's psychiatric stock in trade are fear, (demonstrable) anxiety, depression, and (alleged) insomnia. These commodities are systematically used to secure medication, favorable program recommendations, and ameliorations of custody. Dave's level of disturbance is real; in the words of a classification analyst, "he obviously has deep psychological, emotional problems;" a psychiatrist notes, "this man is in a constant anxiety state since his admission to the penal system." But equally real is the flagrant manipulation pattern based on Dave's disturbance — particularly, the threatened risk of completing suicide.

Dave's folder is studded with injunctions to custody by mental health staff, such as "I have notified the security person to keep a close watch on Dave because he may try to hurt himself again;" "this man should be considered a definite suicidal risk . . . . I would suggest to treat him gently and avoid punishment at this stage;" "in view of the inmate's past history of [suicidal behavior] and mental disorder, it seems advisable to the writer not to place this man under undue pressure. Otherwise, it is difficult to predict what this man will do. Moreover, I believe he should be given back his kitchen job . . . one of his major grievances;" and "I feel if at all possible, he should be out of the metal shop, but of course this is up to the assignment board."

There are also notations such as "patient manipulates environment in order to get habit forming drugs;" "he has been on Dalmane for over seven years in other institutions and certainly is addicted to it. I feel this man is manipulating to get Dalmane;" and "diagnostic impression: addiction to Valium and Dalmane;" these notations appear in the folder in the later stages of Dave's career.

Because of Dave's combination of pathology and manipulativeness, he is viewed as a test of prison and mental health staff forbearance. His advent at one assignment (the mess hall) is greeted with the entry "the word has spread far and wide that this man is a creep." The document concludes, "as long as [the] inmate behaves himself in the mess hall, I have no objection to his being there, of course; but once he starts to act up, I probably will recommend that he see the psychiatrist." This sequence, of course, ends with Dave "acting up," seeing the psychiatrist, and again making the best of his chronically bad situation.

****

My last example, Frank, has completed a checkered nine-year prison term, including 18 institutional transfers (five to mental health settings) and 80-plus disciplinary infractions. Upon entry into the system, Frank initiated an impressive sequence of disruptiveness — incidents such as "throwing food at an officer;" "broke bed — used pieces for weapons — smashed light fixture in cell," alternating with incidents of self-insulation. With respect to the latter, there are report entries such as "he refused to come out of his cell today," "the Sgt. informed me that Frank was just standing in the center of his cell;" and "he came up to the desk and mumbled something inaudibly . . . he refused to speak . . . and he left."

Frank's paradoxic flight-fight pattern has been in evidence, in unabated cycles, for nine years. Frank's explosions are so frequent that they include his diagnostic interviews. During one interview Frank is offered an apple (a generous gesture or a projective test borrowed from Genesis?) and "after receiving the apple from the psychiatrist, he washed it in the sink and then quickly turned around and threw it at the facility psychiatrist. Frank then proceeded promptly to slap the facility psychiatrist about his face." Other interviews move from unresponsiveness and incoherence into towering rages.

Frank's explosions have been punctuated with after-hours yelling, throwing and smashing of objects, and persecutory beliefs freely (and loudly) expressed. Such behavior has contributed to Frank's growing unpopularity among peers, as well as among staff. One forgets that the bulk of Frank's time is occupied with episodes of quiet restlessness, muteness, unresponsiveness, and inactivity (including refusals to eat), and reports of quiet hallucinations—such as "voices which tell him, 'Brush your hair.'"

At the expiration of his sentence Frank had to be released. A final entry in Frank's folder reads:

> Frank was discharged (maximum) from prison and did not want to leave the institution. Dr W., the institutional psychiatrist, tried to talk to the inmate and the inmate struck him in the side of the face, knocking his glasses off. Inmate was requested by Department of Corrections personnel to leave the premises on several occasions. He would leave temporarily and kept returning. Eventually . . . . the inmate was arrested for harassment and given 15 days in County Jail.

No happy endings

Frank is admittedly an uninviting client, and so are Ed, George, Ben, and thousands of others who are similarly situated. Such persons are as uninviting when they terrorize school yards and prison yards as when they contaminate neighborhoods or vegetate under medication in hospitals.

The uninvitingness of setting and person, of course, are mutual. We cannot cope with Frank who cannot cope with his world — or at least, with the settings that he disrupts and disturbs. Frank's settings can — within limits — help themselves. They can expel their Franks and Eds and Georges (always with cause and to other settings) or secrete them to neutralize them in in-house places of exile, for statutory terms. These are holding patterns and they are unstably, warily, and uncomfortably sustained.

The Franks and Georges who find their world inhospitable have no recourse. To Ed, Frank, and their peers, social settings are dumping grounds, variations on inhospitality, always painful, uncongenial, mystifying, irritating, and harsh. The options Frank and his peers have are non-options — to alternately lash out and retreat, to fight without hope of winning, and to flee without hope of escaping.

To avoid the dilemma we must suspend our concern with Frank's or Don's obnoxiousness, with the "management problem" Frank or Don presents. The DDI bus must somehow be made to stop. It must stop long enough so that we can resonate to the bankruptcy that underlies the individual's disruptiveness. This means that we must understand his or her cornered explosions as well as the self-insulating efforts we conventionally associate with psychological extremity.

Eventually, we may generate new ameliorative settings and restorative settings for Frank and Ed and Ben. For we must care for the walking wounded, driven to extremes by a despair that transcends and surpasses the range of the familiar — of mental illness in its more passive and congenial manifestations.

20

Managing the Disturbed Disruptive Prisoner[*]

AS NOTED in Chapter 19, to talk about disturbed disruptive inmates is different from talking about disturbed AND disruptive inmates, which suggests that the inmates are blessed with two coinciding but independent attributes, such as brown eyes and flat feet. The notion is that the fact that the prisoners are disruptive is related to the fact that they are disturbed, and that one cannot address their disruptiveness without taking into account their psychological condition. By the same token, it follows that those who minister to the mental health of the prisoners must consider the problems they create for the prison. The management of the inmates should by implication be coordinated and interdisciplinary in nature.

What happens, by contrast, is often a game designed to get the prisoner as rapidly as possible out of one's own corner into that of the opponent. It goes without saying that this does not do much to sweeten the prisoner's disposition, though there are some disturbed persons who benefit from frequent changes of scenery.

Reasons for referring prisoners to other staff are obviously not malevolent, and

---

[*] Paper prepared for delivery at the University of Washington, Department of Corrections Workshop, Seattle, 8 December, 1994.

justifications for doing so are usually impeccable. The prisoners are unsavory, the problems presented are obdurate, and there are job descriptions one can invoke to keep from having to face problems that it is up to others to solve. The most skilled mental health staff can consequently become virtuosos at invoking off-putting diagnoses for inhospitable clients. The diagnosis antisocial personality disturbance is often used because it is almost a synonym for disgusting, unregenerate bum. Moreover, any self-respecting offender qualifies for such a diagnoses. Whatever the medium, the message to be conveyed is that a person who repeatedly engages in destructive conduct is a candidate for disciplinary dispositions and not mental health ministrations. This position is taken even where the behavior looks a trifle exotic, because chronic destructiveness—on the face of it—is more salient than eccentricity.

If the person's behavior is more than a trifle exotic, the name of the game becomes "stabilization," which can be attained in practice with a short period of massive medication, which deletes florid symptomatology. This instantly converts last week's raving psychotic into this week's custodial problem. "In remission" means cured, and over to you, chum.

On the other side of the net in this game we have a divided or ambivalent team. On the one hand there is grousing about the mental health staff's transparent dereliction of their ostensible responsibility—about the fact that disturbed prisoners are returned with disquieting celerity in the same shape in which they left. On the other hand, there is the view that an infraction is an infraction, a serious infraction is a threat, a history of infractions makes one a menace, and there is no point in quibbling about the quaintness or unorthodoxy of one's motives or one's intellectual limitations. Moreover, consistency of punishment translates into consistency of advertised deterrence. Setting fire to one's cell poses extreme danger, and it is behavior that must discouraged at all cost. The harshness of a disposition is a message addressed as much (or more) to prospective firesetters as it is to the perpetrator of the act. One feels that severity must be made commensurate with the danger posed by the offense to make the prospect proportionately discouraging, even if it is inconceivable that someone sane enough to respond to deterrence would burn down his or her cell.

Given multiple infractions followed by multiple punishments, the game reliably escalates. It does so for two reasons: First, one must send the message that a pattern of serious misbehavior is worse than occasional misbehavior. Second, the failure of dispositions to deter infractors raises questions about their efficacy, and suggests that we must move to a higher order of dispositions. If mental health issues have not been raised in relation to disciplinary infractions, we now have a very disgruntled disturbed prisoner sitting in a maxi-maxi prison. And if the prisoner at this stage throws excrement at guards to express his disgruntlement, the last thing on those guards' minds is the precarious state of the prisoner's psyche.

Should questions about a segregated inmate's state of mental health be nonetheless broached, we now face a chicken/egg problem of major proportions. Was the prisoner disturbed when he committed his infractions, and did he stay more or less disturbed thereafter? Did the prisoner deteriorate in response to our ministrations somewhere along the line? Or did he deteriorate and would have deteriorated anyway? There is, of course, a fourth possibility, which is that escalations of punitive arrangements and runaway technology can drive even nondisturbed prisoners—or relatively nondisturbed prisoners—over the edge (Haney, 1993). One envisages the possibility, for example, that an individual who sees himself at war with the system might fall apart when he feels cornered, vanquished and resourceless. It does not help that by the time the prisoner has run out of options, so has the prison.

I don't think we ought to be surprised by the notion that consistent mismatches between a person and the environments in which that person is placed can attenuate the line between mental health and mental nonhealth. In this connection, a category of prisoner about whom I once became concerned is what I called the "wandering Jew," a label that has nothing to do with religious affiliation. My concern was sparked by prisoners who had years before participated in prison disturbances, including some in which officers were held hostage. These prisoners had acquired an unsavory reputation at the time of the incidents in which they had been involved. This reputation had remained inviolate over the years, and followed the inmates into each new setting into which they were transferred, causing them to be regarded with unvarnished reserve and suspicion. The prisoners had long ago run out of prisons in which they could start out with a fresh slate and the benefit of doubt. Some tried to live up to their reputations; others looked anything but dangerous. However, institutional memories are long, and risk assessment is obdurately tied to past behavior. People who have changed may thus never get the chance to prove it.

A similar fate seemed to have befallen some prisoners who had become involved in disputes which had made them unpopular colleagues. In their case, reasons for transfers had to do with the need to separate them from unforgiving enemies who might regard them with hostile intentions. Again, risk estimates were not subject to reality testing, and I can't help wondering how many prisoners continue to live in groundless fear, or are sequestered or transferred *ad seriatim* based on mythology and a touch of delusion.

By this assertion I do not mean to suggest that protection decisions need to be grounded in documented reality. If a person lives in fear that fear must be respected, and a setting that is perceived as a safe haven must be provided, so that one can begin to address the person's feelings of anxiety and helplessness. But this is different from reinforcing and feeding paranoia or playing into personally destructive mythologies. The first order of business is to verify—if possible—whether grudges are alive or defunct. If they are defunct, one ought to document the fact that they are. And where conflicts exist, they ought to be faced; some may lend themselves to mediation. Enemies can confront each other, and one can create opportunities for social learning by having contenders work through their disputes to reach understandings and effect reconciliations.

I have suggested (Chapters 12 and 18) that the genesis of social learning opportunities should be part of any intervention for interrupting the careers of disturbed disruptive prisoners. As I indicated in Chapter 12, a social learning opportunity is a setting in which patterns of behavior of residents are surfaced in detail and studied and confronted, and alternative patterns of behavior are explored and rehearsed—and where this is done using the peer group as a vehicle of change. I mean thereby a process that does not rely on studies of past behavior *per se*, but includes attention to current behavior that reflects, expresses and exemplifies those historical patterns. This implies that the grist of social learning experiences should very much include the individual's own concrete behavior in the here-and-now—his or her behavior at work and in other encounters with prisoners and staff. Social learning is inconceivable if the prisoner lives in segregation and has no encounters with anyone. It is also inconceivable as a didactic enterprise disconnected from program involvements and life in the prison to which the enterprise is appended.

Social learning is not an intellectual exercise, but must have an unfreezing, experiential, emotional component. As a social learner you must not only understand that you keep screwing up, and see how you keep screwing up, but must be sufficiently disgusted with yourself to stop doing what you have been doing. This process requires reliable and sustained feedback and support for change. The change-related support ought to come with rewards for constructive behavior as it starts manifesting itself (Chapter 7).

The basic concern in pattern analysis of behavior is with the question "why"? One of the attributes of patterns of disturbed disruptive behavior is that they are more richly motivated than patterns of disruptive behavior. The reason why disruptive prisoners are referred to mental health staff by custody staff is that the staff don't understand why they do what they do. When a routinely disruptive prisoner assaults another inmate, we say "he enforced a gambling debt" or "he took part in a gang fight," which is a simple explanation. But when a prisoner assaults a fellow prisoner and reports "the devil made me do it" we have difficulties explaining his actions, and feel queasy about him. By contrast, the garden-variety disruptive prisoner's actions strike staff as subserving uncomplicated motives because staff see these actions as volitional exercises designed to achieve rational ends—or at least, ends that are rational for predatory or gang-affiliated prisoners.

Many prison staff strain to avoid facing the richness of prisoners' motives by pretending that their behavior is cold, calculated and volitional where it is not. Self-destructive acts that express back-to-the wall despair are characterized as manipulative or attention-getting gambits contrived to achieve routine tangible benefits. Tantrums that express helplessness are translated into premeditated acts of retaliatory aggression. Such a characterization makes it easier to punish the person for what he has done but keeps us from addressing problems that may undergird his or her behavior.

Where disruptiveness is chronic we can simplify the question "why" by reacting to manifestations of behavior one at a time. We can refrain from inquiring why a man keeps doing what he has been doing, despite the fact that it gets him locked up and/or extends his time in confinement. The closest we come to an overarching explanation is to attribute obduracy to repeated exercises of volition. This becomes an aggravating factor in the dispensation of dispositions rather than grounds for referral to mental health staff.

Pattern-analytic questions arise in all instances in which destructive or self-

Managing the Disturbed Disruptive Prisoner

destructive behavior is repeated over time. This means not only that staff can ask themselves "why" questions about the redundancy of patterns, but that inmates can ask themselves those questions. More significantly, it means that inmates can ask themselves those questions with the help of staff, which can lead to regenerative resolves and changes in behavior.

If the process is repeated with sufficient diligence, staff can acquire a storehouse of knowledge about disruptive behavior. They can become experts in the subject, and train others to be experts. Much of the substance of this training—at least in the short run—can consist of case studies in which the dynamics of disruptiveness of individual inmates is illuminated. Over time, commonalities of patterns are generally discovered, and can be discussed. The same process leads to cumulated knowledge about changes which enable disruptive prisoners to become nondisruptive.

The issues to be faced in pattern analysis not only include those of personal motivation, but also those relating to stimuli that evoke those motivations, i.e., to prison settings. Though some prisoners remain uniformly recalcitrant all of the time, others act out less under some circumstances than in others. Such respites offer clues to motivation, as do situations that seem to increase psychological problems or escalate misbehavior (Chapter 21).

Regime and social climate crucially affect inmates, but even levels of physical stimulation can make a difference. There are schizophrenics who thrive in segregation, though the prevailing wisdom is that such settings invite decompensation. Changes of stimulation can affect prisoners for the better or worse. So can protracted lack of change.

Some inmates are aware of the conditions that set them off or calm them down. Others are oblivious to the fact that they react differently in different situations and similarly in similar situations. There are also staff who assign inmates to settings with limited regard to their past reactions to the same sorts of environments.

Most to the point, correctional environments can be strategically deployed to affect behavior. At minimum, we can speculate about the extent to which a prisoner is ready for a more challenging environment when we test his resilience or coping competence. Conversely, we have to stand ready to extricate prisoners from settings that will pose challenges they are unlikely to meet. We must also assess environmental challenges in deciding how much support from staff the prisoner will require at given junctures.

The management of disturbed disruptive prisoners hinges on the deployment of staff, including mental health and custody staff. The more disturbed the inmate, the richer the staffing level the inmate will require, but without engaging in professional overkill.

The effectiveness of civilian professionals depends in part on their willingness to work in teams with officers. The analogy that comes to mind is that of orchestration, with correction officers functioning as the string section. The invocation of other instruments depends on sonorities to be achieved (with psychiatric brass used sparingly), but the key criterion must be harmony, which requires instruments to play in close and consonant fashion.

And what about thematic content? In managing disruptive prisoners we seek to reduce the level of their disruptiveness; in treating disturbed inmates our goal is to ameliorate symptoms and prevent self-destructive acts. Our concern in approaching disturbed disruptive prisoners, however, must be a composite, interrelated, combinatory one. To reduce disruptiveness, we must address symptoms, which include acting out and self-destructive behavior. In helping inmates as patients, we must consider the harm they do, and are likely to do, to others.

Part Five

Addressing Prison Violence

THE WARDEN of a model reformatory once explained that her prison's fence was designed not to keep prisoners in but intruders out. Because prisons are inaccessible to the public, they lend themselves to mythification. This tendency is magnified with regard to prison violence, which is sensationalized in the media and the public mind (Chapter 21), and romanticized by prison graduates with literary pretentions.

If prison violence were as endemic as some believe, or as cold and deliberate, there would be little we could do to prevent it. But in prisons as elsewhere, violence is perpetrated by some persons in some situations; there are patterns that can be understood and addressed (Chapter 24). Prisoners who commit violence can be studied and worked with (Chapter 23), as can the subcultures (gangs or cliques) which predispose their members to violence (Chapter 22).

Key ingredients of a program that rehabilitates violent offenders ought to include the following: (1) a staff who can model civilized behavior, whom the inmates like and respect; (2) opportunities to arrive at an understanding of one's behavior; (3) chances to work out alternative response patterns which don't include losing one's cool and taking offense at slight provocations, or taking advantage of others; (4) a group culture which prizes the constructive resolution of conflicts; (5) regular analysis of interpersonal behavior (who does what to whom); and (6) support for those who manifest maturity and self-control.

It is also important to attend to the systematic selection of clients who are assigned to a program. Participants have to be sufficiently alike to justify a common approach; they have to get along with each other and with staff—who in turn must be "matched" to the prisoners. As for staff, humanists contend that in selecting one's staff, credentials and professional affiliation are less important than aptitudes and predilections in dealing with others. A correctional agent in particular must be perceptive and empathetic, constructive and fair, with an ability to respond firmly if it is necessary, or compassionately if it is possible.

21

Prison Violence in Perspective*

I HAVE sometimes asked captive audiences for vignettes or scenarios that come to mind when one says "prison violence." Given the classrooms in which I usually pull that sort of stunt, the incidents I obtain tend to be stark, ideologically-tinged caricatures. The vignettes feature villains, and sometimes heroic figures, are very dramatic and gory, and illustrate some point, such as that prisons are no good, or that people who run prisons are no good, or that prisoners are no good. The riots that are described are last-ditch stands of noble revolutionaries, or the predations of savages run savagely amok. Sadistic guards beat principled inmates, or vice versa. Jailed crime overlords commission executions, your standard shiv-in-the-back-in-the-laundry scenario. Gangs square off in the yard, and rapes are commonplace, despite pervasive, encompassing surveillance.

Prison experts can hopefully provide less primitive perspectives based on experiences that are relevant to the problem. But violence experience is statistically rare,

---

*This paper is an expanded version of a presentation at the 1992 Annual Conference of the Howard League, published in *Perspectives on Violence*, edited by Elizabeth E. Stanko (1994). Reprinted by permission of Quartet Books and the Howard League for Penal Reform.

which means that most of us share war stories that are stale and somewhat long in the tooth. Where our storehouse of experience is richer, we have led suspiciously ill-starred lives, or been less-than-innocent bystanders in some of the encounters we describe. The point about prison-violence experience that matters is its unrepresentativeness.[1]

Romanticizing violence

Prison life is not continuously suffused with imminent violence. This fact is hard to accept because it is drab and unexciting. Correction officers like to get up and go to work telling themselves that their lives are at risk and that they are brave. This sounds better than to say, "Here goes another day of handing out towels in a locker room." Prison officials like to make speeches about incipient riots to show how efficient they must be to prevent them. Such speeches are more scintillating than recitals of paper clips one has ordered. Prisoners like talk of violence as a testimonial to the resilience that one needs to negotiate the prison.

In such telling, violence is romanticized and acquires spurious dignity. By contrast, most incidents of violence in prisons are irrational and grubby and pedestrian, and lack panache and drama. Escalations that are apt to lead to bloodshed originate in the silliest issues of most miniscule import. Persons fearful of others strike preemptively at more fearful adversaries. Yet-unshaved children posture and bluff and have their bluffs called. The most non-tough of men act tough until they think they are tough, and believe that others think they are tough. They bridle and fight, and invariably lose, when their mythical toughness is impugned. Disturbed and brittle people explode, lashing at whoever is nearest them.

But violence is as violence does: Blind rage does targeted harm. A rumor in prison can kill me: I may hear that you wish me ill, and take a knife for protection; you take a knife because you hear that I carry a knife. One of us may die, and the other be segregated for life, based on a mythical grievance.

Riots are often food for streamlined legends. Many riots grow serendipitously, like inchoate fungi, but officials who respond to them can play games against make-believe adversaries in command posts with maps on the wall, and portable radios into which they whisper bellicose messages. The adrenaline of riot-combatants can pleasurably flow, and reporters can pretend they are war correspondents. Prisoners can also become excited, but are generally apprehensive, befuddled, mill around looking lost, and wonder what will happen next. Of such stuff, heroes and villains are made, and the tide of corrections can turn.

The tide of sociology can also turn on riots and the effort that is made to make sense of them. But many riots that are available for study are apt not to make obvious sense (unless one reads sense into them) and to be different from each other. Statements that accommodate diverse collective disturbances can read like tautologies (e.g., instability leads to chaos) or sound like they are negotiable: Riots occur when people are oppressed. But riots also occur when people are less oppressed than they were before, due to a revolution of rising expectations. (But do not expectations of prisoners vary over times? Can our next riot be ascribed to decrements in lowered expectations? Or is it possible that some riots can be less functional, and carry less import, than analysts assign them in stimulating retrospects and post mortems?)

Violence lends itself to incestuous games: I romanticize your clumsy encounters, and you dignify mine; I enhance the import of your aggressivity, and earn counterpart stature. It is a no-lose game, but it is ultimately destructive. As an acknowledged inmate gladiator, you gain stature, but spend months in solitary confinement. As a punitive staff member, I become Defender of the Public Order by assigning stiff penalties to your silly explosive outbursts.

I am implying that there is a great deal of fantasy in perceptions of prison. Prisons make ideal arenas for the projection of aggressive urges because they confine persons we envisage as being repositories of runaway impulsivity. We collude to create the dangerous image of prisons. The crime-fighting system magnifies the threat to which it reacts, to earn its disproportionate share of shrinking budgets. The press sensationalizes petty crime to enhance its dwindling readership. Criminals act dangerous, which is better than being the inefficacious vagrants that many criminals are. Clinicians add to the problem by dispensing diagnoses of sociopathy with indecent abandon.

The prison as stereotype

Only occasionally is the farce obvious to inspection, but projections are impervious to glimpses of reality. Ideas for prison reform die, evidence notwithstanding, because the public sticks to satisfyingly titillating stereotypes. An example, a decade ago, was the coeducational prison, which was a promising innovation that invited visions of orgies behind walls. A sample story of those days began with the announcement "A 'Paradise Island' of sex and drugs flourished in the coed . . . State Prison, where some inmates made $24,000 a year running a computer consulting operation from the prison, according to wiretap transcripts. Drugs, sex, liquor and gambling are easily obtainable inside the prison, an institution which was literally run by its inmates." This article went on to say that "the free-for-all atmosphere ended ... when state police shut down the computer, hauled away male inmates and seized a variety of contraband" (*Prison Vice*, 1982).

The raid at issue was awesome. The attacking force was huge, comprising ten officers per inmate. It was "the largest shakedown raid on a prison population in (the state's) history." The historic campaign was launched in the early hours with an army of police on expensive overtime pay. Great secrecy surrounded the operation, except for television stations that had been alerted. The inmates were painfully impressed. One female prisoner reported: "I woke up with this guy's forearm on the back of my neck, pushing my head down, his knee in my back; he yelled, 'All right, don't move' . . . I had on a transparent night top, and a sanitary pad . . . All I saw was these guys with sticks and helmets . . . they could've said, 'Get up, put on your housecoat, come out, put your hands behind your back (for handcuffs),' and I would have complied." Naked and half-naked prisoners were strip-searched by female officers. There was no chance for them to hide the narcotics allegedly flooding the prison. And what was the heralded result? The yield was eleven pills and seven pharmaceutical containers of white powder, none of which proved to be "controlled substances," according to sheepish police investigators (Taylor and McMillan, 1982).

But this did not curb the enthusiasm of the security-conscious officials. The state prison service proclaimed that its action "was really meant to send a tough message to inmates in a loosely run, perhaps out-of-control prison." The state's top prison official went further, and announced that the raid was "a chance to send a very strong message to the criminal community" (*Ibid*). He proceeded to close one of the last model coeducational facilities in the country, noted for advanced vocational and visiting programs, and for a humane, progressive climate.

Machismo and violence

Ironically, coeducational prisons reduced the incidence of prison violence, because they normalized the prison environment. Violence feeds on machismo, which feeds on authoritarian prison regimes and obsessive masculinity concerns of lower-class males (Chapter 22). The subcultural hang-up is exacerbated where entire generations of young men grow up in single (female) parent households and enter economies that don't provide constructive things for men to do.

In prisons, the young male's need to demonstrate competence through toughness is exacerbated as we play cops and robbers with prison deviants. The prison buys into, and reinforces, hypermasculine norms. I would be rich if I had a dollar for every correction officer who advised timid inmates to counter intimidation with shows of force. And it makes matters worse if the prison punishes inmates for the impossibility of calibrating such advice.

The problem includes an all-too-frequent parallel in the subcultural assumptions of keepers and kept, as in warped institutions other than prisons.[2] A nonsubculturally-warped prison, by contrast, would be one that rewards officers who show compassion and sensitivity and excel in responding to problems and concerns of their charges. A nurturing, supportive and regenerative stance in such a prison would be neither sentimental nor silly, because one statement one can make about many offenders is that they demonstrate a fairly consistent incapacity to negotiate life (Zamble and Porporino, 1988; Toch and Adams, 1989), and can therefore stand a great deal of help. Imprisoned offenders need competence-building support, and the fact that the offenders have successfully offended is no counter-argument, because crime is mostly a low-skilled occupation or a no-skill occupation.

Nurturance is also a weapon for undermining violence-related perspectives, which include the offenders' assumptions about the custodial world. The viability of this strategy is testified to by Jimmy Boyle, the "most violent prisoner in Scotland," who described its effects in inimitable prose. Boyle (1977) recalled that upon arrival in the Berlinnie Unit (a therapeutic community setting) "I was *asked* by the screw if I would come around and sort out my personal property with him. I went, and while we opened the parcels containing old clothing he did something that to him was so natural but to me was something that had never been done before. He turned to me and handed me a pair of scissors and asked me to cut open some of them. He then went about his business. I was absolutely stunned" (p. 230). A second guard Boyle encountered made matters worse by giving him a cup of coffee that he berated himself for accepting (p. 231). He mused that "it was strange during this period because there was a great amount of hatred in me for all screws, yet some of the unit staff would approach me in a way that was so natural and innocent it made it difficult to tell them to fuck off. Something inside me, in spite of the pent-up hatred, would tell me that there was something genuine within them. I knew I didn't really want to recognize this part of the screws. I preferred to see them all as bastards, this would have been so much easier for me" (p. 37).

There is no percentage in making things "easier" for guard-hating convicts if one can disconfirm their preconceptions without being foolish. No one would argue that an officer should have given Boyle a pair of scissors if he was enraged and loudly protesting his transfer to the unit. Screws must engage in screw-like behavior when occasions call for it. But endemic paranoia is self-confirming, and wasteful.

Concerns about security

I recall a conference in a warden's office that was disrupted by a call from the reception area of the prison. A desk officer requested—and received—backing for his refusal to let a teacher bring a geranium to brighten her dingy office. The executive team of the prison (who had sounded like a group of flaming liberals minutes earlier) unanimously opined that flower pots made good repositories for weapons. They cited a regulation that proscribed vegetation in correctional facilities. There indeed is such a regulation. But there is also a tier in the high-security prison for women in the same state with a table that is covered with house plants. The inmates on the tier lovingly tend these plants, trying to convince them to grow. The person in charge of the prison and her staff regularly admire the valiant efforts of the inmates and the plants. Any prisoner attempting to bury a knife in a flower pot would be lynched by her peers for treasonous behavior. (If nothing else, a knife could damage the roots of the plant.)

My point is not to downgrade a concern about the proliferation of weapons in prison, but to suggest that disproportionate and obsessive concerns with security invite counterpart measures of evasion, and unnecessarily diminish the quality of life. No inmate I have talked with has ever said to me, "I needed a weapon but was unable to secure one." Endless ingenuity is exercised by prisoners to protect themselves against other prisoners. The solution to this problem is not comprehensive surveillance, which is physically unattainable except in concentration camps. The solution lies in short-term efforts to provide sanctuary and mediation, and longer-term emphasis on community-building in institutions.

I am not unmindful as I write this statement about security of the fact that I could be accused of ignoring the threats that some predatory individuals pose to the prison community. I do not wish to minimize this problem; I not only know that a few disproportionately do violence to the many, but have spent time with such individuals reviewing their careers in blood-curdling detail (Toch, 1969). It is in part because I have this experience that I am not sanguine about saturation approaches that promiscuously target the problem. I suspect the last thing we want to do is to declare war— to treat the inmate population-at-large, including would-be victims of aggression, as potential aggressors, or make ourselves inhospitable to requests for assistance. We must deprive predators of allies—either active allies or passive allies who stand by while the predator predates, and who could not conceive of crossing inmate-staff lines to discourage victimization.

Building community

One reason I have mentioned the word "community," despite its admittedly mushy connotation, is that it denotes the climate that one would need to generate fellow-feeling among prisoners and open lines of communication between prisoners and staff, such that the battle against victimization can be joined.

Prisoners must feel comfortable about sharing information with staff about what is happening to them. In a cops-and-robbers atmosphere this cannot be done. One can talk to a protector but not to an enforcer who contaminates one's relationship and makes it suspect. No prisoner (nor anyone else, for that matter) wants to "fink," "sneak," "grass," "rat" or "inform," but officers who see themselves as crime fighters develop cop-informer relationships with inmates. The precedent such officers set casts a pale of suspicion over any prisoner who talks to an officer about prison-related events. This suspicion is reinforced by the fact that victims may seek protection, which is also accorded to suspected informants. Moreover, victims tend to be low-prestige inmates, who are inviting targets of rumor-spreading.

Security-conscious staff press prisoners to identify aggressors, and the aggressors then become candidates for sanctions. This makes the distinction between seeking assistance and informing quite evanescent. But none of this needs to happen. Hypothetically, an officer could take an aggressor aside and ask him whether he wants other inmates to help him with his propensity to pick on people smaller than himself, or whether he needs assistance to overcome his homosexual predilections. The officer could offer to secure assistance from a bully's mother, or could consult a group of prosocial prisoners about ways of discouraging predatory behavior short of lynching the bully. The point of these examples is to suggest that different reward systems for prison officers, and innovative training for them (including seminars that focus on incidents in their institutions that they can relate to), can encourage the sort of behavior in which ingenuity is used to find ways to discourage aggressors and assist targets of aggression.

Enriched options become available in enriched settings, where community-building has occurred. The officers in such a setting can encourage a victim to call a community meeting in which the aggressor can be confronted. The officers can evolve and play roles that transcend custodial roles, to the benefit of inmates and themselves (Briggs, 1973).[3] Enriched settings can also take on regenerative tasks of the kind that used to be called "therapeutic" — as in "therapeutic community" (Jones, 1962; Toch, 1980; Chapter 18).

The last implementation effort of this kind that I remember, however, fizzled out after a promising start (Chapter 28). The prison system supported the effort, but was unable to find the living-program space a self-contained unit requires. One point worth mentioning in this regard is that this aborted intervention was cheered on univocally by the disciplinarians in the system, staff members who send inmates to segregation units and work in the units. These staff members were frustrated by the fact that they have to run a turnstile operation for a few individuals who spend their sentences segregated "on the installment plan," as the staff members put it. The dilemma, as seen by the staff members, is that there is no recourse except to use the disciplinary system to address problems that are not thereby resolved. To not use the disciplinary system in this way means to ignore (or to seem to ignore) acts of violence. It also means that fairness can become an issue if discretion is invoked to accommodate inmates with emotional problems. Prisoners have to be locked up, even if they keep returning to segregation, or become commuters between mental health settings and punishment cells (Chapter 19).

The intervention plan that fizzled would have asked inmate-aggressors to consider the program as an alternative to the punitive segregation career on which they had embarked (Chapter 18). The inmates to be invited were repeaters who had first-hand evidence that their patterns of behavior were not "working," which gave them an incentive to try something else. The hope was that they might like the opportunity to learn more about themselves, and be part of an experiment that might accomplish something worthwhile.

When a prisoner is faced with learning in prison it involves a trade-off between the devil, a known deprivation of freedom, and the sea, which offers hope and unfathomable danger. I empathize with the difficulties of making such a choice. But it is the sort of choice victims of violence in prison must make every day, when they accept stimulus deprivation to obtain their margin of safety.

Learning from violence

A recent newspaper account tells the story of an inmate who elected a rigorous three-month military camp regime as an alternative to a three-year prison term. The choice was reasonable, and many other inmates have made it. But some persons—including the young man at issue—cannot tolerate the control and authority that is imposed by the program. In this case (mercifully, one of few), the result was a tragedy.

The inmate entered the program on a Friday and faced the test of his resilience on a Monday. He encountered the uncompromising military regime, exploded with indignant anger, and ended up in a towering rage. The newspaper account notes that he "had been yelling at guards in the mess hall and was ordered to take his dinner tray outside and eat his meal in the yard." "It was supposed to give him time to cool down," a prison spokesman said. "But apparently he wasn't cooling down." In fact, the inmate was working himself up into a tantrum-like condition in which he assaulted prison officers who emerged from the dining hall. He died as apprehensive officers attempted to immobilize and handcuff him face-down on the ground (Germain, 1992).

The incident was placed under scrutiny to ascertain if officers had overreacted in the way they subdued the inmate, since it is customary to parcel out culpability when a tragedy occurs. But reviews of emotionally charged events seldom accommodate the raw emotion—in this case the uncontrolled rage of the inmate and the panic of the officers facing the rage—of the encounters in question.

One can argue that a tragedy is wasted unless one can learn from it, and I think that what one learns can transcend the holds one should have used in handcuffing a person. One must ask about the unfolding of the incident. What initially set the man off? How did his anger escalate and run out of control? Could any miscommunications have occurred? If officers did not understand the inmate (or vice-versa) were these mistakes compounded by further misunderstanding? Did the man signal distress before it turned to serious anger? Did he seem to feel unattended to, disrespected, hurt, discriminated against, crowded, insulted, unfairly dealt with? How did he express initial disgruntlement, and who did what in return? How did the man perceive the "time out" intervention? As he saw it, did it compound his grievance? Did he seem to feel exiled, or contemptuously dealt with?

How did other inmates and staff perceive the inmate during the incident? Did they see him losing control? Did they see him nursing a grievance? Did they see him as irrational? Did they ignore the content of his message (other than hostility), by centering on the form the message took? How much hold did they think the inmate had over his feelings? Did they appreciate the extent of his agitation? How were the inmate's final actions interpreted? Did he look dangerous to inmates and staff? What was the magnitude of the threat perceived at this juncture?

One can reconstruct the situation further, tracking the young prisoner through his last day, or his arrival at the institution. Such reconstruction is called a "psychological autopsy" (Toch, 1992). It permits one to ask questions that transcend the incident and the person. One thing staff members of the camp would want to know is: Are there program candidates (manic depressive individuals, for example) who should not be accepted in the program because they might not tolerate it? Does one need new lead-ins or orientation to ease entry into the program for some inmates? Could "time out" be differently framed or introduced? What can one learn from this experience about the management of anger and the expression of anger? Must a discipline-centered program engender anger, and cause anger-control problems for its participants? What about the preludes to explosive episodes—the catalytic experiences that initiate them? What about cues and danger signals, and what do we do when we see them?

Such learning can be afforded to staff in groups, or to inmate-staff task forces. A militaristic regime can especially benefit from the latter: Inmates can be told, in effect, "we use discipline because we think it will do you good. But we respect you and are concerned about not doing you harm. We value your thinking, though we remain uncompromising about activities we demand you undertake." Shared experiences can humanize any disciplinary settings in which mental health-related episodes upset other segregated inmates. Information that helps inmate-spectators digest traumatic events can go a long way toward preventing rumors, such as the sort of "screws-beat-the-guy-in-the-next-cell-to-death" rumor that frequently precipitates riots.

On the whole, few officers in prisons injure inmates unless officers and inmates are in an agitated state and situations run out of control. This is not to imply that one can condone or excuse violence by anyone against anyone in the prison, whether officer or inmate. But it is a truism that blaming and exculpating is best done once we understand what has occurred. If we blame a person for a caricature of what he or she has done, our message to the person is lost, and he or she cannot profit by it. The reasons given to inmates for punishing them are thus critical. It is important not to add insult to injury: It is one thing to say, "we recognize you felt cornered and helpless when you set your cell on fire, but you expressed your helplessness in a life-threatening fashion." It is quite another thing to say, "we discourage prisoners from setting fires," implying premeditated arson by the inmate. It costs nothing to tell an inmate that one knows he reacted in fear, in defense of pride or in response to perceived injury. It helps the inmate to see himself punished for what he has done. The inmate is not told, "we don't care whether people threaten or insult you." He hears, "we know you were provoked, but we think you handled the provocation in a way that is unacceptable. Violence does not solve problems such as yours." We hope the inmate hears, "violence does not solve any problems," which assumes a consistent message.

The message applies to officers' violence as well. Such violence cannot ever be accepted, but must not be reacted to in a way that permits officers to dismiss the message. If we say, "we know very well that the riot experience was painful to you, building your resentment to the boiling point," we can then say, "you were obligated to control those feelings and not act on them when the riot was over." The correction officer may feel that we have asked him to do the impossible, but he knows that his behavior is at issue. He cannot say, "They are describing a sadistic bully, which is not what I am. It proves that they hate all officers and are subjecting us to arbitrary discipline."

Effective action and accurate knowledge must go hand in hand. Violent behavior has to be curbed, in prisons and elsewhere, based on understanding of violence. Such understanding must not downgrade provocations to violence nor assign them justificatory import. The task is to teach aggressors that there are other ways to respond to frustrations and provocations and affronts, and that these ways are more mature, civilized, constructive and effective. The point that aggressors must understand is that violence is not merely punished, but that it does not solve the problems to which it ostensibly responds.

Notes

1. In 1990 in the US a total of 65 prisoners were killed by other prisoners. The average daily census for the American prison population in 1990 was 690,771. An inmate's chance of getting killed by another inmate during an average day in prison was 1 in 4,000,000. The prison suicide rate for 1990 was double the inmate homicide rate. Some 1,500 inmates (1,462) died of disease—one-third from AIDS. Clearly, health problems in prison (among other problems) are more worrisome in terms of prevalence than violence problems.
2. An interesting contention is that of a subcultural affinity between prisons and fashionable boarding schools. Mortimer (1983), for example, has one of his characters proclaim, "When a chap's been to Lawnhurst, Mr. Rumpole, he can't really feel afraid of prison" (p. 131). Morton describes a school-inmate normative system he refers to as "The Code."
3. In the United Kingdom, experiments include enriched units in Scotland, and at Grendon Underwood and Wormwood Scrubs.

22

Hypermasculinity and Prison Violence*

IN A RECENT book, Victor Hassine (1996), a long-term prison denizen, described what he called the "Inmate's Dilemma." He writes that:

> In the life of an inmate, if you catch someone stealing from you, you're compelled to deal with it physically . . . If someone steals from you and you decide to report him to the guards, all that will happen is that the thief will go to the Hole for a while. Soon he'll be back in population and ready to seek revenge. Revenge in prison can take place years after its initiation. It generally occurs when you are vulnerable and the avenger happens to be around. This reality will leave you constantly looking over your shoulder. Additionally, involving the guards will get you the reputation as a "snitch," which means you will be physically challenged by inmates seeking to make a reputation or pass their own "snitch" label onto you.
>
> If you choose to ignore the theft, the man will steal from you again and tell his friends, who in turn will also steal from you. Eventually, you will be challenged for more than just minor belongings (p.23).

---

*This chapter was prepared for *Masculinities and Violence*, edited by L.H.Bowker (Sage Publications, in press). Used here by permission of the editor.

The passage illustrates a number of subcultural attributes of prison violence. It points to the fact that male inmates subscribe to a normative system which holds that under certain circumstances a prisoner must respond with physical force. The prisoner must particularly do so if he is slighted, affronted or taken advantage of. Securing help is ruled out, as is the alternative of overlooking the slights or affronts or victimization to which one has been subjected. This fact is related to another shared assumption about prison violence, which is that failure to take action justifies future victimization. In prisons, vulnerability attracts predation and fear invites exploitation; such rules are accepted as givens by the prisoners.

To the extent to which a male officer subculture exists in prisons, some of its norms feature counterpart beliefs to those of inmates. One such assumption, for example, is that assaultive prisoners must be "taught a lesson." A 1996 report about the New York detention system, for example, suggested that "tenets of street justice—revenge, retaliation, establishing dominance—appear to guide the behavior of at least some correction officers" (Purdy, 1996). Documents detailing retaliatory incidents in jails "[suggested] that the prisoners had been injured in accidents, such as falling over furniture" (*Ibid*). A local officer union president defended the judicious use of such force:

> "We just don't go in there and beat the crap out of someone just to establish control," he said. But he said "The atmosphere is a jungle type atmosphere, it's survival" and when an officer is hit by an inmate "You have a right to defend yourself by punching him or grabbing him."

Punching is a fairly common response. Internal jail records, written by jail officers, show that in one incident, an inmate in the disciplinary area approached an officer "with clutched fists" and in response, the officer "punched the inmate several times in the face." Two weeks later, an inmate "verbally threatened and then pushed" an officer who then "responded with punches to the face and body" (*Ibid*).

The same logic as that used by officers extends to retaliatory prisoner assaults on staff. In one New York incident, for example, "an inmate sliced two guards with a razor blade" (Gurnett, 1996). The prisoner felt affronted when he was removed from a kitchen assignment following a fight, and he generated sympathy from peers. Thus, "while officers were escorting the inmate back to his cell, another prisoner apparently slipped him a blade" (*Ibid*). The friend who armed the perpetrator in this incident had seemingly decided that the humiliating experience to which his colleague was being subjected called for physical redress.

Violence and a culture of masculinity

Themes such as these subcultural themes are explicitly and self-consciously associated with masculinity in the minds of prisoners and staff. Worthy men are presumed to defend their honor when it is assailed or impugned; they are obligated to "take care of their problems" and they are expected to deter victimization through demonstrations of pugnaciousness. Affronted men are expected to persevere in the face of odds (such as those in the last example) and to take uninviting risks. Unworthy (and by implication, feminine) men are by contrast liable to ignore affronts, to show apprehensiveness when in danger, to admit helplessness and to seek assistance. Since they show themselves incapable of physical retaliation when the occasion calls for it, this demonstration of incapacity justifies their victimization.

In cultures of masculinity, the demonstrated willingness to fight and the capacity for combat are measures of worth and of self-worth. One could cite a number of explanations for this across-the-board fact. The most basic explanation is anthropologico-historical (or historico-anthropological), and has to do with gender roles and obligations in primitive societies. It would follow, for example, that hunters and defenders of villages should gain self-esteem from demonstrations of prowess at hunting and defending.

Such assumptions leave open the question of why modern man would follow in his ancestral footsteps, given that he can now obtain food neatly packaged, and that his spouse may do most of the obtaining. It is obvious that gender-related socialization can be the means whereby male investments are preserved, but that women may also feel continued investments in male aggressivity.

Subcultures of masculinity and violence

The shaping of gender-related attitudes is most explicit in single-sex peer groups such as fraternities, locker rooms and gangs, including delinquent gangs. In such settings the indices of esteem and self-esteem tend to coincide. The rowdiest fraternity men and toughest delinquents become heroic figures and role models for others to emulate. Caricatures of maleness are consensually touted, and (sometimes fraudulently) advertised. Credible (or even incredible) achievements in physical combat and sexual conquest are rewarded with status, esteem and collective admiration.

In the case of predelinquents or precocious delinquents single-sex peer groups emerge early in preadolescence, and to great effect among boys least likely to experience a rich homelife and a budding scholastic career. These descriptive facts relate to the form and the content of single-sex peer influence. The form—the salience of peer esteem as a criterion of self-esteem—can derive from the fact that the group fills a vacuum, that peers are substitutes for the adult support which is absent, unwelcome, or both. The content of the normative system can evolve as a way of dealing with abject failure implicit in the sacrifice, unavailability or unachievability of conventional prestigious and satisfying goals (such as becoming school valedictorian). In other words, the emphasis on what can be easily achieved—such as stealing someone's lunch money—compensates for what is out of reach. As a bonus, the indices of esteem that evolve are calculated to offend authorities and adults who impugn one's self-esteem (Cohen, 1955).

The genesis of the male prisoner culture

Early books on prisons used words such as "importation," "deprivation," and "mixed model" in explaining how salient themes of the prisoner culture had evolved. The word "mixed" was of course a meaningless word unless one first understood what was meant by importation and deprivation.

Hypermasculinity and prison violence

Deprivation theorists pointed out that prisons offer a quality of life redolent with restrictions, frustrations and affronts to self-esteem. They noted that some of the attributes of the prison environment are pettily circumscribing and gratuitously demeaning, and that others are reminiscent of the way children are treated by indifferent or suspicious adults. They reasoned that this fate of "deprivation" shared by all prisoners to varying degrees must be accommodated by adjustments that enable prisoners to salvage some semblance of pride and dignity, to the extent that the situation might permit. In the prisoner culture—as in the case of gangs—indigenous indices of esteem would need to be shared and would have to be immune from encroachment. In lieu of the respect and self-respect lost through imprisonment, status would have to be attained among peers and imperviousness or autonomy from staff (Sykes, 1965, Clemmer, 1940, Goffman, 1961).

Both goals could be reached through displays of manly virtues. Imperviousness calls for stolidity, aloofness and a John Wayne or Clint Eastwood facade. Status calls for demonstrations of bravery or fearlessness, toughness, physical prowess, and loyalty to one's kind. It is not coincidental in this connection that prisons have been single-sex and predominantly male. Indices of inmate esteem and self-esteem would thus gravitate toward norms of the sort that evolve in all-male groups—in other words, toward caricatures of masculinity. (In female prisons subcultures would evolve caricatures of femininity, which lie beyond the scope of this chapter.)

The fact that the male prisoner cultures resemble other male cultures that accentuated masculinity norms suggested that pre-imprisonment concerns and experiences could affect reactions to deprivation. The term "importation" was coined to describe differences in the prison adjustment of different groups of prisoners, consonant with the way these groups had adjusted to life before coming to prison (Irwin and Cressey, 1962; Irwin, 1970). In most instances this meant that the outlooks and habits of the prisoners could vary with the way they went about the business of coping or offending in civilian life. The carry-over extended to young men who had grown up in reformatories, and had evolved extreme subcultural orientations. There were also groups such as gang members who had brought the norms of delinquent gangs into the prison.

Reformatory graduates—or "state-raised youths" as they were called (by Irwin, 1970)—would prove especially problematic and troublesome. Such youths would approach peers with a dog-eat-dog perspective, testing for vulnerability and fears they could exploit. They would dwell on the threat of rape, have no sense of fair play, and perpetrate violence in groups. Gang members similarly would have a proclivity for group-based aggression and would engage in illicit pursuits (such as drug trading) that carried the potential of violence.

The youngest offenders were most prone to violent encounters with fellow-inmates, to be disproportionately resistant to authority, and sensitive to "disrespect" from prison staff. This chip-on-the-shoulder stance would increase the probability of incidents of conflict between officers and prisoners. Counterpart sentiments among younger staff (such as, "never take guff from a convict") similarly increased this probability.

The hypermasculine world view

The perspective of young prisoners—and of some young officers—neatly conforms to the stance of hypermasculinity described in the psychological literature. The state-raised youth especially resembles the psychologists' portrait of the so-called "macho man" (Mosher and Tompkins, 1988):

> Head held high, daring anyone to match his bravery, toughness, and callousness, the young macho celebrates his pride and arrogant contempt for the weak and submissive inferior. Like any warrior, he assumes power, pride, and glory as his entitlement; the vanquished reap the fear, distress, and shame that once was his.
>
> Intolerant of any ambiguity in the dichotomous classification mandated by the criterion of his ideals, he understands the world is divided into the strong and the weak, the masculine and the feminine, the emotionally callous and those who weep, the proud and the shamed, the brave and the cowardly, the excitement-seekers and those basking in safe and dubious enjoyment. He understands; his ideology of machismo tells him so (p. 69).

The ideology of hypermasculinity illuminates an important theme in prison violence, which is that the fearful—those showing apprehension—are inviting targets of predation. Two objectives can be achieved when one assaults a man who is fearful: (1) one shows contempt for the man's demeaning "femininity" while (2) one reassures oneself that one is different (i.e., nonfearful) from one's target. As Mosher and Tompkins (1988) point out, "fear is a deadly affect for successful warfare, being the most serious enemy within. It is assigned to the enemies to be defeated.... A man must not weep, but rather make his enemy cry out in surrender" (p. 63).

While Real Men are never supposed to show fear, or any other "unmanly" emotion (such as mushy compassion), violence allows for the display of feelings such as retaliatory rage. In the words of Mosher and Tompkins (1988):

> The "inferior feminine" emotion of distress is, thus, transformed into the "manly" emotion of anger. The rule becomes: "Big boys don't cry, they have temper tantrums"... The rules of the script are liable to be nonconscious, but, if conscious, the rules might be, "Don't cry, be tough, have contempt for those who cry" and "Don't cry, get mad, and make them cry instead" (p.67).

In the hypermasculine world, character contests occur in which status is conferred on those who best live up to the prescriptions of the masculine script. This frequently entails systematic peer "testing" of bravery and willingness to engage in combat when one is affronted or threatened:

> Gaining admission to a male peer group in a subculture of macho youths requires fighting your way in. A place in the pecking order is pugilistically promoted. You have to have "heart."...
>
> Although victory is sought, it is more important to demonstrate courage and toughness through the willingness to fight (*ibid.*, p.72).

New prisoners are especially subjected to hypermasculine character contests, and these create scenarios such as the "Prisoner's Dilemma" described by Hassine. Gresham Sykes, in his classic *The Society of Captives*, points to a Catch 22 aspect of

these contests which makes the prison world perpetually unsafe. He writes:
> An important aspect of this disturbing problematical world is the fact that the inmate is acutely aware that sooner or later he will be "tested"—that someone will "push" him to see how far they can go and that he must be prepared to fight for the safety of his person and his possessions. If he should fail, he will thereafter be an object of contempt, constantly in danger of being attacked by other inmates who view him as an obvious victim, as a man who cannot or will not defend his rights. And yet if he succeeds, he may well become a target for the prisoner who wishes to prove himself, who seeks to enhance his own prestige by defeating the man with a reputation for toughness (Sykes, 1965, pp. 77-78).

Violence and the hypermasculine life cycle

Hypermasculinity and violence reach their zenith at relatively young ages, and research suggests that both behaviors nowadays tend to reach their statistical peaks much earlier than they did in the past (Blumstein, 1995). But sooner or later hypermasculine men must age, and must face their decreased capacity and propensity for violence. This process of aging, according to Mosher and Tompkins (1988), creates reliable and lawful transitions in the perspectives or scripts of hypermasculine men. These transitions have particular relevance for the long-term prisoners, who face an average of ten to fifteen years in confinement.

Mosher and Tompkins see the young hypermasculine man following a *counteractive script*. Counteraction means that "challenges by male adversaries require escalating violence to be more manly ... The rule: escalate anger, daring, callousness until dominance is established" (p. 79). "Experiencing the invulnerability of youth, the young macho relies on his strength, dominance, toughness, callousness, aggressiveness, violence, virility and physicality" (p. 80).

But "as physicality declines, ... the macho man becomes vulnerable to the shameful discovery that he is not as fearless and as free of distress as he has claimed" (p. 81). This discovery, according to Mosher and Tompkins, leads to the *defensive script*, "which is often a substance-abusing script. Alcohol and other drugs are simultaneously 'manly,' and excuses for the 'unmanly.'" But unwanted unmanly (or feminine) feelings can be experienced by the macho man when he is not anesthetized, and lead to states of depression, pessimism and hopelessness.

One result can be fantasy, in which the man "believes that he can save the meaning of his life by heroically losing it" (p. 81). Such fantasies culminate in what Mosher and Tompkins call the *pseudo-reparative script*, embodied by the motto "death before dishonor." The script presupposes some variation on the "hero's death," which "can rescue a failing macho and transform the meaning of his life from failure-at-living to that of a *real man*. Songs will be sung around the campfire, myths bear tribute to his courage and stoic acceptance of his manly fate" (p. 82).

The enactment of one such scenario is described in a *New York Times* article about Clinton Prison in upstate New York (Purdy, 1995). The inmate in question had spent many turbulant years in confinement, where he had proved exceedingly troublesome. The incident at issue had been videotaped:

The inmate... refused to leave his cell, and officers wearing gas masks can be seen on the videotape spraying tear gas, and then hitting his hands with batons and riot shields to break his grip on the bars. The videotape shows him being driven across the prison yard to the hospital, held down in the back of a station wagon by an officer's legs. When he yells out, an officer is seen wrenching his head back and holding his hand over his mouth. At the hospital, the officers stripped him naked and put him in a shower. He was then put face down on the floor, wet and naked, with his hands cuffed behind his back, his feet shackled and an officer's knee pressed against his back. On the videotape, he continuously yelled, "My name is Felix George. They're going to kill me." He then shouted his prison identification number. After his injuries were treated at the hospital he was left alone and naked in a cell.

Three days later, he was found dead, toilet paper stuffed in his mouth and up his nostrils. An independent board of doctors has ruled his death a suicide.

Addressing violence in the prison

Mosher and Tompkins suggest that hypermasculine men who approach maturity may be ripe for interventions that enable them to discover that "inferior, feminine affects are rewarding and acceptable," and lead them "to consider the rules for how to be a man—a *mensch*—without being a macho man" (p. 82). The task may be daunting, but becomes less daunting over time, with the demonstrated failure of the hypermasculine approach to life in general, and prison life in particular.

Mosher and Tompkins see the outcome of change in the aging macho as a *reparative script*, which "would require the macho to embrace life, and, thus, to embrace the culturally proscribed feminine gender script." The implication of this prescription is that:

> To integrate a truly reparative script, the macho must question his identity and ideology and magnify the suppressed affects here-to-fore pejoratively assigned as "inferior and feminine." The longed for loving, pacific, relaxed communion with "inferior, emotional" fellow humans can indeed be reparative of the macho script (p. 82).

Bo Lozoff, an ex-offender who operates a prisoner assistance program, has written that the macho convict code has become a "cowardly rule of silence" which is inhumane and should be supplanted by a humanistic code (Lozoff, 1995, p. 32). He writes that "a new convict code must be an ideal that speaks to the best in us rather than the worst . . . If conformist life on the streets has become 'Use people and love things,' then the convict code should proclaim, 'Use things and love people,' and prison life should be an example of it. . . . We need a code that allows people the maximum opportunity to become human beings, not one which keeps us and them stuck in the worst parts of ourselves and our past" (p. 70).

Such ruminations, in relation to prisons and prisoners, sound utopian. But in corrections hypermasculinity is a recipe for no-win stalemates. Solitary confinement for young prisoners becomes draconian over time. The punishing experience engenders bitterness and cements recalcitrance.

Hypermasculine men occupy segregation cells long after their aggressivity is attenuated and their reputation still deserved. However, their conceptions of integrity force such prisoners to stage displays of hollow, unconvincing rage. Their counterparts—the guards—follow repressive scripts that become similarly autonomous. Hypermasculine nightmares evolve in the shape of indefinite segregation in super-maximum or "maxi-maxi" confinement settings. In such settings there is often no human contact between captors and captives, and no escape from destructive and self-destructive games (Haney, 1993).

But de-escalation is theoretically possible, as is reparation of the sort that Mosher and Tompkins prescribe. Experiments that neatly fit the bill have been carried out in the Scottish Prison Service, starting with a pioneer effort (the Berlinnie Unit) in 1973. Long-term segregees are placed into intensive, community-centered treatment settings, in which staff work closely and intimately with the prisoners. The object becomes to prepare the inmates to recapture their humanity and to rejoin the prison mainstream.

The work is staff-intensive, and it is costly, because much damage has to be undone. But salvaging human beings who would otherwise be lost, and who would often stay segregated for life, makes the investment defensible and worthwhile. Reparative work also can be a stimulus for innovativeness. There are training benefits in working in such programs, and there is much to be learned in the process.

At earlier stages of the hypermasculine career, the challenge lies in preventing the evolution of obdurate subcultures. A first step taken by the Scottish Prison Service is that of working with prisoners coming into the system, to promote constructive adjustment to the prison. Several months of counseling and charitable work are combined into an orientation ("induction") experience. Thereafter, efforts are made to promote environments in which the prisoners can openly relate to the staff. Prison careers then end with reintegration experiences for the long-term prisoner who is close to release into the community. This effort includes democratized, collaborative living arrangements which provide rehearsals of interpersonal skills (Chapter 10).

The political climate in the US today may be inhospitable to the reparative script exemplified by the Scottish experiment. Hypermasculine themes are prevalent in society, and "feminine" sentiments, such as compassion and relatedness, are dismissed as "liberal," which has become a term of opprobrium. But cultures can and do change, and we may yet reach a point in the future where we can de-escalate our hypermasculine model of corrections.

23

Social Climate and Prison Violence*

THERE ARE two favored perspectives relating to prison violence. One — which appeals to would-be prognosticators — centers on violent prisoners. This view has it that some inmates are consistently violent persons, who happen to be explosive in prison, but are likely to act out in almost any setting. A second portraiture conceives of inmate violence as at least partly a prison product. This view is to some extent shared by prison administrators who think of controlling violence through perimeter architecture, ingenious hardware, and deployment of custodial personnel.

In this chapter, I shall argue for a different context-centered view of prison violence that may offer more positive programming options than those that are conventionally envisaged. The view is also one that may have implications for research and policy.

The advent of the contextual view

In the mid 1960s, researchers attended to prisoner background characteristics,

---

*An expanded version of this chapter appeared in *Federal Probation*, December 1988; reprinted by permission.

Social Climate and Prison Violence

such as MMPI profiles and prior criminality, with an eye toward locating high-risk offender groups. Among exceptions to this trend was a subgroup of a task force in the California prison system. In describing inmate aggression, this group focused on the victimization incident, highlighting the motives of inmate participants that went into producing each incident (Mueller, Toch & Molof, 1965). This sort of analysis illuminated, among other things, the contribution of predation and extortion, homosexual relationships and pressures, debts, stealing, and routine prison disputes to the genesis of violent prison encounters in the mid 1960s.

This focus made possible a new approach to the motivational patterns of chronic, recurrent aggressors, especially trends in the way violent incidents arose for the same individual. The approach involved seeing violence-precipitation as an intersection between personal dispositions and the situational stimuli that invoked these dispositions. In this view, a prison incident could result, for instance, given a perceived affront to an inmate who is oversensitive to such affronts, or from the availability of a tempting target to an inmate who is a habitual bully.

There are probably several ways of defining violence-relevant contextual stimuli. One way of thinking about settings that is helpful is the concept of "social climate" (Moos, 1974; Toch, 1977). In prison, the concern would be with each inmate's immediate world, including prison staff, other inmates, and the physical milieu, as the inmate experiences it and reacts to it. The presumption is that any prison setting in which inmates spend a significant portion of time, such as tiers, shops, and classrooms, has behavior-relevant attributes that stand out for individual inmates. A shop, for instance, may feature a paternalistic or stern foreman, relaxed or firm supervision, a group of street-raised youths or lifers, high or low levels of noise, a playful or businesslike regime. Such factors may be more salient for most inmates than the fact that the shop teaches the plumbing trade, though this learning opportunity is another climate attribute that might be significant to inmates (Chapter 12).

Three fairly obvious points are of theoretical and practical concern: (1) any social climate feature may be critical in the life of one inmate and irrelevant to another (2) the same feature may be welcomed by some and noxious to others, and (3) positive and negative reactions to features of climate can help to spark inmate behavior, including participation in violent incidents.

Contrasting scenarios

How do climate features enter into the genesis of violence? Consider the following examples, some of which are more complex than others:

1. A farm setting in a youth prison is an informal haven for "problem" prisoners because of its low level of supervision, which reduces resentment and rebellious behavior. Inmates who have been troublesome before arriving on this farm become relatively well behaved; however, (a) an inexperienced rural inmate is assigned to the farm; he promptly becomes the target of homosexual pressure; (b) the victim experiences a panic reaction; in an effort at self-protection he seriously assaults one of his tormentors.

2. A recreation room is popular because it offers opportunities for playful socializing; (a) recreational preferences develop into conflicts between two inmates, which produces a fight; (b) the incident-participants are members of ethnic cliques, which become polarized and divide the recreation room into turfs; incidents arise as a result of jurisdictional disputes, and in retaliation for prior incidents.

3. A prison is tightly supervised, except for certain areas which are custodial lacunae; the places-and-times of low supervision acquire standard connotations; for instance: (a) a stairway used for movement from a tier to a mess hall is comparatively unsupervised; it becomes a "gladiating arena" in which aggrieved inmates—some armed with knives—challenge their enemies; (b) in a tier with a tradition of informality, officers open gallery doors on request; the practice is abused by inmates wishing to invade the cells of fellow inmates to victimize them; (c) the prison picnic becomes a drug-trafficking bazaar, with resulting jurisdictional disputes.

I have included examples in which traditional variables — particularly, the extent of supervision — play a role, but my implication is not that we must have prisons in which monitoring is omnipresent. We know that officers cannot be stationed where they are not otherwise needed, on the off-chance that incidents may occur. Deployment of staff of necessity must be uneven, leaving times and places of lower-density supervision. But custody deficits or other formal arrangements of the environment do not produce violence. Incidents arise because the relationships that spring up among people in a subsetting misfire or become sequentially more destructive. The personal motives of violence-prone individuals get mobilized by other people in the environment who press the relevant motivational button. Once anger, fear or retaliatory resolves have been mobilized, meanings assigned to features of the environment — such as the connotation of gladiating of the stairwell—help determine where and when incidents may occur.

Social climate and the aggressors

I have implied that to understand violence means more than to locate prior behavior patterns or consistencies; it also means that we must know the stimuli that invoke the person's motives, the contexts that facilitate or invite them, the group that encourages or applauds them, and the milieu that makes them fashionable.

We must start by asking ourselves how the victimizer arrived at his resolve. Was his goal profit? Retribution? Loyalty to his group? Wounded self esteem? Search for reputation? Escape from danger? The temptation of another's vulnerability? Ethnic prejudice? Resentment of authority? Adherence to a "code?" Where interviews are difficult to do or unproductive, we can often guess at the inmate's motives from information we have about his prior behavior, which may point to patterns; the inmate's folder may also help us to differentiate chronic victimizers from persons whose conduct is more of a product of specific situational forces.

But situational context is always of relevance—even with chronicity. A bully must be deprived of access to inmates with victim-attributes, and in a setting that is

Social Climate and Prison Violence

exclusively composed of self-styled "toughs" the predatory inmate's pattern is less likely to be elicited. Similar impact may be achieved by promoting solidarity among victim-prone inmates, because bullies pick on isolates, or by promoting anti-bully norms among the bully's peers.

Violence-promotion by climate features

Our point about situational context is not that the context produces the incident but that it increases or reduces the probability of incident occurrence. If our view holds, it follows that incident prevalence can be increased or decreased through contextual interventions, even though motives may be manifestations of personality traits. Contextual facilitation of violence in prison occurs in several ways, some of the more obvious being:

1. *By providing "pay offs."* One can reinforce the motives of aggressors by conferring status or other types of rewards for violent behavior. In some cases the rewards are obvious, as when the aggressor secures peer admiration. Elsewhere there are more "hidden" reinforcers, as when "punishment" sends a predator to a status-conferring segregation setting.

2. *By providing immunity or protection.* Violence in prison benefits from a "code of silence" (Chapter 21); however, the significance of the protective code is compounded by inmate staff social distance, by taboos against "ratting," by fear of retaliation, and so forth (Goodstein, 1979). Legalistic solutions to the victimization problem are encumbered by difficulties in securing reliable information from witnesses and victim-complainants. Prisons share this difficulty with other "subcultural" settings, such as those of organized crime.

3. *By providing opportunities.* The prison world features predictability and routine in physical movement, custodial supervision and staff reactions. The inmate aggressor is in the same position as the residential burglar who knows homeowner vacation patterns, and can plan the time and locus of his predatory forays. Predictability, of course, cuts both ways; by studying incident concentrations, we can re-adjust supervision patterns; staff re-adjustments can produce short-term amelioration, followed by new incident clusters once the staff responses become predictable.

4. *By providing temptations, challenges, and provocations.* Climate features may unwittingly spark victimization, as does the red flag that mobilizes the bull. Prison juxtaposes "strong" and "weak" inmates, members of rival gangs, dealers and consumers of contraband, homosexual rivals, debtors and creditors, racketeers and "marks." Such stimuli are often built into population mixes, or into personal characteristics of inmates; others are taken up as optional roles. For instance, there are gangs that spring up in prison in reaction to other indigenous groupings. These prison gangs engage in mutual retaliatory exercises in which each serves as the occasion for the other's violence.

5. *By providing justificatory premises.* Most inmates have more or less serious reservations about other inmates. Fellow inmates may be viewed as natural enemies or as personally contemptible, or in extreme cases they may be "dehumanized" to make them "fair game" for predation or exploitation. To the extent to which this is the case, controlling population mixes separates or combines persons who are predefined by others as potential victims and violent contenders.

Research and program implications

I do not wish to ship coal to Newcastle. I advance some recommendations familiar to prison staff; others suggest formalizing what is already being done, and affirming its value:

1. *It is important to understand violence "hot spots" and low-violence subenvironments.* I am not suggesting that formal research must be routinely deployed, but that inquiries into the reasons for "cold" violent incidents — those no longer being processed — be undertaken. One form of such inquiry that strikes me as useful relates to settings in which violent incidents are frequently generated, or where violence is scarce.[1] Parallel investigation can trace the institutional careers of violent inmates for "high points" and "low points" in their incident profiles. Staff and inmates in violent subsettings — including incident participants — can be interviewed for clues about the high or low level of violence in their settings. Given everyone's stake in minimizing trouble, there is incentive for problem-centered information sharing that has no punitive consequence.

   Available statistics about unique subsettings — their types of inmates, schedule of activities, levels of interaction, population movements, patterns of supervision — can be collated, and compared to statistical details relating to other subsettings, and information about incident participants. Such data are clues to violence motives, and may serve to check or validate data from interviews. Moreover, statistics fed to inmates and staff can help them understand their violence problem.

2. *One can help inmates and staff in high-violence settings to address their own violence problem.* We note elsewhere in this book that solutions that originate with those affected by their implementation are least likely to mobilize resistances. Moreover, persons in conflict-ridden subsettings have a stake in reducing localized danger and disruption. So, frequently do groups of violent individuals. Staff and inmates can be charged with documenting the reasons for violence patterns, and asked to recommend policy changes to neutralize violence patterns. This must obviously be done with the understanding that documented and practical suggestions will be implemented.

3. *One must create support systems for victims and potential victims.* The most common measures used to deal with violence target aggressors; by

Social Climate and Prison Violence

segregating them, however, prison enclaves can be created in which levels of violence can become disproportionately high. Victim-centered strategies can stigmatize inmates, or can exile the prisoners in settings with program voids. Less drastic options entail creating new settings in which victim-prone inmates can be mixed in with others to receive services for programmatic purposes. Activity-centered inmate groups can provide victims with peer support and with respectable staff links.

4. *One can constitute crisis intervention teams.* Such teams are an example of support measures that can be invoked where the violence problem is still "hot." Teams can be made up of persons who are trained to mediate or defuse violent conflicts and to refer participants, if necessary, for professional assistance.[2] Such teams can range in composition from chaplains to custodial officers or inmates. One can also "debrief" violence participants to prevent lingering disputes from flaring up after the protagonists leave segregation settings and return to the yard.

5. *One can use violence-related data in staff training and inmate indoctrination.* This approach requires no technology beyond collation of relevant information. For feedback purposes, such data should be as setting-specific as possible (Chapter 25). Training content would consist of statistics and illustrations that sensitize staff and inmates to situations they are likely to encounter in areas in which they live or work. Moreover, standard curricula can be enriched or supplemented by updated information about prevailing interpersonal problems or group tensions, and about solutions that have been tried and that have worked. Inmates and staff can also be informed during their induction about problems they might expect in their assignments, so as to avoid dependence on trial-and-error learning.

None of these strategies will "solve" emerging problems. No matter what any of us do, low-visibility disputes can arise and dedicated predators can create occasions for predation. The goal is the reduction of violence through the creation of a climate that understands its own occasions for violence and begins to defuse them. When one accomplishes this goal, residual violence will be "person centered," and can be addressed as such.

Notes

1. One use of data feedback relates to fear of violence (secondary victimization), a topic I have not touched upon because it deserves detailed examination. Fear relates imperfectly to violence; this means that we may be afraid without cause, or unafraid where apprehension might be functional. Information about violence that does occur in a setting can be a corrective to irrational apprehension. Similarly, fear can be mapped, and such data can be discussed as one makes a direct effort at fear reduction or fear alignment.
2. Teams of this kind have been successfully used for suicide prevention in prisons and jails.

24

The Violent Prisoner*

WE CAN start to think about the dynamics of prison violence by reviewing the career of an inmate who has been repetitively violent in the prison. As this man's story unfolds in official documents, we can discover that he has assiduously assaulted prison staff members, and that his first assault on a correction officer occurs early in his sentence. This incident is described as follows:

> The inmate spit on the wall and stairs while coming off his gallery on the way to the mess hall. A correction officer attempted to counsel him and he struck the officer in the left cheekbone, then dove into the officer and secured a body hold on him and attempted to bite him in the neck. The officer slammed the inmate into the bars in an attempt to free himself, also pulled the inmate's hair to get his teeth off his neck. Other inmates came to the officer's aid and pulled the inmate off and restrained him until help arrived.

A staff member who interviews the inmate while he is awaiting disciplinary disposition writes that "he is more concerned about his return to school and plumbing class than he is over the possible disposition of the [incident]." Later, in the segregation unit, the inmate is described as "very moody," and, as an example of his

---

*This chapter is excerpted from a contribution to *Clinical Approaches to Violence*, edited by Kevin Howells and Clive Hollin (Chichester: John Wiley and Sons, 1984). Reprinted by permission.

The Violent Prisoner

moodiness, staff note that "from time to time he would throw garbage and other items out of his cell." Even later the inmate's "moodiness" takes a turn for the worse, and an officer files a disciplinary report contending that "the inmate reached through the bars and slapped me across the face . . . I proceeded up the gallery while the inmate was hollering that I had changed his cigarettes."

Within the next few days the prisoner sets fire to his cell, and after a period, an officer files a report which reads:

> While letting out the above inmate for the yard, he refused to be pat frisked. I told him either to submit to the frisk or return to his cell. He then threw a punch at me and hit me under the left eye. [Another officer] grabbed him from behind and we wrestled him to the floor.

The two officers involved in this attack require medical attention and must take compensation leave, but the inmate off-handedly explains that "I don't like being told what to do. I was only fighting with the officers." Three days later another disgruntled officer records:

> While passing by the inmate's cell to dispense mail to [a neighboring cell] the inmate threw a container of urine at myself hitting me in the right shoulder and back of the head. I continued on and dispensed the mail. As I was leaving this area I again had to pass by the inmate's cell and was hit again by a second cup of urine. This one hit me in the back of the head.

There follow incidents in which the prisoner announces that he does not like his accommodations. In one such incident:

> He said he wanted to be moved. I gave him three direct orders to return to his cell. Each order was given at a slow count. After the third order I pressed my personal alarm. [Two sergeants and six officers] came to assist. The inmate was put in his cell by force using hands, arms and body to get the inmate to his cell. The inmate tried to resist and attempted to assault the employees involved. After he was returned to his cell he spat in my face.

The next encounter occurs in a hospital observation cell two days later. On this occasion:

> The inmate started beating the cell door, shouting statements that were incoherent. After this he beat his chest with his fists stating, "I am a Puerto Rican and you can't hurt me. Me tough." He made more verbal threats that he would get me and stated he hoped I slept good tonight because, "some day I'm getting you."

Another incident also takes place in the observation ward. An officer reports:

> When the inmate came out for a shower he immediately assaulted me. I opened the cell door with my left hand and the inmate came out of his cell swinging with both hands. I was able to block the blows but he scratched my neck with his fingernails while swinging. I pushed the inmate against the wall. [Another officer] used a neckhold and I used an armlock to put the inmate on the floor . . . While in this position the inmate said, "You mother fucker, I will kill you someday because I am doing 26 years and I don't care" . . . We then picked the inmate off the floor using our hands, and put him back in his cell.

Four days later, in the early morning, still another report is filed, which notes that:

> The inmate started yelling, throwing his pillow and mattress around, banging on the door and walls, and throwing water from his toilet. A nurse advised [that she proposed] to use medication by injection authorized by the doctor. When the door opened, the inmate refused to lie down and came at the officers. An officer used a shield to push the inmate to the wall. [Three other officers] held the inmate's arms and placed him on his bed. The inmate offered little resistance as the nurse gave him an injection. He was released and the officer left the room. The inmate threw toilet water at the officers [as they were] leaving.

A disciplinary hearing is held covering the last set of reports. Staff at this juncture are concerned about the possibility that the inmate might need mental health assistance, and indicate they would like to see him transferred to a setting where such assistance was available.

A consulting psychiatrist interviews the prisoner and records:

> The inmate told me that he was constantly getting in fights with people but justified this by saying the he was always the victim of other people's unpleasantness before he hit out. He said that for the most part his problems were with the corrections officers . . . He strenuously denied being crazy. I could find no evidence of any mental illness today and think from my interview and the information on his file that this man is merely an explosive psychopath. I do not think that any psychiatric treatment is likely to make any difference to his behavior. However, he is so extremely intolerant of any type of frustration he is likely to prove a continual disciplinary problem in this situation and I would concur with the recommendation made by [the physician] for transfer, if and when this can be arranged.

The inmate eventually is thus sent to a new institution with a note from a counselor, who advises that:

> If the writer may coin a phrase, this subject is suffering from a "hate the police officers" syndrome.... His response toward any person that might represent authority is almost Pavlovian, in that the stimulus is the sight of the authority figure and the response is hate and aggressiveness.... He is a prime candidate for a psychotherapeutic community in the event that such a unit is established in the system. His present attitude is such that he will spend the majority of his remaining period of incarceration in special housing unless he has a very drastic change in attitude.

The man indeed starts by spending several months in the segregation unit of his next prison. Here the first entry records that "the subject has been suspected of urinating on the floor, and when he talks, he talks in mumbles and frequently to himself." The next entry notes that "the subject was placed in a Plexiglas covered cell over the weekend because of allegedly spitting at a correction officer. He has been moved to a stripped cell at this time and seems to be behaving rationally." Two weeks later the segregation counselor writes:

> His body appearance and cell are disgraceful at best, and he continues to request that he be transferred to Puerto Rico. He again was advised that this is relatively impossible to do, and he then stated that he would like to go down to population in this facility and participate in the programs. In view of his mental situation it is this interviewer's impression that he will be with me for quite some time.

After the inmate has spent three months in segregation and his deportment has

The Violent Prisoner

surprisingly improved the counselor requests that the inmate be moved out, and he is sent to another prison, where three months later he receives another long segregation sentence for an episode which is described as follows:

> An officer approached the inmate who was washing his clothes in the utility sink and told the inmate to either take his shower or lock in his cell. The inmate stated, 'When I finish washing my clothes I'll take a shower.' The officer again stated his order to the inmate. The inmate left the sink and proceeded toward his cell with the officer following him. The inmate turned quickly, and using his fist struck the officer on the right side of the face. The inmate then grabbed the officer around the neck and started choking him. The officer broke loose and the inmate attempted to strike him again. The officer defended himself, and when the inmate grabbed his coat, the officer pushed the inmate into his cell and locked the door.

After the prisoner completes his segregation term he is transferred to a different institution, where he spends several months accumulating a satisfactory work record, but is repeatedly locked up. He finally drops out of programs, claiming that he is taken advantage of by other inmates. But he also commits fewer dramatic violations, and this pattern continues at the next prison to which he is sent, where his most salient offense consists of marking his cell walls with a pen, explaining that he "didn't like the way they looked."

Finally the inmate is assigned to a newly established program for victim-prone prisoners "so that he would have the opportunity of participating in therapy." The program staff write:

> Since entering the unit the resident has posed certain administrative difficulties. He appears to be of limited intelligence with emotional problems of long standing, as well as having a great deal of difficulty with the English language. The resident for the most part has demonstrated a positive attitude toward program participation. His motivation has been limited by stress from other inmates and a difficulty with the language barrier... He has received a number of misbehavior reports since his last parole board appearance. However, in fairness it would be advisable to evaluate the most recent reports. [On one occasion] he was written up for destruction of state property when he cut into his mattress and made a pillow from the stuffing. Destruction of state property cannot be tolerated, but one must understand that for a period of time in the block we did not have enough pillows for all our residents, and the inmate may have requested a pillow and been denied. He admitted to the adjustment committee that he did not have a pillow, and he needed one. [On another occasion] he received a misbehavior report from the recreation leader in our mandatory physical education program for refusing to participate in a floor hockey game. The inmate, according to the report, attempted to explain to the recreation leader that he doesn't know how to play hockey. Several residents have experienced difficulty while participating in some mandatory competitive sports, while in this program. Previously the inmate received a misbehavior report for failure to follow a direct order. This order was given by the correction officer, telling the inmate that he had to go to the gym program when the inmate had informed the officer that he did not wish to go. He has received one other misbehavior report when he interfered with an officer by hollering his cell location in the presence of other inmates. A brief explanation of these misbehavior reports has been given so that the parole board

may be able to see the inmate as an individual of limited intelligence with a definite communication problem who has demonstrated a difficulty following institutional procedures and processes which have resulted in misbehavior reports... The inmate has been able to decrease the number of misbehavior reports and decrease the seriousness of those reports.

Actually the man's pattern of difficulties has been tempered, and when he leaves the prison he stands transformed from an incredibly recidivistic assaulter into a clumsy and somewhat volatile individual, who is seen as having nuisance value, and who invites pity from staff. It is hard to tell, of course, whether any fundamental change has occurred beyond the fact that after four or five years it has at some level dawned on the man that his pattern is self-destructive, and that the parole board can keep him in prison a good deal longer if he continues brawling with every officer who makes him feel resentful.

The term "brawling" is used advisedly, because, as this man sees it, his conflicts with officers are "fights." In other words, they are disputes which are settled physically, as disputes must be settled among men. This view is partially shared and reinforced by the officers, who repeatedly describe in vivid detail the wrestling holds they have deployed to neutralize the man, although they obviously resent his tendency to attack officers without adequate warning and the damage he does before one knows what he is about. The man is said to have "communication problems," and these are reciprocal. Observers do not know when he feels mortally affronted because they no more understand him than he understands the concerns of those around him. The central issue often appears to be that the man feels himself treated like a child, and that his version of machismo holds that no man must be ordered about by another man, and that it is demeaning and insulting to be told to do things, particularly when you have explained why you do not wish to do them or would have explained if you could have.

The issue of the man's alleged reactions to uniforms does not necessarily enter the equation because the man sees encounters between himself and officers as personal, and perceives custodial instructions as originating in whims and expressions of disdain or disrespect. When the man feels disdained or disrespected in this way he reacts at the first available opportunity, which makes his behavior unpredictable, because his reaction does not necessarily coincide with the move that originates the offense to which he reacts.

In the first incident, for example, the officer does not know that the inmate is puzzled and enraged because the officer has taken a plastic spoon the inmate thinks he will need for his meal. The officer also does not heed the inmate's initial expression of resentment, which consists of spitting on the floor, and the attack follows after the officer lectures the inmate about prison sanitation rules, which the inmate (who does not understand most of this lecture) perceives as adding insult to injury. In a second incident the officer is oblivious to the fact that the inmate is enraged because he has ordered one brand of cigarettes and has been mistakenly given another, an act the inmate regards as deliberate and contemptuous.

When the inmate must rely on officers to obtain what he needs (or thinks he needs) such as cigarettes, contact with a sergeant or a psychiatrist, or permission to wash his clothes, he feels that this dependency is in itself demeaning. Thus when his requests are not immediately responded to, the humiliation becomes more serious, because not only has he had to ask for something but also those who have compromised his manliness by making him a mendicant now deny his requests, to show him who is in charge. He also sees himself receiving the same arbitrary and demeaning messages when officers present him with forced-choice situations (such as "submit to the frisk or return to your cell") which do not include the option (go to the yard for recreation) that he elects to exercise.

Since the inmate feels that officers make unacceptable demands and knows that his own verbal skills are deficient, he usually concludes that there is nothing further to be said, a fight ensues and his subjection by (occasionally overwhelming) force reinforces his perspective. The fact that he keeps losing these fights because he is badly outnumbered has no bearing on the principle involved, which is that a man must fight when he must fight, and that it is better to fight and lose than to permit oneself to be belittled and emasculated by being ordered about like a child, having legitimate requests denied or having somebody else's will prevail in a contest of will, which denotes childish subservience. To be wrestled to the ground by greatly superior forces is not to be considered unmanly and is not a cause for shame, particularly if one can indicate, by spitting at one's retreating enemy or by otherwise declaring oneself inviolate ("You can't hurt me. Me tough") that suppression is not tantamount to surrender.

It is true that the man does begin to intuit something of the authority structure of the prison, although it takes a great many months of segregation to get to the juncture where he no longer reacts with rage to what he regards as belittling and rejecting moves of officers. This does not mean, however, that even at this juncture the man accepts or understands the demands the prison makes on him, which include not skipping meals and appearing at work on days when he does not feel like working, or taking showers he feels he does not need.

The man's violations at this stage show fewer refusals to conform, and he has learned to temper his indignation when he is admonished, because he has learned that officers enforce rules rather than invent them to humiliate inmates. This means that a man's honor need not be at stake when he is asked to abide by a prison rule or when he is taken to task for nonconformity.

Depicting a violence pattern

I have reviewed a somewhat redundant career in exhaustive detail to illustrate methodological as well as substantive points. The methodological issue revolves around the specification of the pattern, which can be the core of the clinical enterprise when we deal with violent offenders. Kozol et al., (1972) take this position, and indicate that "of paramount importance is a meticulous description of the actual assault... The description of the aggressor in action is often the most valuable single source of information" (p. 384).

With recurrent violent behavior the prime concern must be with patterned information, which covers consistencies of perspective and motive across a person's violent incidents (Toch, 1969, 1986). Such consistencies can be situational (phenotypic) or may relate to underlying (genotypic) dispositions (Allport, 1961). Phenotypic commonalities consist of inventories of the circumstances in which the person aggresses, such as the common characteristics of individuals he selects as victims (Monahan, 1981). Genotypic consistency underlies phenotypic consistency. It can accommodate situational diversity, but this does not mean that where superficial commonalities exist we need dig no deeper. Incidents in hospitals, for example, often occur at given times of the day, such as in the morning or when staff shifts change (Lion and Reid, 1983). This fact tells us little, however, until we translate time and place into changed levels of environmental impingement, which lead us to infer that some patients feel overstimulated when their environment becomes enriched, making them irritable and over-responsive to trivial demands. We similarly learn little from the fact that our prisoner assaults prison guards until we consider the connotations the officers' interventions hold for the inmate, which explain the intensity of the rage reactions with which he responds to seemingly innocuous instructions.

To arrange events in chronological order, as we have done in our example, is helpful on a number of counts:

1. Temporal patterns often call attention to the effects of environmental changes which contribute to violence or ameliorate pressures to which the person reacts. A prisoner, for example, may discontinue violent reactions when he is segregated (our inmate does not), which suggests that the relative isolation of confinement is paradoxically beneficial in his case (Suedfeld, 1980a). Another person may be involved in a great deal of violence in an age-homogeneous prison for younger inmates, but may reduce his involvements in a prison that contains an older population, which provides clues to the peer temptations and pressures to which the inmate has reacted.
2. Chronologies often point to time-bound internal states, such as tensions, fear and anxieties. Disturbed inmates, for example, frequently act out at entry into the prison system or when they face impending release, which mobilizes subsurface anxieties.
3. Time-bound reductions of aggressivity can also provide clues to the ameliorative impact of serendipitous experiences, which we can only systematically mobilize once we have identified them (Bandura, 1986).

Our case study illustrates that motives and dispositions of even patterned offenders can change over time. In our inmate's case, in fact, the change is extreme, involving an attenuation of behavior from recidivistic aggressivity to helpless confusion. Although most changes we encounter are not as significant as this, improvements over time are nonetheless prevalent. Young prisoners, who are most involved in violence, thus reliably improve their deportment over the course of their prison terms (Toch and Adams, 1989). Such changes, which at one time were regarded as anticipatory reactions to release from prison (Garabedian 1963), are attributable to varying combinations of maturation and adaptation to the prison.

Deploying therapeutic assistance for violent prisoners

The inmate we have discussed had been enthusiastically referred for mental health assistance on numerous occasions but had been consistently adjudged non-

The Violent Prisoner

disturbed. The only circumstance in which a formal diagnosis was entered involved a psychiatrist who diagnosed the inmate as suffering from an antisocial personality disturbance. As noted in Chapter 20, this diagnosis is an expression of clinical disapproval. Moreover, persons diagnosed in this way are deemed refractory to treatment (Hare, 1981; Cleckley, 1976), which means that the diagnosis discourages, rather than encourages, referrals of the patient for mental health services.

There is no consensus about whether all (or most) prisoners such as our inmate are to be regarded as emotionally impaired and/or as entitled to mental health services. An affirmative answer is provided, among others, by Vernon Fox (1958), who wrote that "the types of offenses committed by each individual may be psychiatrically diagnosed according to the area in which the individual finds conformity most difficult," since "the specific nature of the offenses committed by each individual is partially dependent upon the personality structure of the offender" (p. 324). Fox's connotation of "diagnosis" includes standard taxonomic categories but obviously transcends them, since Fox would recognize that few violence-involved prisoners formally qualify as psychiatric patients. What Fox suggests is that we sidetrack recidivistic inmates from the ministrations of the conventional disciplinary process (which has, by definition, failed to modify their conduct) and place such inmates in therapeutic settings, such as the one that was invoked for our inmate. Fox (1958) suggests programs that would "permit emotional maturation to occur in a controlled environment" (p. 326). Among the arguments one can advance for the strategy (which is similar to the proposal described in Chapter 18) are that:

1. Almost any special setting would be infinitely more humane than the prevailing practice of *ad seriatim* solitary confinement (Jackson, 1983).
2. The stigmatizing connotation of being "emotionally disturbed" can be spared to the clients of a surrogate punitive program.
3. The goal of seeking to enhance the interpersonal competence of violent offenders is, on the face of it, the most constructive use we can make of time they must spend in a controlled setting.
4. The organization of interdisciplinary settings promotes invaluable cross-fertilization. This attribute may be particularly useful in prisons, where clinicians often operate in self-contained ghettos. The condition can be inferred, for example, from a survey conducted by the federal prison system, in which psychologists complained to interviewers that "they were not being allowed to participate enough in the correctional process," while administrators "requested more involvement in the overall correctional process through consultation, staff training, and general program development" (Powitzky, 1978).

The disciplinary process and the violent offender

Inmates who commit violent infractions tend to be severely punished. Several issues arise in connection with the enactment of sanctions:

1. The process is offense-centered rather than person-centered, which means

that underlying psychological patterns such as the one that we have outlined for our offender cannot be taken into account.
2. The process does not consider the impact of punishment on the offender, including the possible fact that punishment in the past has only made the person's behavior worse.
3. The process is legalistic and tends to equate fairness with the standardization and inflexibility of sanctions.
4. The process is concerned with the harm the offender has done rather than with the causes of his behavior, and defines the punishment it assigns as a warning to other prisoners who may contemplate comparable malefaction, such as assaulting officers.

The retributive-deterrence framework is not only antithetical to the treatment perspective but also implies that treatment approaches can subvert the order maintenance goals of the prison, by being concerned with the motives of offenders rather than the harm that they have done. It is true that if treatment succeeds, the inmate becomes less of a threat to prison staff and/or to other prisoners, but these effects are incidental to the purpose of treatment, which is to help the person to abandon maladaptive patterns of conduct (Chapter 18). Treatment also differs from behavior control by being person-centered, sensitively flexible and (if defensible) humane.

The contrast is mitigated in practice by a number of facts:

1. Discipline as practiced is invariably more flexible than it is in theory; penalties are, at times, suspended. Segregation stays are shortened in midstream, and lost prison time is restored if behavior improves.
2. Disciplinary staff have been sensitized to problems of mental illness, and may refer some inmates to mental health personnel where such personnel are available.
3. Disciplinary staff find it hard to ignore the recalcitrance of behavior patterns, and the fact that available sanctions have failed to modify behavior in the past.

Such considerations make it possible to propose special interventions for violent inmates, especially interventions as options that can be exercised by disciplinary staff themselves when they feel that conventional dispositions are inappropriate (Chapter 18). Treatment interventions can either be defined as punishment "moratoria" (Fox, 1958) or as contractual experiments during which penalties are suspended, subject to reinstatement if the offender rejects treatment or fails to respond to it.

The psychodynamics of prison violence

The psychology of violence has not advanced to the point where a taxonomy of violence-proneness is available, but two themes are candidates for inclusion in such a taxonomy, and a third enters when we consider motives for assaults on staff. The two principal themes are (1) developmental immaturity, impulsivity and egocentricity; and (2) compensatory reactions to low self-esteem. The third theme (to which we have alluded in our case example) relates to issues of autonomy/dependence.

DEVELOPMENT DEFICITS

Reviews of prison incidents suggest that much of the violence in prisons is a manifestation of impulsivity and lax impulse control. Another way of characterizing such patterns is that they reflect deficient socialization, which leaves the individual fixated at impulse-ridden and opportunistic stages of personal development (Loevinger, 1976).

The purest impulsivity patterns are those that describe persons who engage in repeated behavior that is designed to satisfy their needs in a direct and primitive way. Such persons may encounter others who are similarly oriented, and resolve rivalries through physical combat. A more reliable propensity is predatory aggression, in which the person regards others as objects of need satisfaction, and uses violence or threats of violence to intimidate, extort, expropriate or bully those susceptible to intimidation, who may also violently resist being victimized.

A third impulsivity pattern involves a susceptibility to reacting with aggression to comparatively minor frustrations (Chapter 18). When persons of this kind are disappointed or obstructed in the pursuit of their goals they often engage in explosive aggression, which expresses blind anger and rage. A different quality (back-to-the-wall despair) characterizes violence where the person feels that situations close in on him, leaving him feeling impotent. (Limited verbal skills, as in our example, can be contributors to this pattern.)

One variation of the violent impulsivity theme reflects the "stimulus-seeking" propensity that has been underlined by Eysenck (1964). This propensity is one that we described as "Russian Roulette" behavior, because the person takes risks in the service of short-term goals and excitement, and does not care that he inevitably gets into trouble, or at least does not draw lessons from the fact. Other impulsive offenders engage in consistently nonreflective, childlike, self-serving and irresponsible behavior, but eventually discover that their behavior generates unwelcome repercussions. This discovery, unfortunately, often mobilizes unhealthy defenses, and the person indulges in self-pity rather than self-reflection.

COMPENSATORY VIOLENCE

Much violent behavior is designed to cement a person's sense of self-esteem, either by trying to build a reputation or by defending against feelings of low self-esteem through compensatory behavior (Adler, 1927; Toch, 1969). In the most direct manifestation of this pattern the person aims to demonstrate toughness or pugnaciousness in an attempt to achieve candidacy as an individual to be admired by his peers. A second pattern is somewhat represented in the case we have reviewed. It has to do with feeling easily disparaged and affronted, and reacting violently when one thinks oneself offended or slighted.

Some persons function as members of a violence-prone group, and act with and on behalf of this group and in defense of its values. However, to the extent to which the person meets his group more than half-way, compensatory features may overlap this pattern. Irrespective of group membership, for instance, the person may see himself as a gladiator, and may regard violence as a skill and a preferred way to resolve conflicts, which makes him engage in combat readily and casually to resolve interpersonal disputes. Pattern admixtures involving neuroses are also sometimes encountered. One such pattern involves the use of violence to preempt anticipated unpopularity. Such violence occurs where the person expects to be rejected and reacts with provocation and hostility in anticipation of rejection, thereby documenting his assumptions.

Compensatory violence includes the display of a wide range of psychological mechanisms, and many of these defenses can make the person uninviting. For instance, some violence-prone individuals who have low self-esteem feel unable to compromise or retreat from rigidly defined positions, and equate this stance with defending their sense of worth.

AUTONOMY/DEPENDENCE

Given the authority structure of prisons, it is not surprising that prisons evoke regressive behavior that is concerned with dependence upon or independence from parental figures, such as persons in authority. For prisoners who engage in such behavior, as does the inmate whose career we have reviewed, the issue of dependence/autonomy is emotionally charged, because it relates to definitions of adulthood which include emancipation on the one hand, and loss of support on the other. This issue is a paradoxical one, and includes patterns in which the person alternates between dependent and violently rebellious behavior, depending upon whether he feels his needs are met or frustrated.

Other inmates take a very consistent and systematically rebellious, defiant and challenging stance toward persons in authority. Some such inmates are particularly concerned with rejecting personal constraints, such as the autonomy constraints that are endemic in the prison. These persons feel that no one has a right to infringe on their autonomy, and react angrily to all infringements, whose rationale they cannot understand or accept. Being apprehended and punished can compound the problem for such persons, because this experience is reminiscent of childhood (Sykes, 1958).

A final note

We cannot here presume to offer programmatic or therapeutic prescriptions, except to note (as we have done) that inmates often mature in prison, and that assistance in accelerating this endeavor is not misplaced. We have also suggested that where misbehavior patterns prove chronic (as too frequently they do), continued disciplinary processing is not an appropriate response.

Beyond these points, we have suggested that violence can be a subject as well as object fof analysis. Patterns such as the one we have described can help make sense of individual violence, but, more to the point, they can help a violent person make sense of his violence, when he is ready to do so. In this endeavor, humane staff can be a powerful asset, if such staff show personal acceptance, making it clear to the offender that while they reject his conduct, they respect his capacity for self-understanding, regeneration and eventual reform.

25

Creating a Niche*

WHILE ON a working vacation in Scotland I was able to spend two stimulating afternoons with a thoughtful, soft-spoken and charming intellectual[1] who had become a living legend. My host's name was Tom McCulloch, and his accommodations are unusual. He has a prison unit to himself, and he was watched over by three correction officers twenty-four hours a day. He has lived under these conditions for some twenty years.

One problem is that Tommy McCulloch is doing his best to feed the view that he has violence potential by disseminating scenarios of violent acts that he might be induced to commit if he is driven from his unit. And McCulloch knows that he need not say much along such lines to evoke anxiety and fear. As late as 1992, newspapers called him "maniac," "psycho ax killer," "the Mad Axman," and "Scotland's most dangerous man." The judge who sentenced him in 1976 labeled him "an incurable psychopath" before decreeing that he must never be released.[2]

---

*This chapter is a modified version of a presentation at the Second International Conference on Treatment and Diversion of Mentally Disordered Offenders in Tempe, Arizona, 10 November, 1993. It is here reprinted (with permission) from *The Journal of Psychiatry and Law*, Winter, 1993. I am indebted to Tom McCulloch and Joel Dvoskin for their reading of drafts of the chapter.

McCulloch admits that he wants to stay in isolation. But he insists that the reason he talks of his potential for violence is to show that he is a realist who does not fool himself, and does not wish to create dissonance or confusion. In a note he wrote after our first meeting, he told me:

> The "popular" perceptions of me, regardless of the reality, are what will shape the manner of others' address to me. Those perceptions are profoundly negative.... Because I cannot change that negativity ... I have to remain a man capable of meeting the consequences of that profoundly negative dynamic. We must address the future in the light of those "realities" and shape it to exclude the negative implications it is possible, without a great deal of imagination, to see developing. If that leads to my "nest," as you termed it, being transformed to my environmental disadvantage, then that is better than the "gamble" that more "developmental" options offer. I have countless reservations on every front, every bit as disturbing as the reservations of the authorities, especially those of the men who have to work directly with me.

Of course, we cannot be certain that Tom McCulloch would never be violent again, and we cannot afford to be less than certain. But McCulloch is saying that *he* is not sure, leaving the impression that what he is not sure about is what we are not sure about. And it is in this regard that I have ventured an alternative hypothesis, though McCulloch is the world's leading expert on McCulloch, and may well be right in his self-analytic assumptions.

What I infer that Tommy McCulloch is not sure about—and cannot afford to be unsure about—is his ability to handle the level and complexity of stimulation to which he would be exposed in the prison yard. This includes interactions with persons who are not visiting staff—or foreign psychologists, for that matter—who drop in for tea, or guards whose faces and routine are familiar. "I am a loner," McCulloch says, "I have always been a loner." He implies that he may have little in common with other prisoners, but that they can involve him in escalating prison conflicts in which he can end up doing things he does not want to do. He does not partake of outdoor exercise. "I may leave my room when there is a point to it," he says, but sees no point. "There is no purpose in going out," he writes, "if it is just to walk up and down or round in circles on my own in the little area behind the block."

McCulloch repeats time and again that what he most values is structure and predictability. He writes that "the need for 'control' over my environment was always a major factor in my make-up, my inability to get it created great instability in my youth. The years I have spent in isolation have compounded, to a degree I can't begin to estimate, that need." In some scenarios he invokes images of being moved under sedation, and becoming a vigilant spectator to out-of-control events, such as riots.

Clearly, part of the concern is with having feelings stirred up, including angry feelings, which might inspire unscheduled physically destructive or self-destructive acts. At this point, in this setting, such behavior is unthinkable. Tommy writes:

> I have emotional volatility, but it is, I believe, in control. Undoubtedly, pathologically so ... and that of course is a problem in the disturbance of the "nest" scenario (or

Creating a Niche

"Cocoon scenario" as I favor). I just live in hope that as we address that we can provide enough checks and balances to maintain the "stability" I retain.

Where Tom McCulloch would like to remain, he governs and modulates his level of stimulation. An officer who knows him has observed that he is not an omnivorous intellectual, but (like the rest of us), culls from what he reads and sees on TV the grist for specialized mills.[3] McCulloch's existence is self-regulated, with help from his keepers. He enlivens his daily routine to keep himself occupied and to feed his imagination. In the past he has made toys ("His animals were really alive," staff fondly recall, "no two of them alike—all originals, all expressive"). Today, McCulloch works on a chronicle of his prison, HMP Peterhead. Such endeavors let his mind range, within self-defined limits. More crucially, the external structure in the unit and the corresponding internal structure—Tommy McCulloch's perspective on the world — are calculatedly sane and congruent.

What I suspect Tommy cannot be sure about is what could happen to the confines and flexibility of this perspective, should the floodgates open, and should he lose control over the type and level of stimulation to which he is subjected. I think the issue is not merely one of facing confusion, or threats, or dashed hopes, or the Great Unwashed of the yard, or feelings that might arise as a result of confusion or threats, or unwanted social pressures but rather the prospect of an emerging need for a conspiratorial view of things, the possibility of losing a sane view of the world, whose dispassionateness is Tommy's pride and joy. McCulloch once protested when a parole board broached a routine review. He saw their invitation as an assault on his sanity, since he must stay in prison.

McCulloch reminisced to me about a prison warden who had faced him with an injunction he would not justify or explain, which caused him (McCulloch) problems. What happened, McCulloch said, was that he was going through a "paranoid phase" at the time which made misinterpretations possible. Paranoia imposes structure on information by distorting it. This poses a danger to one who has tenuously achieved a measured, dispassionate, and tolerable view of himself and his fate.

Tommy McCulloch would like to remain a self-governing isolate. He insists he does not mind his keepers, but would be delighted to dispense with them to make his unit more acceptably cost-effective.[4] Technology, he thinks, could solve the problem.

But can a prison afford to let one of its prisoners remain a hermit to help the prisoner preserve his sanity? Can a prison accommodate different versions of precarious equilibria to help inmates survive? Can a prison accommodate specialized needs for specialized environments where such environments are not nurtured or promoted (as in McCulloch's case) by the prison itself? As a case in point, should we mainline or mainstream a McCulloch for his own benefit? Reintegration as an end-in-itself is nonsensical, McCulloch argues, and not worth the risk. And if reintegration is supposed to mean the chance for growth or development, what if horizons expand in solitude, but shrink under stimulation?

Let me hasten to say that I know many prison inmates whose resources and resourcelessness contrast sharply with those of Tommy McCulloch, and whose version of survival differs from McCulloch's.[5] But the details of what is tolerable and of what one does when the environment is not tolerable matter less than the principle that the level and type of stimulation matter, and that flexibility of programming is the means whereby sanity can be preserved.

One of my former associates, John Seymour, wrote an insightful essay on what we called *niches* in prison. "Even where environmental conditions appear most malevolent," he noted, "men create, seemingly from rocklike or diaphanous material, a fabric of life. Such adaptation also occurs in prison"(Seymour, 1977, p. 179). Seymour said that a niche is "a microcosm that rarely guarantees happiness but usually guarantees survival." "The world of the vulnerable inmate," he wrote, "is limited to the dimensions of prison that are relevant to his concerns." "These concerns," he wrote, "highlight required subenvironments, sanctuaries, or *niches*. A niche is a functional subsetting containing objects, space, resources, people and relationships between people. A niche is perceived as ameliorative; it is seen as a potential instrument for the relaxation of stress and the realization of required ends. It is this quality of niches that stimulates the creative process of niche search and niche identification" (pp. 180-181).

Seymour made several statements that pertain directly to Tommy McCulloch. "Where inmates demand Structure," he wrote, "it is not chaos that they bemoan, it is the prison's failure to control things that need controlling.... Inmates often search out arenas in which constraints may be self-imposed, or where organization controls dominate and monitor or modulate behavior.... Niches may be perceived by inmates as defenses of the boundaries of self.[6] They enhance their ability to escape from violence; reduce the unpredictability of the inmate world; modulate such environmental irritants as noise and incursions upon thoughts and activities; ... provide predictable access to areas and possessions; produce more lawful restrictions of autonomy or activity; and facilitate the effective management of time" (pp. 188-189).

Seymour implies that niche-search and niche-allocation is a process that benefits prisons as much as the prisoners. Vulnerable inmates who are not placed in environments that are congruent with their needs and coping skills are apt to experience problems. And we make matters worse when we respond to the problems that thus arise with a process that does not differentiate (except at extremes) between premeditated acts and maladaptive behavior that results from coping deficits (Chapter 18).

The inflexibility of the prison's response at times leaves us with an unspeakable mess. Segregation settings become repositories of men and women who are transparently disturbed, including patients whose declamations keep other inmates awake, and thus create tension. Prisoners whose offenses are transparently irrational (such as inmates who smear themselves with excrement or set their cells on fire) are processed in terms of the impact of their acts, rather than having the despair that prompts their acts attended to (Chapter 24).

For the sake of equity, let me add that the inflexibility of the mental health system is no less a problem than the rigidity of the prison regime. Mental health professionals defend silly sectarian boundaries and the taxonomic systems that sustain them.

Creating a Niche 205

Though the range can be expanded by pathologizing prisoners who require help (such as nondisturbed prisoners who are contemplating suicide) the range can also be constricted by attaching labels such as "malingerer," "attention seeker" or "antisocial personality" to clients who are found aversive.[7] Prisoners who act out and/or prisoners whose offenses are particularly offensive (as were McCulloch's) are most apt not to have their vulnerabilities credited. By the same token, wheels that do not squeak are apt not to be ministered to with ameliorative grease.

The line between mental health jurisdiction and prison management is particularly troublesome because the most powerful therapeutic modality that is available to us is the prison milieu, which includes regime attributes, sociometric composition of settings, and the type of staff assigned to the settings. Mental health services that are rendered in a vacuum, or in prison contexts that are ignored, are apt to have their effectiveness (if any) neutralized by influences over which mental health staff have abrogated control.

The solution I have suggested before is closer partnerships. Problem inmates often need team approaches, because they have combinatory problems that defy jurisdictional boundaries. A person who is emotionally labile and intellectually limited and socially disadvantaged and subculturally marginal has no neat credentials to offer. His claim to assistance results from the fact that in the absence of such assistance he is apt to have trouble adjusting, and is apt to create problems for fellow-inmates and staff.

The taxonomies that have struck me as most helpful are those that describe the inmate in terms of his or her current adjustment problems and their underlying dynamics (Chapter 14). The focus admittedly overlaps with conventional diagnostic classification—especially so, where difficulties the prisoner experiences in the institution are serious, and replicate difficulties he or she has experienced in the community. But the inmate's pattern of maladaptation may be discontinuous, since the environment is discontinuous. Moreover, different pathologies can produce overlapping adjustment problems, while a given pathology can create different prison problems for different inmates.

This brings me back to Tommy McCulloch, a man who has spent years in a psychiatric hospital and has committed a criminal offense of surpassing seriousness. Tommy's hospital stay is to some extent relevant, because his view of threats to his survival centers on hospitals as the embodiment of this threat. The magnitude of Tommy's offense is also relevant, because it frames his view of himself, and colors the way others perceive him. But the main problem Tommy and the system face at the moment is different: It is the fact that Tommy has a prison to himself and is guarded by three officers. And Tommy regards this prison as a niche, which he feels he needs for survival.

The challenge is to make Tommy's niche less draconian and hermit-like than it is. In doing so, one need not tamper with niche-attributes Tommy prizes, nor inspire anxiety in staff and occasion adverse press coverage. (Recently, a proposal for Tommy to appear at a prison open house sparked a revolt among guards, and inspired the headline, "Danger Man Fury at Prison.") Change can be incremental, and can occur after notice and consultation. The object of the game must be to enrich Tommy's range of human contacts. A selling point is that one can help Tommy enhance the products he creates. His work on prison history can be improved through consultation with historians, and can benefit from record searches. Tommy could add an oral history component. This enterprise could involve interviews with staff or ex-staff of the prison, former prisoners, and old community residents. Escorted field trips are an option, if and when they are deemed viable.

Human contacts can be designed to range in the benefit they offer to McCulloch and the public. McCulloch—who is immensely concerned about education—could offer hortatory lectures to the young, which he can record on videotape. "No one is so useless," McCulloch has pointed out, "that they can't at least serve as a bad example for others." And McCulloch could share his legendary penchant for making endearing animals, by teaching his skill to retarded patients, fellow-inmates or children. He could visit mental health settings to assuage his concerns about gratuitously intrusive therapy, and so forth.

Another solution would let McCulloch contribute to a prison management function, increase his contact with staff and de-escalate the level of supervision to which he is subjected. These conjoint goals could be accomplished by locating training facilities in McCulloch's building, letting him provide support services to officers who design training modules and run in-service courses.[8]

For a man like McCulloch, one value of such interventions would be to increase stimulation, including social stimulation, while enhancing veridicality of perspective. One could at the same time help McCulloch demonstrate his capacity to behave nonviolently under reduced supervision. "I may be a burnt out case," McCulloch has written, "but is it to anyone's advantage to try and find out?" He has to understand that the answer is "yes," if one can try to do so safely.

As for a prison system, it has to be able to show that legitimate concerns of the public can be addressed without resort to practices that are cost-ineffective as well as uncivilized and detrimental to the psychological survival of its charges.

Notes

1. Tom McCulloch is largely self-educated, because early assessment in the school system relegated him to a non-academic (pre-vocational) track.
2. McCulloch is serving a natural life sentence for a triple homicide committed during an escape from a psychiatric facility, in which the victims included a patient and staff member of the hospital, and a police officer.
3. Tommy McCulloch's interests include the operation of the mental health and criminal justice systems, and specialized subjects such as the effects of pornography (which he tends to discount). But McCulloch is also an amateur historian, and a student of public affairs and public policy. An area of recently acquired expertise is that of computer-assisted communication and instruction.
4. McCulloch's guards are custodial overkill, but the officers serve as sounding boards and social reality checks. McCulloch regales his guards with excerpts of his writings for their

comment, and talks with them about a variety of subjects. He conducts seminars in his room on topics such as the death penalty, which the guards favor. With respect to this issue, McCulloch has told the officers that "protestations that it isn't 'me' they vote to have hung, it's the principle they pursue, is to deny reality." The officers listen to such arguments with tolerant amusement bred by familiarity.

5. Most prisoners who opt for self-segregation beyond the level required by their assignment tend to have a prepotent concern about issues of physical safety. Self-segregation also often occurs among schizophrenic inmates.
6. The concept here alluded to derives from Goffman (1961).
7. The diagnosis of antisocial personality is currently very much in vogue, and the concept accentuates hypothesized differences between offenders and nonoffenders. By contrast, a practicing prison psychiatrist has recently written that his experience "has led me to believe that the differences between the best of us and the worst of us are smaller than generally imagined" (Goodwin, 1993, p. 19).
8. At the time of reprinting of this paper, the prison training unit had been relocated to permit these activities to occur.

Part Six

Research and Reform in Corrections

THE ACADEMIC discipline of corrections is not just a body of knowledge; it is also a profession, which seeks to apply knowledge to effect improvements in the world. The desire to apply knowledge determines the way we go about building knowledge. It directs our choice of problems to be investigated (so that we ask, "Would the findings make a difference?" as well as "Is the problem interesting?"), and our mode of inquiry (because we want results that are "consumable" as well as defensible). It prompts us to disseminate knowledge to those who can deploy it, as well as to subjects of research, who consequently feel less exploited by researchers (Chapter 26). Subjects can become part of the corrections research process if we involve them in the discussion and analysis of findings. Subjects—or persons like subjects—can become researchers themselves (Chapter 27).

One can boast of professional success when knowledge has been applied to beneficent effect. Unfortunately, reforms that are attempted or enacted do not necessarily survive over time (Chapter 28). There is also much change that takes place that is not based on knowledge, or that is out of conformance with the advice offered by students of corrections. Such facts are discouraging, but are also incentives for studying the process of change, so we can intervene more effectively.

26

Prison Research and Prison Reform*

AS A RULE, reports of in-house research make poor bedside reading. Corrections research compendia are apt to contain multi-columned tables that display changes in population or incident frequencies from one year to the next. Such statistics are mostly confusing, and the changes are likely to be evanescent, hard to explain, and devoid of exciting implications.

A bright green report

Expectations are low when one opens a bright green volume issued by the Scottish Prison Service as Occasional Paper No. 1/1992. One is pleasantly surprised when one discovers that the authors (Ed Wozniak and David McAllister) tried to survey all staff and prisoners in Scottish prisons, which meant travel to recondite, difficult to reach, places. For the authors, it also meant meeting with groups of inmates to discuss survey questions. Later, it meant compiling consumable summaries of

---

*This chapter appeared as a "News of the Future" column in *Federal Probation*, June 1993, and is here adapted and reprinted with permission.

findings—two for each prison. The researchers took the trouble because they felt that one should "establish a regular, systematic mechanism through which it will be possible to discover the views of staff and prisoners on a range of issues" (Wozniak and McAllister 1992, p.9).

Why did these researchers feel that one should set up this mechanism? Because — they said — it would let prison managers know what staff and inmates thought *before* they did any planning. Wozniak and McAllister tell us that:

> All [Scottish] prisons have developed strategic forward plans over the past year which outline the direction in which they propose to change and develop and detail specific targets which they hope to achieve. The plans for each prison have been drawn up by senior management teams after careful consideration of the survey results based on the views of both staff and prisoners on aspects of service delivery and their ideas on changes in their prison (p.10).

Wozniak and McAllister acknowledge that feedback of survey results to top management runs short of being Organizational Development, and they have committed themselves to "reporting back the findings to staff and prisoners in each prison to permit discussion to take place about the findings . . . to ensure that staff and prisoners . . . felt part of the process and were being consulted at all stages" (*Ibid.*) This is a new and different approach to prison administration, which is traditionally top down and hierarchical.

But Scotland is unashamedly undergoing reform, and newspapers carry headlines such as "Prisoners can now choose where and how to spend time" (*The Herald*, 1992). The inmates are referred to as "consumers" of correctional services. There is talk of prisoners making responsible choices, and of prisons furnishing "a range of opportunities to permit prisoners to accept responsibility for their behavior and enable change and personal development." There is also talk of an "enhanced role" for staff, and of "the critical role staff will have to play in implementing the new strategy" (Scottish Prison Service, 1990).

This is heady stuff, and it makes doing relevant research exciting, because what one does can constructively matter. Wozniak and McAllister wanted their respondents to understand this fact. In introducing their study to groups of inmates, they "engaged in extensive and lively debate about the merits of co-operation in the exercise." The liveliness is illustrated by comments from inmates such as "We've heard all this before. We fill in forms and that's the last we hear of it. There's lots of talk about change, but I don't see any evidence of it" (Wozniak and McAllister, 1992, p. 46).

Survey results

Staff in Scotland's prisons prove surprisingly supportive of change, and willing to participate in it. For instance, "in response to an open ended question about developments in the role of the prison officer, staff mention that they particularly want to be able to deal on a personal level with prisoners and be in a position to help with drug and alcohol problems, mentally disturbed offenders and prisoners with HIV and AIDS" (p. 20). Nine out of ten staff members (92 per cent) endorse sentence planning for inmates; 65 percent welcome a prison ombudsman's office; 75 percent favor new prison rules. Only one development—legal representation at grievance hearings—is opposed by staff.

But staff have doubts about their own role in planning. Most have not felt consulted, informed or dealt in in the past; half (48 per cent) assert that "senior staff have little grasp of what goes on in the prison," and more than half (56 per cent) charge that managers do not listen to suggestions (Wozniak, 1992). Interestingly, though, "fifty-four percent agree that management *in their prison* places a high value on staff participation, and only 18 per cent disagree" (Wozniak and McAllister, 1992, p. 32). In some prisons, virtually all officers feel they are participating. In others, only four of ten officers say they are consulted.

With respect to expanding staff roles—what some call "job enrichment"—the Scottish climate is receptive. Wozniak and McAllister report that:

> Many staff, particularly younger recent recruits express disappointment that they are still turnkeys and little else. The suggestion of a shift in the staff role toward greater involvement with prisoners and greater responsibility which is likely to devolve to the staff through schemes such as sentence planning are welcomed (p. 41).

Scottish prisons have had problems in the past, but at this point staff see little tension in prisons. The officers feel they get along with prisoners. Eight of ten inmates concur, and 95 percent report no problems with fellow-inmates. A minority of prisoners (one in five) feels unsafe; some say they are afraid of officers.

Prisoners have reservations about conditions of confinement. One concern is with arrangements for family visitation. Three of four prisoners (76 per cent) rate conditions for children's visits poor; four of five (78 per cent) complain there is no privacy; two thirds (67 per cent) feel visits are too short. Prisoners also complain about prison food and medical care. Wozniak writes that "some of these areas may seem trivial and mundane when contrasted against the prisoners' loss of freedom but for many prisoners the true acid test of change in the SPS will be measured by improvements in areas such as food and laundry and not in the implementation of major schemes such as Sentence Planning or Personal Officer Schemes" (Wozniak, 1992, p. 11).

Wozniak's point is well taken. Tangible improvements are easy to see, and augur well for reform. Basic needs must be satisfied before higher needs are invoked. And this point applies with equal measure to the guards, who complain they have no space or privacy, and are needlessly moved from prison to prison. Significantly, the guards are concerned about the inmates' needs. Almost all (96 per cent) want improved sanitation for inmates; most (76 per cent) favor expanded family visits and home visitation (63 per cent). Guards are therefore far from resistant to improvements in the lives of inmates.

What of the prospects of participatory planning? Staff say they want it, the system is officially committed to it, and data are available for planning to occur.

System-wide planning

One level of planning involves systemic questions. How can visiting conditions across the country be improved? How does one go about involving officers in the counseling of inmates? What programs do we offer prisoners? How do we gauge their interests and preferences? Where are assignments that satisfy these interests?

A good way of gaining participation in such planning is through task forces. Different ranks—including customers—can be represented on a task force. One can also try for added stratification, such as geographical coverage, or one can seek representation by size or type of prison. Task forces can be subdivided into mini-task forces to do detailed planning and report back to each other. Most important, task forces can do studies, or can commission studies, if they need more information.

For example, in line with the "basic needs first" postulate, a Scottish planning task force could put family visits and staff transfers high on its agenda. The initial survey shows that guards join inmates in their concern about family visits. Could guards help by gathering information about transportation or the monitoring of visits? Could they help liaise with agencies willing to sponsor bus transportation for children and spouses?

What about staff transfers? Is the problem structural and constrained? Are all assumptions that have been made about the transfer system valid? Are they engraved in stone? Must older guards, with families, suffer as they do, or is there a way to arrange less frequent rotation of married staff? Is there possible virtue in the stability of staff assignments?

If inmates are to have "choice" it means that one must inventory inmate preferences at intake into the system. One must have options available that relate to preference profiles. (One cannot ask an inmate to opt for education or for training if one has no teachers to teach him or train him.) The opinions of prisoners who leave on parole might help predict those of entry cohorts. Pre-planned flexibility can help to keep options in line with demands. Task forces can help implement proposals. They lend them the credibility that comes with representative membership. Solid documentation—such as survey data—helps to sell proposals.

Local planning

In local planning, surveys can be not only catalytic, but on occasion, cataclysmic. Take the item, "Senior staff in the prison have no idea of what actually goes on." Concurrence in Scotland is 48 percent, and ranges from 69, 68, and 62 to 16 percent at the facilities (Wozniak and McAllister, 1992, p. 19). Feedback can hypothetically take the form, "in your prison, over two-thirds of respondents said senior staff does not know what goes on. You are way out of line on this item."

Or, assume that as a manager you are told that the survey majority "describe the levels of cleanliness, repair, etc. as either fairly good or OK," but that your prison is the exception, and that eight of ten staff members rate your halls as dirty (p. 15). Or, assume that your prison is one of three in which inmate-staff relations are not ranked uniformly highly (p. 28). Or that only one percent of your inmates rate your food as edible (p. 52).

In survey feedback, such data can be embedded in other data. One can say something like, "Your prison stands out as a safe institution, but your staff are not sure that you fully appreciate the problems they face" or "Yours is a harmonious facility, but your inmates feel that the food service can use attention."

The goal is not to sugar-coat the prison's problems, but to convey the fact that responses to single questions are not of unseemly concern to the system's Central Office. Survey answers cannot document adverse conclusions such as, "the guards at Jonesville don't get along with inmates," or "the warden of Kumquat is a dictator," or "Mountain View is unsafe." The best that surveys can do is suggest hypotheses, such as "young violent offenders shipped to Jonesville may pose temporary problems." Such hypotheses must be checked at the prison level.

Feedback is a way of stimulating thinking among survey respondents. Ideally, it leads to self-questioning, followed by self-study and self-reform. A prison researcher who runs feedback sessions must walk a fine line between pinpointing deficits (which can lead to anger, denials and defensiveness), and glossing over problem areas highlighted by the survey. If sensitive issues arise, the researcher may face acrimony, and have to work through accumulated feelings about topics such as supervision, transfers and family visitation. He must try to orchestrate his sessions so that he can at some point move from catharsis to serious problem solving.

Research and reform

While serving in the military I was involved in military research. My forte was studies of rank-and-file morale. After one such effort, our group received a note from a high-level officer, which said "my men have better things to do than to fill out your **** questionnaires!"

I discovered that research acceptance can be precarious, but so is the claim research can advance to making a contribution. The claim is most vulnerable where the research function is insulated, or where research is self-insulated by choice. There are researchers who say, "I only do what is theoretically relevant." By this they can mean, "I don't care what agency staff think of my work because my heart lies in academia." The output of such researchers often consists of mathematical exercises no lay persons can understand. Their idea of feedback is to present a paper to fellow-methodologists, preferably abroad.

Some corrections researchers have never talked to an inmate. Officers may make them uncomfortable. Data are collected (if at all) by others. Data analyses may be painstakingly done, but the use of the data is left to enlightened administrators who have graduate degrees in mathematical statistics. Other researchers are compilers of numbers. Numbers that might lend themselves to inferences are lost in a profusion of insignificant numerological detail. All tidbits are pedantically summarized, in sentences such as "there was a slight increase in the number of brown-eyed inmates from suburban areas convicted of robbing convenience stores."

My own concern is with different researchers, who want to be involved in efforts to improve their agencies and want to make the prisons more humane. Many such researchers (unlike their colleagues) are not cynical about the system and what it can accomplish. Their rewards come from seeing reforms enacted that are based on research findings, and documenting the success or failure of reforms through research.

Researchers such as these benefit from the permeability of boundaries between staff and line functions. They need to be accepted by prison workers and by the inmates, and to garner credibility. They need to involve staff members and prisoners in their work, and to have it seen as relevant. And they need to take part in the dissemination and utilization of findings.

Such researchers may be in short supply in graduate schools that breed elitist conceptions of research and pessimistic views of reform. Good researchers are also in short demand by agencies that discourage experimentation and the crossing of bureaucratic frontiers. In this sense, the story of Wozniak and McAllister and the Scottish Prison Service is doubly refreshing. It shows us what can happen when motivated researchers work in an innovative system, and it suggests that if it happens there, it can happen elsewhere as well.

27

The Convict as Researcher*

SEVERAL YEARS ago, I was involved in a study of the social psychology of violence. In studying violence inside prisons we operated with a resident research staff that combined sophistication, practical experience, and the ability to inspire confidence in our informants. Our group in one prison, for instance, consisted of six men whose graduate training added up to 83 years of confinement. Their competence to study violence in prisons was obvious since five of them also qualified as subjects.

Our top researcher was an interdisciplinary social scientist for whom I cannot find enough praise. His name was Manuel Rodriguez, and his academic background consisted of an eighth grade education, a term in the US Army Supply School, and a short course in automobile repair.

But Rodriguez had other qualifications. Before the age of 18 he was arrested for malicious mischief and assault. Later he was sentenced for such offenses as armed robbery, burglary, firearms possession, narcotic addiction, and drunk driving. (I might

---

*This chapter originally appeared in *Transaction*, 1967 (pages 72-75), and is here adapted and reprinted with permission from Transaction Publishers; all rights reserved.

confess that since joining us he was arrested again, this time for driving without a license while engaged in research.)

Rodriguez had spent 15 of his 36 years behind bars, mostly in the California State Prison at San Quentin. As an inmate Rodriguez became interested in our research topic. He describes the beginning of his interest as follows:

> I was assigned to the weight-lifting section of the gymnasium. Most of the more violence-prone inmates come here to blow off steam at one time or another. It is also sort of a refuge where an inmate can get away from the pressures of staff scrutiny and the yards. We try to keep violence nonexistent, if possible, in this section. This was part of my job, although it was not explicit. In many cases — as a peacemaker — I had to convince both would-be combatants that they could retreat without losing face or pride. Most inmates contemplating violence will usually go to a respected member of the prison community for advice on "Shall I kill this guy or not?" I and a friend of mine were two of these persons so respected. When these guys who are straddling the fence between violence and nonviolence came to us we began to actively prescribe nonviolence.

Rodriguez started out as an informed layman, with a completely pragmatic concern with violence. But he ultimately became a sophisticated violence researcher. His transmutation began in early 1965 when he was selected as a trainee in the New Careers Development Project directed by my collaborator, J. Douglas Grant. This revolutionary program was aimed at converting standard clients of professional services (such as Rodriguez) into dispensers of professional services — or at least into intermediaries between clients and professionals. Research work seemed to be one sort of activity relevant to such transmutation. Inmate Rodriguez was thus put to work, during his training period in prison, on the first stage of our study. His work included research design, as well as code construction, interviewing, and coding. After Rodriguez was released on parole, we were happy to hire him as a staff member.

Outside, Rodriguez acted as our principal interviewer. He interviewed parolees with violent records and citizens who had assaulted police officers. He was not only a sympathetic and incisive interviewer, but became unusually successful in stimulating interest among potential subjects. He is 5 feet 10 inches tall and weighs 175 pounds. He generally wears shirts that allow an unimpeded view of two arms full of tattoos. In addition, when we began the police assaulter interviews, Rodriguez grew a bushy moustache to make himself look — as he put it — more "subcultural." This prop undergirded an invitation to participate that started with the words, "We are not a snitch outfit," but then proceeded to a thoughtful, honest exposition of our objective.

In our study, we tried to blur the line between the observer and the observed. Each of our interviewees was invited to sit down with us to conceptualize the data obtained from him. Each one was asked to help find common denominators in the particulars obtained in the interview. Each one received the same opportunity we did to play the social scientist and become a minor partner in our enterprise. We felt this was the ethical thing to do, but we obtained some material of extraordinary sophistication from these nonprofessional collaborators.

The Convict as Researcher

Results and rapport

Why did we choose to rely on nonprofessionals? How did they serve us better than the usual research associates and assistants with the conventional technical and academic credentials?

First, and most obviously, they were able to establish trust where we were not, to get data that we could not get, and to obtain it in the subjects' own language. I think I can best illustrate this advantage by excerpting a brief passage of one of our prison interviews. The respondent here is a seasoned inmate whose reputation was solidly based on a long record of violent involvements. The interviewer was one of our nonprofessional researchers — another prison inmate:

> Q: Was it the next day that you were going through the kitchen line and that he approached you and said he was coming down and wanted his stuff, and you better be there with it?
>
> A: He said he was coming to get me, and I better be ready. The inference was — Was I going to be ready?
>
> Q: So you went back to the kitchen and got a shank [knife] and then went to your pad. Now this dude who was doing the talking to you now, this is the one who you were playing coon can [a card game] with? The next morning one of the dudes approached you?
>
> A: The next morning. The same dude. When I came out of my cell in the wing this guy approached me. He lived in the wing.
>
> Q: What is his message?
>
> A: His message is just a play, and they were playing a pat hand. It wasn't anything different from the day before. I told him.

This excerpt fits into a standardized interview schedule that was designed to tease out sequences of interpersonal moves leading to violence. But it also is a snatch of conversation between two persons discussing a subject of mutual interest in the most natural and appropriate language possible. In this type of interaction, data collection occurs with no constraint, and without translations designed to please or to educate the researcher.

Another advantage to be obtained in the use of nonprofessionals is the benefit of their unique perspective in data interpretation. A well-chosen lay researcher can often be in a position to correct naive inferences by less experienced professionals. In one dramatic experience one of my research partners, inmate Hallinan of San Quentin, chided me (in graceful prose) for drawing a hasty and incorrect conclusion from an interview we had conducted:

> Your interpretation seems to be influenced by the subject's storied loquaciousness rather than the incidents themselves. Is the subject's behavior, as he claims, the result of his being an Indian leader, and having to intercede in their behalf, or is it because of his need to establish a personal reputation as a prison tough guy? I choose the latter interpretation; an interpretation based on how the subject has behaved, not how he thinks he has behaved . . . .
>
> An Indian functions within the rigid framework of rules. "There are family

codes, tribal codes, and Indian laws," is how he puts it. But there is also . . . a joint code that he is well aware of: "The cons have their own rules, and one of them is that they step on the weak."

The first incident that the subject becomes involved in is the rat-packing of an Indian child molester in order to ostracize and punish the molester, and also to solidify his position among the low-riders. So, rather than being a leader of these Indians, he is using his Indian blood to further his own ends. He wants to be a tough con, someone to be feared and respected. "The new guys that come in, no one knows about them. Once you get a reputation you have to protect it." The above statements, and others similar in nature, were made by the subject during the course of the interview. [Their] significance is self-evident.

How does the subject go about building a reputation? As he says, fighting for home boys, and interceding for other Indians? No. Of the ten incidents — actually nine, because No. 1 and No. 9 are the same — No. 6, no violence occurred; No. 2 involved helping a friend, although the details were vague; No. 7 was a fight of his own making; No. 9 he was attacked; and No. 10 was the rat-packing incident. The remaining four involved custody. He was proudest of No. 8. In regards to this incident the following dialogue occurred:

Q: Do you think this incident helped your reputation?
A: It sure as hell did. I knocked down the Captain.
Q: How did you feel just before you knocked him down?
A: Like a big man.
Q. During?
A. I sure am doing it right this time.

The subject is also proud of the fact that at one time he had spat on the warden . . . . Obviously the subject feels that these things scare people . . . .

The word circulates that he has fought with the "bulls," implying that he will jump on a convict with little provocation. The facts are never pursued, but accepted prima facie, because those who pass on these rumors and exaggerations are the very ones who are most impressed by them. The rumor returns and the subject begins to believe his own yard reputation . . . .

Our subject has completed the building of his reputation, petty though it is, and now he and his low-rider friends can observe and honor it. Not that the cons on the yard do, but the subject feels that they do, and this is all that really matters. If anything he is tolerated, not respected and feared as he would like.

It is obvious that inmate Hallinan is not only furnishing me with a lesson in perspective, but is also demonstrating that he can compete with professionals in his methodological acumen and his ability to vividly summarize and communicate research conclusions. And although this analysis is unusually literate, because inmate Hallinan has invested much prison time in creative writing courses, much can be learned even from our most unlettered collaborators.

There is another aspect to the use of nonprofessionals which relates to a less tangible and more general advantage. Most social researchers sense some difficulty in the initial approach to subject populations of vastly different backgrounds from their own. Some react at this juncture with an elaborate process of ingratiation or "gaining of rapport" in which the research is presented in the (presumably) best light. This posturing is often transparently insincere and always wasteful. Worse, it usually achieves merely a wary and delicate stalemate, during which only a hit-and-run raid for data is possible before the subjects discover what has happened to them.

Avoiding exploitation

During rare moments of honesty, we may admit that even when we induce subjects to cooperate, our dealings with them are seldom the exciting adventure we tell our students about. I say this because I suspect that the real problem is not one of communication and social distance at all — it may have nothing to do with culture or dress or the use of more or less vivid vocabulary. It may be that our subjects understand us only too well — that what we ask is unreasonable and unfair. After all, at best we are supplicants, and at worst, invaders demanding booty of captive audiences. In return for a vague promise or a modest remuneration we expect a fellow human being to bare his or her soul or to make revealing and potentially incriminating statements. The "communication" is one-way — the researcher maintains his or her position as a recipient of nonreciprocated information.

We also make our informant aware that we are not interested in him or her as a person but as a "subject" — a representative of a type, or a case, or a constituent of a sample. He or she knows this because he or she is being approached as the inhabitant of a ghetto or a prison, or a member of some other study population. And most research subjects know that their interests are being subordinated to our own. How can they share our objectives, after all, if they mostly cannot see the results of the efforts in which they have participated?

I speak with considerable humility here, because I almost once again made the mistake of taking my Viennese accent and my parochial concerns into prison cells and police stations, expecting to secure frank answers to prying questions. I had done this sort of thing in the past and shall probably do it again. But this once, Grant and I followed an alternative course, and it supplied us with linkage across cultural gaps, with motivated informants, with substantive expertise, with heightened analytic power, and with the feeling that we had been defensibly fair.

I shall not pretend that these benefits are automatic and free of risk. Like professional researchers, nonprofessional participants in research must be selected with care. Unintelligent or completely illiterate persons would be of limited use, as would social isolates. A cynical, exploitive, or immature outlook can create a poor prospect for programs that have the usual training resources. This is also true of rigidly held preconceptions, though to a lesser extent.

On the other hand, too close attention to selection criteria may produce a staff of quasi-professional nonprofessionals. They may be rejected by the subjects of research. Not being trusted, they may have relatively limited useful knowledge or insight, contribute little, discover they are marginal members of the team, and develop poor motivation.

Even careful selection will not altogether eliminate these possibilities. The nonprofessional must get training that is not only directly related to research but also can provide a meaningful role definition. Some of this training may be of the sort routinely encountered in graduate schools; some may be more characteristic of supportive social movements. The nonprofessional researcher must be, in a sense, a convert. He or she may have to acquire a revised persona, a new set of values, and new models and friends while remaining in close touch with old associates. The professional merely places others under the microscope, but the nonprofessional must integrate his or her own life experiences into the data. While the rest of us can view research as a job, the nonprofessional may have to see the involvement as part of a personal transmutation.

What training, then, should the nonprofessionals get? First, there is research indoctrination, in the purest sense of the word, awakening curiosity, which in our case involved the desire to reach latent meanings or patterns. One must try to inculcate suspicion of the unrepresentative and unique and a phobia against premature interpretation. Obviously, one must also provide tools — intensive practical instruction in the use of the steps to be employed, in our study including interviewing techniques, content analysis, survey design problems, and data processing. This training must not only include general information about the process and content of the research but also social skill training of the kind necessary to work with sensitive groups.

But the most critical challenge is to our self-conceptions. Will we treat the trained nonprofessionals as partners and colleagues and respect their integrity and abilities? We have a right to preserve the nature of our own contribution, but we must also be prepared to become receptive members of our own team.

Nonprofessionals, if given the opportunity, can help us shape ideas, formulate designs, and analyze results. We can continue to provide intellectual discipline and a sense of perspective. For the rest, we may find ourselves in the unaccustomed position of being students to spirited and able teachers — and the benefits will be reflected in the quality of our research, as well as in the resolution of ethical dilemmas that currently often leave social researchers with a bitter taste in the mouth after they are done.

28

The Impermanence of Planned Change in Corrections*

THOSE OF US who feel we have originated beneficent interventions in corrections often exhibit scars in the shape of discontinued innovations and residuals of enterprises that are only remotely — if at all — related to the presumably bold visions that inspired their inception. This chapter explores one aspect of this process — the staying power of successful innovations.

Contrasting presuppositions of innovators and counter-innovators

It should be obvious that one reason why self-styled innovators invite disillusionment is that they share the presumption that it is in principle possible for innovations to have long-term effects. In this respect they most sharply diverge from the perspective of criminologists who presuppose that "nothing works." This perspective allows for the notion that interventions work at first because of a Hawthorne Effect (the flattering attention attracted by new experiments) but presumes that every interven-

---

*With J. Douglas Grant. This chapter is adapted from a contribution to *Policy and Theory in Criminal Justice*, edited by D.M. Gottfredson and R.V. Clarke (1990). It is reprinted with permission from Ashgate Publishing, Ltd. The authors wish to thank Joan Grant for her support, advice and assistance.

tion stops working when this effect wears off. The same perspective also postulates that everything seems to work when sloppy, self-serving data are collected to document it, but can be shown not to work if one asks for rigorous documentation (Lipton, Martinson and Wilks, 1975). Such skepticism relates to the inherent complexity and obduracy of crime-related problems, and to the presumed primitiveness and oversimplicity of any efforts to improve our responses to the problem (Wilson, 1975).

On the other hand, innovators tend to assume that they have kindred spirits within the system, in the shape of officials who take their assigned missions seriously, and want their operations to become more rational and responsive to public needs. This view is prominently at variance with one that holds that public officials are by nature wedded to the status quo, and regard all new ideas as disequilibrating threats (Shadish, 1984). The first premise differs from the second, however, not only in direction, but in the scope of its coverage, in that it implies no claim about the prevalence of innovation-consumers, nor about the extent of the receptivity and hospitality on which one can count. In other words, no one claims that all politicians are statesmen.

The "inside man"

One reason why innovations can be evanescent is that turnover can occur among officials, and such turnover can include the sponsors of innovations. Critics would argue that this contingency is predictable, since risk-taking (which includes sponsorship of new ideas) adversely affects public careers. This assumption is gratuitous, but sponsorship alone is rarely safe as a way to achieve the long-term undergirding of reforms. The innovator always needs friends in high places to get his foot in the door, but he cannot depend on such links to sustain his innovation over time.

Sponsorship also varies in the degree to which it implies wholehearted endorsements of one's goals. An official who strikes an innovator as hospitably progressive is a person who has what one considers a congenial progressive agenda. Though such an agenda may overlap with one's own agenda, the chances are that it will never coincide with it. The discovery of any overlap one senses during initial encounters leads to intoxicating liaisons, but the fact that one ignores indications of non-overlap means that any resulting marriage becomes one of compromise, in which each party achieves some of his or her goals, but not others. And where substantial goal discrepancies occur, one can confidently predict that the sponsor is the person who will achieve his or her goals, and that the innovator may not discover this fact until his program has been subverted.

The Encounter with the Enlightened Official who Approves of What you Do is an intoxicating experience and there is little this side of heaven that can rival it. This is so because the official is a Commander of Legions who is prepared (he says) to put a platoon, perchance a company, at your disposal. To add flattery to such favor, the sponsor sponsors you because he thinks (he says) you can improve his operation. Such trust earns loyalty and indebtedness, not inquiry about your sponsor's agenda. And it does not invite verification of the fact that what your sponsor thinks you want is what you think you want, which you may feel is obvious, given the presumed identity of your perspectives.

The Impermanence of Planned Change in Corrections

Intersections of perspective next become an issue when the sponsor embarks on an effort to "sell" the intervention to others in his organization. If the sponsor is powerful, the "selling" may consist of mandating adoption, and the result of this can be grudging acquiescence. The prognosis where this occurs is invariably unpromising, because sophisticated subordinates will use or create opportunities to sabotage the fledgling intervention, which they will regard as an alien imposition.

Less authoritative sponsorship carries different but commensurate risks. One such risk is that the sponsor will make concessions to superiors to secure acceptance and, though he or she may regard these concessions as inconsequential, they may seriously emasculate a program. Another risk is that the program may become tied to the sponsor's political agenda, or may fall victim to institutional power plays.

Internalization of premises underlying the innovation

Interventions with staying power must be internalized by their targets, in the sense that the premises on which the interventions are based must fit prevailing preconceptions and make sense to key gatekeepers (Kelman, 1958). This process is easy to gauge where the intervention's premises are simple, but becomes harder to trace where the goals are more complex, so that partial endorsements can be confused with total agreement.

This issue typically arises where the interventionist's premises predefine the process and content of interventions, which can be highlighted at each other's expense (Argyris, 1970). Humanistic change agents, for example, are committed to democracy or participation as a mode of organizational intervention (Chapters 9 and 10). This notion, however, runs counter to the experiences, though not to the expressed philosophy, of managers. Typically, managers concur with the idea of democracy, but may resist the implementation of this idea when it gets translated into action.

Goal displacement

The point that interventions have staying power to the extent to which they are internalized is different from the view that interventions will survive if they are institutionalized, which means that they must appear on a table of organization or otherwise become part of their host organization. To be internalized means that you are adopted both in letter and in spirit as long as your goals make sense to the organization. Institutionalization can mean the opposite of internalization because it can perpetuate interventions after their goals have been abandoned.[1] The presumption here is that goal displacement, which is a corollary of bureaucracy, can emasculate an intervention after it becomes a routine operation in a bureaucracy. The process is described by Merton, who writes that goal displacement means that:

> Adherence to the rules, originally conceived as a means, becomes transformed into an end-in-itself . . . . Formalism, even ritualism, ensues with an unchallenged insistence upon punctilious adherence to formalized procedures. This may be exaggerated to the point where primary concern with conformity to the rules interferes with the achievement of the purposes of the organization (Merton, 1957, p. 199).

If one substitutes the word "intervention" for "organization," Merton's description applies to institutionalized innovations whose form survives at the expense of their content after bureaucratization has occurred.

Goal displacement seems particularly likely to occur where interventions deviate from traditional, classic management or where they presuppose that higher-level needs of low-level organizational members will be mobilized. We have elsewhere (Toch and Grant, 1982) described an intervention that involved correction officers and met with only qualified success. In this intervention, several groups of officers drafted proposals for prison reform, with the understanding — confidently relayed by the interventionists — that favorable consideration would be given to implementing as many of the proposals as possible. Though the organization did extend hospitality, they ended up parceling out the proposals to low echelon officials who were uniformly unimpressed with the participatory origins of the ideas. The proposals were assessed in the context of continuing bureaucratic planning. This meant that the closest a proposal could come to "adoption" was that it could be deemed an endorsement of a move already under way.

The point here is not that change tends to be co-opted, but that it is absorbed into the familiar world of the organization, which is different (or at least, can be different) from the Brave New World of the interventionist.

The constraints of the managerial world

Managers are subjected to a variety of pressures with which the interventionist is of necessity unfamiliar, a fact which is facilitated by the discourse about bold vistas that typically characterizes innovator-sponsor dialogues. Where administrators talk to innovators about organizational force fields — budgetary realities, for example, or competing demands on resources — the innovator's eyes predictably glaze over, and the sponsor's soliloquy may be dismissed as an attack of dyspepsia. The administrator may conversely decide to keep reality-based worries to himself, so as not to dampen the innovator's enthusiasm. By the time resistances surface it may be too late (or almost too late) to address them. On one occasion, for example, a member of one of our research teams unwittingly ran afoul of prison regulations, and the writer was instructed — until he could talk his way out of the escalating situation — to disband a program of inmate self-study groups. Another prison program I have mentioned that was aborted envisaged a self-contained community component deemed critical which required a combined living-program setting. It was tempting to infer from the program's discontinuance that the administrator harbored reservations about the program's philosophy, but for months during the planning phase we had been warned about space constraints and had insufficiently attended to the warning.

Some implementation problems also arise because interventionists come and go, leaving a fragile legacy unprotected after they have gone. Though there are some difficulties which are uncircumventable, there are also demands that may lend themselves to trade-offs if a spokesperson for the intervention could plead its case. It would, therefore, be an advantage if one could assure buttressing, as well as defensible solidity and integrity, for a long-term contribution, before one parted company

The Impermanence of Planned Change in Corrections

with the host organization. We suspect that this means that a powerful figure within the organization — a person who could negotiate organizational realities and who subscribes to the goal of the intervention — ought to be built into its support system. Such an official could be assigned the role of protecting the intervention's existence and integrity and would have to ensure his or her succession in this role if he or she moved to different pastures.

Invoking the leader

One of the authors of this chapter had a memorable experience which involved a site visit following an application for funds to conduct an action research intervention in a prison system. Government representatives met a senior official, who assured them of unqualified cooperation. "What about the wardens?" the visitors asked. The official assured them that the wardens would cooperate. "What happens if some object to the inconvenience and intrusion?" insisted the visitors. "Then," the official said, "we use clout."

The use of "clout" is philosophically uncongenial to humanistic interventionists because of the democratic ethos to which they are wedded. They also resist appealing to higher echelons because they see the chain of command as a given, even where lower echelon conflicts have proved irreconcilable. Most important, however, is the prevalence of stubborn self-confidence and misplaced faith among interventionists, even where experience should suggest that one needs assistance.

Hesitance to invoke higher authority can create a paradox whereby innovations fail though they are supported by committed, innovative top administrators. Several such instances have been reported — and others almost occurred — under a prison administration that was noted for its liberal leanings. In one notorious instance (Studt, Messinger and Wilson, 1968) an innovative therapeutic community that was instituted in a prison failed to survive and a traditional prison regime was reinstituted.

The interventionists wrote later:

> Of primary importance was the fact that the community was never permitted to design its institutions for control in congruence with the values espoused in its welfare institutions ... The sanctioning system imposed from outside the Project was a powerful force maintaining the "do your time" orientation among the unit inmates ... The lack of problem-solving connections between the Project and upper-level administration in (the prison) was in large part responsible for turning the Unit community into an ineffective satellite ... The administration of the larger institution could neither understand nor respond positively to the Project's request for increased responsibility (Studt, Messinger and Wilson, 1968, pp.280-1).

A central administration under which this type of conflict occurs is obliged to support its prison staff, but it is also obliged to keep innovations that it sponsors alive. The chief administrator can acquire the stature of King Solomon if he mediates conflicts such as those between rule enforcement and the dispensations sought by those who run an innovative operation. Intervention in such disputes does not mean "taking sides" but using the opportunity one is afforded to explore the implications of running an intervention with integrity in an organization of integrity. It means defining accommodations that must be made while preserving the compatibility of a new program with the needs of its host organization, so that the former does not become a cancerous growth. Such issues must be explored because they set useful precedents for definitions of the interface between the organization and future programs that require flexibility. From the administrator's perspective it is a missed opportunity if those involved in conflicts throw up their hands and deprive him or her of the chance to review interface problems for integrative solutions.

One difficulty, of course, is that battle lines may harden beyond the point of return, which is a contest the interventionist cannot win. Defeat under such circumstances, however, can be sweet because it carries psychological satisfactions such as a pure conscience and the opportunity for self-righteous indignation. Unlike the administrator, the interventionist can write a nostalgic book detailing a Noble Experiment that was squelched by Forces of Reaction. These books (such as Murton, 1976; Hickey and Scharf, 1980) can discourage future interventions by depicting an obdurate system that is non-amenable to reformation.

The sour grapes syndrome

Interventions that fail to take hold are learning opportunities, if they are properly utilized. Such self-examination would have revealed in the above described prison failure (Studt, Messinger and Wilson, 1968), for example, that the inmate governance system was poorly planned and ill-defined, and that the interventionists had a tendency to "play things by ear," which invited disaster.

Posthumous critical self-examinations are rare, however, and self-blaming is unheard of, which makes learning from failure difficult. Learning also means that one's retrospects must be case-specific, rather than generalizing disillusionment to obdurate environments that fall beyond the circumstances that occasion it. It is understandable that one should undersell one's mistakes or even fail to perceive them, but it is harder to see why most interventionists insist on confusing inhospitable circumstances in one organization with generic structural problems in a range of organizations. All too frequently the lesson derived by the reformer is that his or her reform was foredoomed because all reform is foredoomed unless one permits oneself to be coopted, or unless one survives at the expense of doing anything worthwhile. Such views provide solace but discourage innovations, and cast suspicion on anyone currently involved in reform, whose integrity and/or intelligence are impugned.

The reformer fails to recognize that, if a system is impervious to change, it could have resisted the introduction of reforms, rather than waiting until it could undermine their survival. Prisons that want to remain authoritarian, for example (Hickey and Scharf, 1980), can easily prevent therapeutic communities from being opened, and tradition-bound prisons have no reason to go out of their way to hire self-advertised reformers (Murton, 1976) who must be painfully discharged under adverse publicity.

The disillusioned reformer may also confuse the end product of a long-term acrimonious conflict (which he or she may have done more than his or her share to produce) with outcomes that might have been possible in the absence of escalating conflicts. Such options can only be seen where they are experienced, however, as in crises weathered, including narrowly averted disasters.

One step forward, six steps back

The danger of generalizing beyond non-survival to predictions of future failure is run both by change agents and observers of change. The risk particularly attaches to unfriendly observers who tend to wait in the wings for reformers to fail so they can say "I told you so." The lesson drawn by such observers is that each program they disapprove of has failed because it is based on naive and unrealistic assumptions about what is possible.

A good example of nihilistic inferences drawn by critics pertains to the advocacy of inmate governance in prisons (Chapter 9). Moderate advocates of the strategy mostly believed that the autocratic management of prisons could be ameliorated if prisoner representatives could have input into decisions that affect the quality of life in the prison. Fogel (1975), for example, argued that "We begin with the premise that prison is not the ideal setting for a democracy, but that it could be democratized . . . there is no reason, as in the case outside prison, why we cannot deepen the engagement of the governed in their own governance" (p. 209).

Howard Gill, a pioneer in the establishment of American inmate councils, saw them as furthering the rehabilitation of his offenders. A historian of Gill's institution (the Norfolk Prison Colony) points out that:

> Mr. Gill realized that, in attempting to rehabilitate maladjusted men and in reorienting them to fit into society on their release, it was essential that they should be brought under principles almost antithetical to those of a bastille prison in which everything conspires to take the last vestiges of responsibility away from the men. Norfolk, on the other hand, sought to give the men as much responsibility as they could stand (Yahkub, 1940, p. 84).

The journalist Serrill (1982) traced a portrait of Howard Gill in which he notes that Gill "succeeded in establishing a prison community extraordinary for its time. Most rules were made and enforced by the inmates themselves" (p. 27). Yet Gill's experiment has been adjudged a failure, by (among others) Rothman (1980), who writes that "its view of a harmony of interests, its readiness to treat the individual not the act, would appear to contradict whatever lessons an historical record can provide" (p. 421). The "lessons" at issue have to do with Gill's personal fortunes (he was fired by conservative legislators) and with Rothman's belief that the prison by its nature must be a non-democratic institution.

Gill's redoubtable prisoner councils experienced periods of lassitude, and stages during which inmate "politicians" gained temporary ascendancy. Such junctures, however, were interspersed with extremely effective inmate groups, which weathered and overcame all sorts of crises.

A more recent attempt at prison self-governance had disastrous results, though it was highly touted at its inception. In a study of this program, for instance, Regens and Hobson (1978) found that inmates who had participated in the experiment had improved perceptions of self-esteem and self-competency compared to non-participants, and showed greater acceptance of law and authority. The positive findings were presumed mediated by the involvement of the participants in self-government, with those most involved showing the greatest change.

The denouement of this experience has been summarized by DiIulio (1987), who writes:

> Among those who came to rule the prison were the "Bikers," a prison gang which, when not terrorizing other inmates or the staff, extended its members the privilege of racing their motorcycles in the prison yard. The experiment ended when the internal situation became so chaotic that public pressure mounted to regain control of the institution (p. 37).

The failure of this program not only turned the clock back in its own prison system, but fed the cumulating argument that "the more freedom inmates have, the more unsafe prisons will be" (McCoy, 1981, p. 193). This view is expressed by DiIulio (1987) who concludes that:

> Where inmates come to participate in the formulation and administration of prison policy, prisons change little or become worse. There is not a single example of a system of inmate self-government — formal or informal — in a higher-custody prison that has resulted in a safer, cleaner, more productive facility. Where prison officials have been unable or unwilling to run the prison without the assistance of inmates, the quality of prison life has suffered, often resulting in the rule of inmate predators (p.38).

DiIulio's assessment is widely shared. The dictum that you are free to try again does not describe opportunities open to reformers such as democratizers of prisons. For such reformers, unhappy endings are invariably adjudged preordained, and regarded as documentation of the non-viability of theories on which their reforms are based. The non-survival of reform efforts perceived in this fashion not only lowers the probability of change in the settings in which they occur, but makes analogous changes less likely to be attempted elsewhere. This makes it hard for reformers to profit from experience, which includes applying the lessons they have derived from their unsuccessful experiences. "Sadder but wiser" reformers are not in heavy demand, which may make them bitter enough to share the cynicism of their critics.

The difference between the nihilistic perspectives of critics (who question change premises — arguing, for example, that "inmates are incapable of democracy") is different from that of disappointed reformers (who blame resisting forces, as by claiming that "the system is not ready for democracy"). Both perspectives, however, are unhelpful, because they avoid the questions that could permit us to profit from experience (such as "what strategies could we use to ensure quality participation in our next prison experiments?") which require critical self-examination.

Learning from experience

Token economies have been used in efforts to resocialize offenders. In one such experiment, Ross and McKay (1976) began working with a small number of delinquent girls who were unmanageable in an institution and who had not responded to a variety of therapies. The introduction of the behavior modification program brought about dramatic improvement in behavior within the institution, and the girls' adjustment in the community proved "remarkable, persistent and impressive" (p.392). The pilot results were so encouraging that the program was extended to a 50-bed facility, and a long-term treatment-research program was begun. After the results of the pilot studies, however, those of the more formal program were seen as disappointing and perplexing. In the first phase of the program, the treated girls did worse than the control group, both in the prison and after release. In the second phase (of a now modified program) the treated girls did better than the controls in confinement, but continued to do worse after their release.

The investigators re-examined their pilot studies. The girls in these studies had become familiar with reinforcement techniques and had used them to influence their peers. The third phase of the program introduced this variable by adding a peer therapist component to the token economy program. Compared to the controls, the girls in this phase did very well in the institution. In the community, they did worse.

With a commendable willingness to rethink their premises, the investigators concluded that it was the original token economy program that might be the problem. They ran a fourth phase involving the peer therapist component alone. The results were significant and impressive. The girls in the treatment program performed well in terms of institutional adjustment and did far better in the community than their matched controls.

The investigators had found the limitations in their original behavior modification program. They had found a way of utilizing peer group interaction to bring about pro-social behavior. And they had found the answer to a question that they had not initially raised: Institutional adaptation does not necessarily predict behavior in the community. This study thus made significant contributions to knowledge development, irrespective of the permanence of the institutionalization of the program.

A similar sequence of insights was reported by Phillips, Phillips, Fixsen and Wolf (1973), who worked with delinquent boys in Achievement Place, a family-style treatment home. Phillips and his colleagues report:

> After three years of trial and error and careful evaluation we had developed what we considered to be a successful home. We had worked out a behavioral treatment program that produced significant changes in the skills of six to eight boys who lived in the home. We were convinced, on the basis of several controlled studies, that we had found a usable model for almost any community, one that would help make potential criminals into productive citizens.
>
> We ran into trouble, however, in our first attempt to replicate the model in another community ... The token economy had been our chief object of study in the early years, but we came to realize that it was not the heart of the program.
>
> The heart of the program was the teaching, social interaction component. It is unfortunately true that a token system by itself doesn't teach the most important, social skills. Teaching involves an active give-and-take process — instruction, demonstration, practice, feedback. This process was the secret behind the success of the first Achievement Place. However, it was only through our original failure to replicate the model that we discovered its importance (Phillips et al., 1973, pp.329-30).

The authors of Achievement Place have more recently suggested a strategy of finding boys a permanent place in a real home with specially trained "surrogate parents" (Chance, 1989). Two decades of research brought the interventionists from an emphasis on behavior modification to concepts of bonding and social control.

Jesness (1979) discussed institution-wide treatment programs in two California Youth Authority institutions, one involving behavior modification and the other transactional analysis. Outcome measures showed no significant differences between the two treatments (though there were indications of treatment/inmate-type interactions), but both institutions experienced decreased recidivism rates compared to their prior performance and the performance of comparable institutions. This suggested that the crucial treatment variable may have been participation in a totally experiment-oriented institution. Even such a Hawthorne (benefit-of-attention) Effect could be perpetuated by continuing an experimental, innovative climate.

These studies exemplify the payoff of self-inquiry and self-criticism. Innovators who have continued to experiment tend to discover the heart of their program. Hearts are the things from which concepts, principles and models are developed, both in interventions that last and in those that do not.

Losing battles, or losing wars?

In the mid 1950s, one of the authors conducted a field experiment at a navy installation, the Camp Elliott Retraining Command (Grant, 1957; Sullivan, Grant & Grant, 1957; Grant & Grant, 1959; see Chapter 11). Several interventions were built on the idea of utilizing peer study groups as a means of affecting delinquent behavior. The group leaders included both the program staff (a psychologist, an educator and a social worker) and noncommissioned officers with no specific mental health training. The experiment had received enthusiastic support from military officials. However, all was not well on the local level. There was a good deal of concern from professional staff about the studies' implications for professional psychotherapy and counseling. The most vicious attack came from an Education Officer who submitted a letter to the Commanding Officer of the base stating that the lay (noncommissioned officer and peer) therapeutic interactions going on in the study groups were damaging the mental health of the subjects.

Not quite undaunted, we moved on to a series of efforts to deploy other clients (we called them the "products of a problem") and non-professional and lower echelon staff in developing strategies for coping with the problems they were familiar with and/or had exemplified (Grant, 1980; Pearl & Riessman, 1965; Spencer, 1963; Toch, 1967). These efforts met with varying degrees of success and a great deal of institutional and agency opposition. None, it is safe to say, changed the face of corrections or mental health.

Yet today, non-professionals, paraprofessionals, peer self-help groups, and therapeutic communities are established components of human services. In one state, for example, mental health patients and ex-patients started working as consumer case managers in the community. The government office supporting this demonstration was headed by a man who in 1966 was a prison inmate and a participant in one of our programs.

The point is that reformers frequently lose battles, but may (intentionally or not) contribute to winning wars. In the prison activity in which we were involved — which was called the New Careers Development Program (Grant & Grant, 1970; Grant & Grant, 1975) corrections agencies at first had agreed to employ the graduates as program development assistants. Some products of the crime problem (ex-criminals) were to be used in efforts to cope with the problem in corrections. Before any New Careerists had graduated, however, a different administration had taken over, and the original employment commitment was not honored.

Concurrently with this lost battle, however, the government embarked on a war against poverty. The legislation outlining this war called for employing the poor in human service roles to address the needs of the poor. The program called for developing career-oriented education and promotional ladders for new careerists as well as developing more effective services for the poor.

Community services aides, teacher aides, mental health aides, welfare aides, nursing aides, legal aides, parole aides and other paraprofessionals rapidly emerged. These paraprofessionals became — and many still are — an accepted resource, though career ladders and adequate supportive education opportunities that were part of the original program are now hard to find. Does that make it another lost battle? Perhaps. Yet it is hard not to see New Careers as a contribution to the effort to establish jobs (if not career ladders) for women, minorities, and/or the poor (Levin and Rumberger, 1983; Ginzberg & Vojta, 1981).

What are we learning?

It should be obvious that change does not proceed in accord with classic social science experimental designs. Models are not developed, implemented, replicated, then institutionalized. Change does not occur in blocks of demonstrated approximations of the truth. Innovators may at times demonstrate better services at reduced cost, but policy and program decisions — even when they are couched in tax-saving terms — are determined by interests other than those of the taxpayer or consumer.

There is an important and hopeful caveat. Although an innovation imposed on an agency from the top or brought in from the outside is seldom whole-heartedly adopted, some self-developed programs continue to be internalized, modified, improved and integrated into continuing operations. It is axiomatic in this regard that institutional ownership of a program is more likely to occur if the program is developed by the institution. But how do we arrange for institutions to prize experimentation and innovation? And what can we propose to increase the competence of social science in developing rational approaches to the delivery of services?

Available alternatives

There are at least six distinguishable, but not necessarily mutually exclusive strategies for improving the staying power of planned change efforts. None of these strategies has proved a panacea. They are:
1. *Develop better dissemination strategies for promising innovations.* This prescription is popular. Unfortunately experience suggests that, though the

possibilities have not been exhausted, the sales approach appears limited as a way of perpetuating innovations.

2. *Limit innovation efforts to modest changes that can be accommodated by existing policy and social structure.* This strategy unfortunately often means safe, non-boat-rocking ventures, which some innovators consider to be both circumscribing and demeaning.

3. *Develop settings hospitable to innovations* (Sarason, 1972). This means concentrating on the organizational structure necessary to allow change to survive, which may be easier said than done.

4. *Develop your own institution.* Tharpe and Gallimore (1979) give us an example of a research-built institution that guarantees an experimental climate to address a specific problem. In tackling the education difficulties of native Hawaiians, the researchers operated their own school, using researchers as teachers. In this special social structure, they conducted successive innovations, modifications and evaluations. Their goal was to build an effective model for ultimate institutionalization in established school systems. The final word on this type of experiment is not in.

5. *Build in a systematic modification of an agency's own program.* At the very least, this means looking for ways to create and maintain self analytic and flexible institutions (Chapter 26).

6. *Concentrate on the development of formal knowledge.* Many change agents have moved back and forth from classroom research to field work, tying down component concepts and principles that cut across interventions. This strategy has obvious merit, but sophisticated concepts do not appear to have more staying power than unsophisticated ones.

Disseminating innovativeness

We began this chapter by suggesting that interventions must be internalized to be adopted. A corollary of this point would be that the internalization of change must continue over time if the intervention is to last. This means that people who are targets of the intervention must keep on subscribing to its premises, which would include — if the intervention has integrity — an interest in whether the intervention solves the problems to which it is addressed.

A compromise approach suggests that "if you cannot beat them, join them." An internalization approach to the same contingency holds that "if you cannot beat them, get them to join you." This model is a prescription for partnership in which the line between interventionist and clients of intervention becomes blurred, and the targets of intervention become interventionists themselves. This goal is not addressed through a top-down, dissemination-of-findings approach. In the words of Wilkins (1984):

> There is a need for communication between those who are managed and the management, between those who are governed and those who govern, between those who decide and those decided about. Collections of data can meet some of

these needs, but they do not provide an effective two-way process (p.123).

Wilkins (1984) makes provision for the fact that participants in innovations may have to undergo personal development. He points out that "if people do not understand a process to an adequate degree, their advice is not likely to be of value" (p. 8). This means that there must be some way of creating a problem-solving orientation, of pooling the scientific knowledge of the interventionist with the local wisdom of change targets to enhance the sophistication of the latter and the responsiveness of the former.

What can the interventionist do to promote such pooling? He or she can:

1. Provide leads for creating settings that support organization-wide participation in continual experimentation and development. In relation to prison governance, for instance, Murton (1976) tells us that "A new prison community is created by forming a coalition between staff and inmates to combine power and expertise in changing the prison to a mutually beneficial environment . . . In effect, staff members say to the inmates: 'Come, let us join hands and climb the mountain together'"(p. 191).

2. Make general concepts and principles available in consumable form as resources for problem-solvers. Inmates and staff who become involved in governance experiments, for example, must get to know what others have learned from analogous ventures.

3. Help conceptualize methods and procedures to be used and developed by lay persons to acquire knowledge of interest to themselves. The inmates might wish to survey fellow-inmates, for example, in shaping the program.

4. Help grass-roots researchers to build an information network of kinds of questions, kinds of leads, and kinds of strategies to be considered for kinds of problems, such as avoiding cooptation or preventing rigged elections in prisons.

5. Provide appropriate kinds of research methods for kinds of questions (Cronbach, 1980; Kelman, 1968; Wilkins, 1965; Wilkins, 1969). What is needed is the precise mix of rigor and vigor that allows reasonably empirically-grounded rational approaches to problems requiring solutions through truth by approximations.

The interventionist as a social scientist can benefit from access to the hunches, understandings and good ideas that practitioners and clients can bring to science, and action development and knowledge development can thus grow together. With mindful participation and partnerships change and development not only has a better chance to advance but can have substantially more staying power.

Note

1. For example, the innovative segregation model described in Chapter 24, as institutionalized in Canada (Special Handling Units) and California (Adjustment Centers), reverted to standard solitary confinement.

References

Abbott, J. H. (1981). *In the Belly of the Beast.* New York: Vintage.
Adler, A. (1927). *The Practice and Theory of Individual Psychology.* New York: Harcourt.
Advisory Council of the Penal System (1974). *Report: Toung Adult Offenders.* London: Her Majesty's Printing Office.
Agee, V. L. (1981). "The Closed Adolescent Treatment Center." *Utah Correctional Association Annual Conference,* 10 September, 1981.
Albany Times-Union. (1991). Editorial: "Why not a maxi-maxi?" 7 June.
Albany Times-Union. (1995) 9 January.
Allport, G. W. (1961). *Pattern and Growth in Personality,* New York: Holt, Rinehart and Winston.
American Friends Service Committee. (1971). *Struggle for Justice: A Report on Crime and Punishment in America.* New York: Hill and Wang.
Argyris, C. (1970). *Intervention Theory and Method Reading.* Massachusetts: Addison-Wesley.
Associated Press. (1988). News release: "In Michigan: Shock versus prison." 12 March, 1988.
Baker, J. E. (1964). "Inmate self-government." *Journal of Criminal Law, Criminology and Police Science, 55,* 39-47.
Bandura, A. (1977). *Social Learning Theory.* Englewood Cliffs, NJ.: Prentice-Hall.
Bandura, A. (1986). *Social Foundations of Thought and Action: A Social Cognitive Theory.* Englewood Cliffs, NJ: Prentice-Hall.
Barbanel, J. (1989). "Accord in mayoral race: Boot camps for criminals." *New York Times,* 19 July, 1989.
Barry, J. V. (1956). "Pioneers in criminology: Alexander Maconochie (1787-1860)." *Journal of Criminal Law, Criminology and Police Science, 47,* 145-161.
Barry, J. V. (1958). *Alexander Maconochie of Norfolk Island.* London: Oxford.
Baum, A. and Valins, S. (1977). *Architecture and Social Behavior: Psychological Studies in Social Density.* Hillsdale, NJ: Erlbaum.
Baxter, J. C. (1970). "Interpersonal spacing in natural settings." *Sociometry, 33:* 444-456.
Beto, J. (1989). "The future of the criminal justice system." Address to the Mid-Winter Meeting of the American Correctional Association in San Antonio, Texas.
Blumberg, P. (1973). *Industrial Democracy: The Sociology of Participation.* New York: Schocken Books.
Blumstein, A. (l995). "Violence by young people: Why the deadly nexus?" *National Institute of Justice Journal,* 2-9 August.
Bondeson, U. V. (1989). *Prisoners in prison societies.* New Brunswick, NJ: Transaction Books.

References

Bowker, L. H. (1980). *Prison Victimization.* New York: Elsevier
Boyle, J. (1977). *A Sense of Freedom.* London: Pan Canongate.
Briggs, D. Chino. (1973). "California." In S. Whiteley, D. Briggs, and M. Turner, *Dealing with Deviants: The Treatment of Antisocial Behavior.* New York: Schocken Books.
Brown, B. S, Wienckowski, L. A. and Stolz, S B. (1975). *Behavior Modification: Perspective on a Current Issue.* Washington, DC: National Institute of Mental Health.
Burtch, B. E. and Ericson, R. V. (1977). *The Silent System: An Inquiry into Prisoners Who Commit Suicide* Toronto, Canada: University of Toronto.
Cather. J. (1987). "Judge cites loopholes for mentally disturbed."*Albany Knickerbocker News*, 10 December.
Chance, P. (1989). "Group homes don't turn delinquents around - but a real home might."*APS Observer*, 2, 15.
Cleckley, H. (1976). *The Mask of Sanity* (Fifth Edition). St. Louis, MO: Mosby.
Clemmer, D. (l940). *The Prison Community.* New York: Holt, Rinehart and Winston.
Clendinen, D. (1985). "Crowded prisons in South lead to tests for other punishments." *New York Times*, 18 December, 1985.
Cloward, R. (1956). "Session four." In H. L. Witmer and R. Kotinsky (eds.),*New Perspectives for Research in Juvenile Delinquency.* US Department of Health, Education and Welfare, Children's Bureau, Washington, DC.
Cohen, A. K. (l955). *Delinquent Boys: The Culture of the Gang.* Glencoe, IL: The Free Press.
Cohen, S. and Taylor, L. (1972). *Psychological survival: The Experience of Long-term Imprisonment.* Harmondsworth, UK: Penguin.
Colorado Department of Corrections. *Master Program Scheduling.* Colorado Springs, CO.
Combined Staff and Wire Service Reports.(1982) "Prison vice: Sex, drugs, in-house bookie." *Albany Times-Union*, 13 February.
Commons, W. H. (1940). "Official manual of the state prison colony." In C. R. Doering (ed.), *A Report on the Development of Penological Treatment at Norfolk Prison Colony in Massachusetts.* New York: Bureau of Social Hygiene.
Coughlin, T. A. (1987). Personal communication.
Coughlin, T. A. Testimony: New York State Assembly Standing Committees on
Corrections and Mental Health, Mental Retardation and Developmental Disabilities, 9 December, 1987. Public Hearing on Persons with Developmental Disabilities and the Criminal Justice System.
Cronbach, L. J. (1980). *Toward Reform of Program Evaluation.* San Francisco: Jossey-Bass.
Cronin, R. C. (1994). *Boot Camps for Adults and Juvenile Offenders: Overview and Update.* Washington, DC: National Institute of Justice.
D'Atri, D. A. (1975). "Psychophysiological Responses to Crowding." *Environment and Behavior*, 7, 27-252.
de Beaumont, G. D. and de Tocqueville, A. (1964). *On the Penitentiary System in the United States and its Application in France* (Reprint Edition). Carbondale, IL: Southern Illinois University Press.
Deming, W. E. (1986). *Out of Crisis.* Cambridge: Center for Advanced Engineering Study. Massachusetts Institute of Technology.
Denenberg, V. and Denenberg, T. (1975). "Prison grievance procedures."*Corrections Magazine*, 1, 29ff.
de Tocqueville, A. (1956) *Democracy in America* (edited by R. D. Heffner). New York: New American Library.
DeWolfe, R. and DeWolfe, A. S. (1979). "Impacts of prison conditions on the mental health of inmates." *Southern Illinois University Law Journal*, 497-533.

DiIulio, J. J. (1987). *Governing Prisons: A Comparative Study of Correctional Management.* New York: The Free Press.

Doble, J., Immerwahr, S. and Richardson, A. (1991). *Punishing Criminals: The People of Delaware Consider the Options.* New York: Edna McConnell Clark Foundation.

Doble, J. and Klein, J. (1989). *Punishing Criminals: The Public's View. An Alabama Survey.* New York: Edna McConnell Clark Foundation.

Doering, C. R. (1940). *A Report on the Development of Penological Treatment at Norfolk Prison Colony in Massachusetts.* New York: Bureau of Social Hygiene.

Dollard, J. et al. (1930). *Frustration and Aggression.* New Haven, CT.: Yale University Press.

Early, K. E. (ed) (1966). *Drug Treatment Behind Bars: Prison-Based Strategies for Change.* Westport, CT.: Praeger.

Edna McConnell Clark Foundation. (1992).*Americans Behind Bars.* New York: Edna McConnell Clark Foundation.

Ellis, D. (1982). *Crowding and Prison Violence: An Integration of Research and Theory.* Downsview, Ontario: York University.

Ellis, D., Grasmick, H. and Gilman, B. (1974). "Violence in prisons: A sociological analysis." *American Journal of Sociology, 80*: 16-34.

Eysenck, H. (1964). *Crime and Personality,* Boston, MA: Houghton Mifflin.

Finn, A. (1989). *The Disciplinary Adjustment of Mentally Retarded Inmates.* Doctoral Dissertation, Albany: State University of New York.

Flanagan, T. J., Brennan, P. G., and Cohen, D. (1991).*Attitudes of New York Legislators Toward Crime and Criminal Justice: A Report of the State Legislator Survey.* Albany, NY: University at Albany.

Flowers, G. T., Carr, T. S. and Ruback, R. B. (1991). *Special Alternative Incarceration: Evaluation.* Atlanta, GA: Georgia Department of Corrections, January, 1991.

Fogel, D. (1975). *"We are the living proof... " The Justice Model for Corrections.* Cincinnati, OH: Anderson Publishing Co.

Fox, J. G. (1982). "Women in prison: A case study in the social reality of stress." In R. Johnson and H. Toch (eds.), *The Pains of Imprisonment.* Beverly Hills, CA: Sage.

Fox, V. (1958). "Analysis of prison disciplinary problems."*Journal of Criminal Law, Criminology and Police Science, 49,* 321-326.

Freedman, J L. (1975). *Crowding and Behavior.* San Francisco: Freeman.

Freeman, R. A., Dinitz, S. and Conrad, J. R. (1977). "A look at the dangerous offender and society's efforts to control him." *American Journal of Correction,* January-February, pp. 25-31.

Freud, S. (1925). Foreword to A Aichhorn's *Wayward Youth* (Meridian Edition). New York: Meridian Books.

Garabedian, P. G. (1963). "Social roles and processes of socialization in the prison community." *Social Problems, 11,* 140-52.

Germain, D. "Inmate death a first at successful 'shock camp.'" *Albany Times-Union,* 23 June, 1992.

Giallombardo, R. (1966). *Society of Women: A Study of Women's Prisons.* New York: Wiley.

Ginsberg, E. and Vojta, G. J. (1981). "The service sector of the US economy." *Scientific American, 244,* 48-55.

Glaser, D. (1964). *The Effectiveness of a Prison and Parole System.* Indianapolis: Bobbs-Merrill.

Glaser, D. (1977). "Institutional disciplinary action and the social psychology of disciplinary relationships." In R. M. Carter, D. Glaser, and L. T. Wilkins (eds.),*Correctional Institutions* (Second Edition). Philadelphia: Lippincott.

References

Goffman, E. (1961). *Asylums: Essays on the Social Situation of Mental Patients and Other Inmates*. Garden City, New York: Anchor.

Goodstein, L. (1979). "Inmate adjustment to prison and the transition to community life." *Journal of Research in Crime and Delinquency, 16*, 246-272.

Goodstein, L., MacKenzie, D.L. and Shotland, L. (1984). "Personal control and inmate adjustment to prison, *Criminology, 22* 343-369.

Goodwin, R. (1993). "Prison Shrink." *Northeast, 123*, December, 1993, p.19.

Grant, J. D. (1957). "The use of correctional institutions as self-study communities in social research." *British Journal of Delinquency, 7*, 301-306.

Grant, J. D. (1968). "The offender as a correctional manpower resource." In F. Reissman and H L Popper (eds.), *Up From Poverty: New Career Ladders for Nonprofessionals*. New York: Harper & Row.

Grant, J. and Capell, F. (1983). *Reducing School Crime: A Report on the School Team Approach*. San Rafael, CA: Social Action Research Center.

Grant, J. and Grant, J. L. (1970). "Client participation and community change." In D. Adelson and L. Kalis (eds.), *Community Psychology and Mental Health: Perspectives and Challenges*. Scranton: Chandler.

Grant, J. D. and Grant, J. (1975). "Evaluation of new careers programs." In E. L. Struening and M. Guttentag (eds), *Handbook of Evaluation Research* Beverly Hills: Sage.

Grant, J. D., Grant, J. and Toch, H. (1982). "Police-citizen conflict and decisions to arrest." In V. J. Konencni and E. B. Ebbesen (eds.), *The Criminal Justice System: A Social-Psychological Analysis*. San Francisco: Freeman.

Grant, J. D. and Grant, M. Q. (1959). "A group dynamics approach to the treatment of nonconformists in the Navy." *Annals of American Academy of Political and Social Science, 322*, 126-135.

Gray, J. M. (1970). "Evaluation of the Army's restoration program." In S L Brodsky and N E Eggleston (eds.), *The Military Prison: Theory, Research and Practice*. Carbondale, IL: Southern Illinois University Press.

Greenberg, D. F. (1977). Introduction, in D. F. Greenberg (ed.), *Corrections and Punishment*. Beverly Hills: Sage Publications.

Greene, J. (1977). "Controlling prison crowding." *Corrections Today, 59*, 52-65.

Gurnett, K. "Two guards slashed at Coxsackie state prison." *Albany Times-Union*, 15 January, 1996.

Hackman, R. J. (1974). *On the Coming Demise of Job Enrichment*. Technical Report 9, Department of Administrative Sciences. New Haven: Yale University.

Hagan, C. R. and Campbell, C. F. "Team classification in federal institutions." *Federal Probation, 32*, 30-35.

Hagel-Seymour, J. (1982). "Environmental sanctuaries for susceptible prisoners." In R. Johnson and H. Toch (eds.), *The Pains of Imprisonment*. Beverly Hills, CA: Sage.

Halleck, S. L. (1986). *The Mentally Disordered Offender*. Washington: National Institute of Mental Health.

Haney, C. (1993). " 'Infamous punishment:' The psychological consequences of isolation." *The National Prison Project Journal*, Spring, 3-21.

Hare, R. D. (1981). "Psychopathy and violence." In J. R. Hays, T. K. Roberts and K. S. Solway (eds.), *Violence and the Violent Individual*. New York: Spectrum.

Harris, M. (1936). *I Knew Them in Prison*. New York: The Viking Press.

Hassine, V. (1996). *Life Without Parole: Living in Prison Today*. Los Angeles: Roxbury Publishing Company.

Hayakawa, S. I. (1962). "Why the Edsel laid an egg: Motivational research versus the reality principle." In S. I. Hayakawa (ed.), *The Use and Misuse of Language*. New York: Fawcett World Library.

Hepburn, J. R. and Albonetti, C A. (1978). "Team classification in state correctional institutions: Its association with inmate and staff attitudes." *Criminal Justice and Behavior*, 5, 63-73.

The Herald, 3 September, 1992.

Herzberg, F., Mausner, B. and Snyderman, B. B. (1993). *The Motivation to Work*. New Brunswick, NJ: Transaction.

Hickey, J. E, and Scharf, P. L. (1980). *Toward a Just Correctional System: Experiments in Implementing Democracy in Prisons*. San Francisco: Jossey-Bass.

Hobart, T. Y. (1984). "Action, not rhetoric, needed on school discipline issue." *President's Perspective*. New York State United Teachers, 20 February.

Irwin, J. (1970). *The Felon*. Berkeley, CA: University of California Press.

Irwin, J. (1980). *Prisons in Turmoil*. Boston: Little, Brown.

Irwin J. and Cressey, D. R. (1962). "Thieves, convicts, and the inmate culture." *Social Problems, 10*, 142-155.

Jackson, M. (1983). *Prisoners of Isolation: Solitary Confinement in Canada*, Toronto: University of Toronto Press.

Jesstress, C. F. (1979). "Was the Close-Holton project a bummer?" Reprinted in R. R. Ross and P. Gendreau (eds.), *Effective Correctional Treatment*, 359-366, Toronto, Canada: Butterworth.

Johnson, R. (1996). *Hard Time: Understanding and Reforming the Prison*. (Second Edition). Belmont, CA.: Wadsworth Publishing Company.

Jones, M. et. al. (1953). *The Therapeutic Community: A New Treatment Method in Psychiatry*, New York: Basic Books.

Jones, M. (1949). "Acting as an aid to therapy in a neurosis centre." *British Medical Journal, 1*, 756ff.

Jones, M. S. (1957). "Commentary." *British Journal of Delinquency*, 7, 307-308.

Jones, M. (1962). *Social Psychiatry in the Community, in Hospitals and in Prisons*. Springfield, Illinois, Charles Thomas.

Jones, M. (1968). *Beyond the Therapeutic Community*. New Haven, CT: Yale University Press.

Jones, M. (1979). "Learning as treatment." In H. Toch (ed.), *Psychology of Crime and Criminal Justice*. New York: Holt, Rinehart and Winston.

Jones, M., Pomryn, B. A., and Skellern, E. "Work therapy." *Lancet*, 343-344, 31 March.

Kalogerakis, M. G. (1971). "The assaultive psychiatric patient." *Psychiatric Quarterly, 45*, 372-81

Keehley, P. (1992). "TQM for local governments: The principles and prospects." *Public Management*, August, 10-18.

Kelman, H. C. (1958). "Compliance, identification and internalization: Three processes of attitude change." *Journal of Conflict Resolution, 2*, 51-60.

Kelman, H. C. (1968). "Rigor vs. vigor: The debate on research philosophy." In H. C. Kelman *A Time to Speak: On Human Values and Social Research*, 141-163 San Francisco: Jossey-Bass.

Kozol, H. L., Boucher, R. J. and Garofalo, F R. (1973). "The diagnosis and treatment of dangerousness." *Crime and Delinquency 18*, 371-392.

Krech, D. and Crutchfield, R. S. (1948). *Theory and Problems in Social Psychology*. New York: McGraw-Hill.

Kuhn, T. S. (1970). *The Structure of Scientific Revolutions* (Second Edition). Chicago: University of Chicago Press.

References

Kurlander, L. T. (1983). *Report to Mario Cuomo: The Disturbance at Ossining Correctional Facility, January 8-11, 1983*. Albany, NY: Executive Chamber.

Langer, E. J. (1983). *The Psychology of Control*. Beverly Hills, CA: Sage.

Lansing, D., Bogan, J. and Karacki, L. (1977). "Unit management: implanting a differential correctional approach." *Federal Probation, 41*.

Levin, H. M. and Rumberger, R. W. (1983). "Impact of technology on education." *Technology Review, 68*, No. 6.

Levinson, R. and Gerard, R. E. (1973). "Functional units: A different correctional approach." *Federal Probation, 37*, 8-18.

Levinson, R. B. (1980). "TC or not TC? That is the question." In H. Toch (ed.), *Therapeutic Communities in Corrections*. New York: Praeger.

Levinson, R. B. (1982). "Try softer." In R. Johnson and H. Toch (eds.), *The Pains of Imprisonment*. Beverly Hills, CA: Sage.

Levinson, R. B. (1994). "The development of classification and programming." In J. W. Roberts (ed.), *Escaping Prison Myths: Selected Topics in the History of Federal Corrections*. Washington, DC: American University Press.

Lewin, K. (1947). "Group decision and social change." In T.M. Newcomb and E. L. Hartley (eds.), *Readings in Social Psychology*. New York: Holt & Company.

Likert, R. (1967). *The Human Organization: Its Management and Value*. New York: McGraw-Hill.

Lion, J. R. and Reid, W. H. (1983). *Assaults within Psychiatric Facilities*. New York: Grune & Stratton.

Lipton, D. S. (1996). "Prison-based therapeutic communities: Their success with drug-abusing offenders." *National Institute of Justice Journal*, February, 12-20.

Lipton, D., Martinson, R. and Wilks, J. (1975). *The Effectiveness of Correctional Treatment: A Survey of Treatment Evaluation Studies*. New York: Praeger.

Loevinger, J. (1976). *Ego Development*. San Francisco, CA: Jossey-Bass.

Lombardo, L. X. (1981). *Guards Imprisoned: Correctional Officers at Work*. New York: Elsevier.

Lozoff, B. (1995). "Revising the convict code--one step further." *Prison Life*, July-August, *32*, 69-70.

Marrero, D. (1977). "Spatial dimensions of democratic prison reform." *The Prison Journal, 57*, 31-41.

Maslow, A. M. (1954). *Motivation and Personality*. New York: Harper.

McCain, V. C., Cox, V. C. and Paulus, P. B. (1980). *The Effect of Prison Crowding on Inmate Behavior*. Washington, DC: Department of Justice, National Institute of Justice.

McCoy, J. (1981). *Concrete Mama: Prison Profiles from Walla Walla*. Columbia, MO: University of Missouri Press.

McMahon, W. G. (1987). Testimony. New York State Assembly Standing Committees on Corrections and on Mental Health, Mental Retardation and Developmental Disabilities, 9 December.

Mead, M. (1983). "Cultural discontinuities and personality transformation." *Journal of Social Issues, 39* 161-178.

Mecklenberg Correctional Center. (1981). *Mecklenberg Treatment Program*. Mimeographed. Boydton, V.A., author. 1 December.

Megargee, E. I. (1977). "The association of population density, reduced space, and uncomfortable temperatures with misconduct in a prison community." *American Journal of Community Psychology, 5*, 289-298.

Megargee, E. (1977). "The need for a new classification system." *Criminal Justice and Behavior, 4*, 107-114.

Merton, R. K. (1957). *Social Theory and Social Structure* (Revised Editon). Glencoe, IL: The Free Press.

Monahan, J. (1981). *Predicting Violent Behavior: An Assessment of Clinical Techniques*, Beverly Hills, CA: Sage.

Monahan, J. and Steadman, H. J. (1983). "Crime and mental disorder: an epidemiological approach." In N. Morris and M.H. Tonry (eds.), *Crime and Justice: An Annual Review of Research*. Chicago: University of Chicago Press.

Moos, R. H. (1974). *Evaluating Treatment Environments: A Social Ecological Approach*. New York: Wiley.

Morris, N. (1974). *The Future of Imprisonment*. Chicago: The University of Chicago Press.

Morris, N. and Hawkins, G. (1977). *Letter to the President on Crime Control*. Chicago: University of Chicago Press.

Morris, N. and Tonry, M. (1990). *Between Prison and Probation: Intermediate Punishments in a Rational Sentencing System*. Oxford: Oxford University Press.

Morse, N. and Reimer, E. (1956). "The experimental change of a major organizational variable." *Journal of Abnormal and Social Psychology, 52*, 120-129.

Mortimer, J. (1983). *Rumpole and the Golden Thread*. London: Penguin.

Mosher, D.L. and Tompkins, D.S. (1988). "Scripting the macho man: Hypermasculine socialization and enculturation." *Journal of Sex Research, 25*, 60-84.

Mueller, R. F. C., Toch, H. and Molof, M. F. (1965). *Report to the Task Force to Study Violence in Prisons*. Sacramento, CA: California Department of Corrections.

Murton, T. O. (1976). *The Dilemma of Prison Reform* New York: Holt, Rinehart and Winston.

Myers, L. B. and Levy, G. W. (1978). *The Description and Prediction of the Intractable Inmate*. Columbus, OH: Battelle.

Nacci, P. L., Teitelbaum, H. E. and Prather, J. (1977). "Population density and inmate misconduct rates in the federal prison system." *Federal Probation, 41* 26-31.

National Congress on Prison and Reformatory Discipline. (1871). *Transactions*. Albany, NY: Weed and Parsons.

National Governors' Association, Office of State Services. (1992). "Total Quality Management initiatives in state government." *Management Briefs (*Attachment). Washington, DC: Author.

National Institute of Corrections. (1982). *NIC Program Plan for the Fiscal Year 1983*. Washington, DC: Author.

New York Department of Correctional Services. (1980*). Downstate Reception and Classification Center, Fishkill, NY*. Draft prepared by Elaine Lord. Albany, New York: 15 January.

New York Times. (1987). 20 September.

New York Times. (1991). 20 February.

Newsweek. "Back to the Chain Gang?" (1994). 17 October, 87-90.

Pearce, J. P. (1994). "An overview of the Scottish prison system." Paper delivered at the Annual Conference of the Middle Atlantic States Correctional Association, Killington, VT., 24 May.

Pearl, A. and Riessman, F. (1965*). New Careers for the Poor: The Nonprofessional in Human Service*. New York: Free Press.

Phillips, E. L., Phillips, E. A., Fixsen, D. L. and Wolf, M. M. (1973). "Achievement Place: behavior shaping works for delinquents." *Psychology Today, 6*, 75-79.

Porporino, F. J. and Dudley, K. (1984). "An analysis of the effects of overcrowding in Canadian penitentiaries." *Program Branch User Report*. Ottawa: Ministry of the Solicitor General of Canada.

Powitzky, R. (1978). "Reflections of a federal prison psychologist." *Quarterly Journal of Corrections, 2,* 7-12.

President's Commission on Law Enforcement and Administration of Justice. (1967). *The Challenge of Crime in a Free Society.* Washington, DC: US Government Printing Office.

Prosecuting Attorneys Association of Michigan. (1989).*Comprehensive Corrections Policies in Michigan.* East Lansing, MI, 18 September.

Purdy, M. W. (l995). "An official culture of violence infests a prison." *New York Times,* 19 December.

Purdy, M. W. (l996). "Who guards the guards? At Rikers, a history of beatings." *New York Times,* 28 January.

Quay, H. Q. (1984*). Managing Adult Inmates: Classification for Housing and Program Assignment.* Lanham, MD: American Correctional Association.

Quay, H. C. (1984). *Managing Adult Inmates: Classification for Housing and Program Assignments.* College Park, MD: American Correctional Association.

Quinsey, V.L. (1977). "Studies in the reduction of assaults in a maximum security psychiatric institution." *Canada's Mental Health, 25,* 21-23.

Redl, F. (1966). "The life-space interview: strategies and techniques." In *When We Deal with Children: Selected Writings.* New York: Free Press.

Redl, F. (1966). "Ego disturbances and ego support." In *When We Deal with Children: Selected Writings.* New York: Free Press.

Regens, J. L. and Hobson, W. G. (1978). "Inmate self-government and attitude change: An assessment of participation effect." *Evaluation Quarterly, 2,* 455-579.

Reveron, D. (1982). "Mentally ill and behind bars." *APA Monitor,* March 1982, 10-11.

Roberts, J. W. (1990). "View from the top." *Federal Prisons Journal, 1,* 27-46.

Rosenhan, D. (1973). "On being sane in insane places." *Science, 179,* 250-258, *180,* 365-369.

Ross, R. R. (1981). *Prison Guard/Correctional Officer: the Use and Abuse of the Human Resources of Prisoners.* Toronto: Butterworth.

Ross, R. R. and McKay, B. (1976). "A study of institutional treatment programs."*International Journal of Offender Therapy and Comparative Criminology, 20,* 167-173.

Rothman, D. J. (1980). *Conscience and Convenience: The Asylum and its Alternatives in Progressive America.* Boston: Little, Brown and Company.

Sarason, S. B. (1972). *The Creation of Settings and the Future Societies.* Beverly Hills, California: Sage.

Scheckenbach, A. F. (1984). "Behavior modification and adult offenders." In I. Jacks and S. G. Cox (eds.), *Psychological Approaches to Crime and its Correction.* Chicago: Nelson-Hall.

Scottish Prison Service. (1990).*Opportunity and Responsibility. Policy Document.* Edinburgh: Author.

Seelye, K. Q. (1994). *New York Times,* 2 November.

Serrill, M. S. (1982). "Norfolk: A retrospective. New debate over a famous prison experiment." *Corrections Magazine, 8,* 25-32.

Seymour, J. (1977). "Niches in prison." In H. Toch (ed.), *Living in Prison: The Ecology of Survival.* New York: Free Press. Republished: Washington, DC: American Psychological Association, 1992.

Shaw, R. "An Explosive Situation." (1983). *Albany Times-Union,* 18 Sept. .

Shaw, R. D. (1995). *Chaplains to the Imprisoned.* New York. Haworth Press.

Smith, A. C. (1979). "Violence." *British Journal of Psychiatry, 134,* 528-529.

Smith, R. (1984). *Prison Health Care.* London: British Medical Association.

Smith, W. A. and Fenton, C. E. (1978). "Unit management in a penitentiary: A practical experience." *Federal Probation, 42*, 40-46.

Special Task Force to the Secretary of Health, Education and Welfare. (1977). *Work in America.* Cambridge, MA: The MIT Press.

Spencer, C. (1963). *Experiment in Culture Expansion: Proceedings of Conference on "The Use of the Product of a Social Problem In Coping with the Problem."* Sacramento, California: Department of Corrections.

Spieker, D. J. and Pierson, T. A. (1987). *Adult Internal Management System* (AIMS): *Implementation Manual.* Washington, DC: National Institute of Corrections and Missouri Department of Corrections and Human Resources.

Steelman, D. (1987). *The Mentally Impaired in New York's Prisons: Problems and Solutions.* New York: The Correctional Association of New York.

Studt, E., Messinger, S. L. and Wilson, T. P. (1968). *C-Unit: Search for Community in Prison.* New York: Russell Sage Foundation.

Suedfeld, P. (1980). *Restricted Environmental Stimulation: Research and Clinical Applications.* New York.: Wiley.

Suedfeld, P. (1980). "Environmental effects on violent behavior in prisons." *International Journal of Offender Therapy and Comparative Criminology, 24,* 107-116.

Sullivan, R. (1992). "In New York, state inmates work or else." *New York Times,* 27 January.

Sullivan, C., Grant, M. Q and Grant, J. D. (1957). "The development of interpersonal maturity: Applications to delinquency." *Psychiatry, 20,* 373-385.

Sykes, G. M. (1965). *The Society of Captives: A Study of a Maximum Security Prison.* New York: Atheneum.

Sylvester, S. F., Reed, J. H. and Nelson, D. L. (1977). *Prison Homicide.* New York: Spectrum Publications.

Tannenbaum, F. (1933). *Osborne of Sing.* Chapel Hill, NC: University of North Carolina Press.

Taylor, S and McMillan, G. (1982). "Lingering questions on the value of a prison raid." *Boston Globe,* 20 February.

Tharpe, R. G. and Gallimore, R. (1979). "The ecology of program research and evaluation: A model of evaluation succession." In L. Secrest, S.G.West, M.A. Phillips, M.A. Redner and and W. Yeaton (eds), *Evaluation Studies Review Annual.* Beverly Hills: Sage.

Time. (1955). 25 July, p. 35.

Toch, H. (1967). "Prison inmates' reactions to furloughs." *Journal of Research in Crime and Delinquency,* 248-262, July 4.

Toch, H. (1967). "The study of man: the convict as researcher." *Transaction, 4,* 72-75.

Toch, H. (1969). *Violent Men: An Inquiry into the Psychology of Violence.* Chicago: Aldine. Revised and republished, Washington, DC: American Psychological Association, 1992.

Toch, H. (1970). "The care and feeding of typologies and labels." *Federal Probation, 34,* 15-19.

Toch, H. (1975). *Men in Crisis. Human Breakdowns in Prison.* Chicago: Aldine. Revised and republished as *Mosaic of Despair.* Washington, DC: American Psychological Association, 1992.

Toch, H. (1977). *Living in Prison: The Ecology of Survival.* New York: The Free Press. Revised and reprinted, Washington, DC: American Psychological Association, 1992.

Toch, H. (1978). "Is a correctional officer, by any other name, a screw?" *Criminal Justice Review 3*:19-36.

Toch, H. (1979). "Perspectives on treatment." In H. Toch (ed.), *Psychology of Crime and Criminal Justice.* New York: Holt, Rinehart and Winston.

References

Toch, Hans. (1980). *Therapeutic Communities in Corrections.* New York: Praeger.
Toch, H.(1980). "Toward an interdisciplinary approach to criminal violence." *Journal of Criminal Law and Criminology, 71*, 646-653.
Toch, H. (1981). "Psychological treatment of imprisoned offenders." In J. R. Hays, T. K. Roberts and Solway, K. S. (eds.), *Violence and the Violent Individual*, New York: Spectrum.
Toch, H. (1986). "True to you, darling, in my fashion: the notion of contingent consistency." In A. Campbell and J. J. Gibbs (eds.), *Violent Transactions: The Limits of Personality.* London: Blackwell.
Toch, H. (1995). "Inmate involvement in prison governance." *Federal Probation, 59,* 34-39.
Toch, H, and Adams, K. (1987). "In the eye of the beholder? Assessments of psychopathology among prisoners by federal prison staff." *Journal of Research in Crime and Delinquency, 24,* 119-139.
Toch, H. and Adams, K. (1989). *Coping: Maladaptation in Prisons*, New Brunswick, NJ: Transaction Books.
Toch, H. and Adams, K. (1989). *The Disturbed Violent Offender.* New Haven: Yale University Press.
Toch, H. and Grant, J. D. (1981). *Police as Problem Solvers.* New York: Plenum Press.
Toch, H. and Grant, J. D. (1982). *Reforming Human Services: Change through Participation.* Beverly Hills, California: Sage.
Toch, H., Grant, J. D, and Galvin, R. T. (1975). *Agents of Change: A study in Police Reform.* Cambridge, MA: Schenkman Publishing.
Trickett, E. J. and Moos, E. H. (1972). "Satisfaction with the correctional environment: An instance of perceived self-environment similarity." *Journal of Personality,* 40, 75-87.
United States Circuit Court. (1982). *Ruiz v. Estelle.*
United States Department of Justice. (1992). *Operation "Weed and Seed." Reclaiming America's Neighborhoods.* Washington, DC: US Government Printing Office.
US Metropolitan Correctional Center: New York MCC (1979). *Suicide Prevention Project: Revised Final Report* (Executive Summary). New York, 9 March.
Von Hirsch, D. (1976). *Doing Justice: The Choice of Punishments. Report of the Committee for the Study of Incarceration.* New York: Hill and Wang.
Vorrath, H. H., and Brendthro, L. K. (1974). *Positive Peer Culture.* Chicago: Aldine.
Wexler, D. B. (1973). "Token and Taboo: Behavior Modification, Token Economics, and the Law." *California Law Review, 61,* 81-109.
Wexler, D. B. (1981). *Mental Health Law: Major Issues.* New York: Plenum.
Wheeler, S. (1961). "Role conflicts in correctional communities." In D. R. Cressey (ed.), *The Prison: Studies in Institutional Organization and Change.* New York: Holt, Rinehart and Winston.
Whiteley, S., Briggs, D., and Turner, M. (1973). *Dealing with Deviants: The Treatment Of Antisocial Behavior.* New York: Schocken Books.
Wilkins, L. T. (1965). *Social Deviance: Social Policy, Action, and Research.* Englewood Cliffs, NJ: Prentice-Hall.
Wilkins, L. T. (1984). *Consumerist Criminology.* London: Heinemann.
Wilson, J. Q. (1975). *Thinking about Crime.* New York: Random House.
Wilson, R. (1980). "Who will care for the mad and bad?" *Corrections Magazine, 6,* 5-17.
Wozniak, E. (1992). "Are they Being Served? A Customer Focused Prison Service." Paper presented at Fulbright Symposium, Stirling University, September.
Wozniak, E. and McAllister, D. (1992). *The Prison Survey.* Edinburgh: Scottish Prison Service.

Yahkub, T. (1940). "A history of the state prison colony." In *A Report on the Development of Penological Treatment at Norfolk Prison Colony in Massachusetts*. New York: Bureau of Social Hygiene.

Zamble, E. and Porporino, F. J. (1988). *Coping, Behavior and Adaptation in Prison Inmates*. New York: Springer-Verlag.

Zupan, L. L. (1991). *Jails: Reform and the New Generation Philosophy,* Cincinnati, OH: Anderson.

Zwerdling, D. (1980). *Workplace Democracy: A Guide to Workplace Ownership, Participation and Self-management Experiments in the United States and Europe*. New York: Harper and Row.

Index

Achievement Place 229-230
Alderson Reformatory 66-69, 73, 88
alienation 95
antisocial personality disorder 151-152, 160, 197, 204
alternatives to incarceration 7-10, 128-130
Attica 8

Bandura, Albert 57, 92-93
behavior modification 56-57, 88, 141, 228-230
Beto, George 45-46
boot camps 7-10, 14, 173
Boyle, Jimmy 170-171
bus therapy 150-151, 158, 173

Camp Elliott Experiment 87-89, 230-231
career model 46-48, 117
case management 31-32, 47-48, 205

chain gangs 45-46, 48
classification 20-23, 55-56, 133
    analysts 121
    as a transaction 107-112
    clinical 123-125
    criteria 21, 117
    inmate input into 111-112
    long term 116-117
    reform 39-40
    stages 108-109
clinical thinking 121-122
cognitive problem solving 143
community 172-173
community based alternatives 128-130, 133
convict code 184, 186-187
corrections
    as an academic discipline 208
    research 208-214
Coughlin, Thomas A. 13, 133-134
crisis management 5, 25, 29, 189

Index

Crofton, Sir Walter 50-51

de Beaumont, Gustave 44-48, 83
de Tocqueville, Alexis 14, 44-48, 83
delinquents 178-179
democracy 74-83
deprivation theory 178-179
differential treatment approach 87-89
disturbed disruptive offenders 86, 122, 126-134, 136-138
    diagnosis 149-150, 154
    discipline 140-141
    management 159-164
    treatment 147-154
drug treatment programs 11, 32-34, 54

education programs 23, 33, 40, 54, 99-106
emotional social learning 143

fear of crime 12-13
Federal Bureau of Prisons 31-33, 41, 89
Fogel, David 52-53
Freud, Sigmund 92, 153
frustration aggression theory 136-137
functional unit management 83

gangs 98, 165, 167, 178-180
gender related socialization 178
Georgia Depratment of Corrections 7-11
Gill, Howard 70, 227
goal displacement 223-224
good time 50, 53, 101
Glaser, Dan 31-32
guards
    and crowding 18-19
    and violence 174-175, 177-178
    duties 18-19, 64-65, 96-97, 122-123
    job enrichment 70-71
    relationship with inmates 31-32

Hayakawa, SI 11-12
hearing officers 140-141

human resource management 68-69, 73
hypermasculinity 170-171, 176-183
    and scripts 181-183
    norms 170
importation 178-179
inmates
    as researchers 215-220
    as consumers 72-73
    classification of 20-23, 32-33, 39-40, 71-72, 107-112, 116-118, 123-125, 140
    Cuban 123-124
    health problems 17
    HIV positive 33
    law suits 55, 57, 59, 69
    long-term 33, 85, 113-118, 176
    mandatory drug testing 2-3
    mentally ill 28, 38-41, 62, 126-134
    multi-problem 136-138
    predatory 22, 32-33, 38, 65, 85, 89, 171-172, 177
    psychological treatment of 85, 90-98
    subcultures 32-33, 40-41
    violent 190-200
Inmate's Dilemma 176-177, 180
innovation 221-225, 231-232
intensive discipline units 10-11
intervention 91, 96, 223-232
    inmate centered 144-145
intractability 152

Jones, Maxwell 93-94, 98, 143, 172
judicial discretion 9, 11, 13-14, 128
Just Community 141
just deserts 27-29

Koch, Edward 9
Kurlander, Lawrence 23-24, 26

learning theory 56-57, 143
Levinson, Bob 31, 33
local planning 212-213

Index

machismo 170-171, 194
Maconochie, Alexander 50, 54, 56, 58
mainlining 126-134
management constraints 224-225
mandatory drug testing 2-3, 14
mandatory sentencing 12, 127
mandatory treatment programs 9-11, 15
McCulloch, Tom 201-207
Mead, Margaret 64-65
medical model 89
mental health-model 42, 90-91, 120-125, 204-205, 127
mental health work 120-125, 196-197
mental health workers 86, 97, 123-125, 138, 159-160, 204
mental hospitals 29, 91, 153
military research 87-89, 213, 230-231
moral education 141

New Careers Development Project 216, 230-231
New York Times 7, 8, 10, 181
neurosis 96
niches 62-64, 201-207
Norfolk Island colony 50-51, 227

overcrowding 16-26
    and idleness 19-20
    and riots 23-25
    and stress 17-19, 38-39, 62-65, 96-97, 140
Ossining Correctional Facility 23-24, 26, 73

parole 9, 28-29, 37, 49, 51-52, 59, 121, 124, 136, 194
participatory democracy 36, 66-83, 227-229
    history of 68-71
    mission statement 81-82
pattern analysis 162-163
peer study groups 230-231
police violence 69-70

prisons
    architecture 37, 40-41, 184
    as secure hospitals 130-133
    as schools of crime 38, 97, 114
    as stereotypes 169-170
    as warehouses 16-17, 23-26
    and politics 4-6
    chaplains 42, 84, 95-96
    coeducational 169-170
    early history 88-89
    effect on inmates 20-21, 37-38
    maxi-max 10, 152, 183
    mental health work in 120-125, 138-143
    quality of survival in 60-65
    reform 35-43, 53-55, 213-214
    social environment 40-41, 60-65, 115-118, 125, 163, 184-189
    subcultures 166, 177-178
    violence 165-169, 173-175, 182-183, 198-200
    womens' 5, 8, 66-68, 171, 179, 228-230
Prison Preference Inventory 111-112
probation 9-10, 13-14, 49
Project Start 56-57
protective segregation 135-136, 140, 173, 182, 204
psychological autopsy 174
psychosis 105, 124, 127, 131, 139, 148, 150-153
psychotherapy 92-95
public opinion 1-4, 12-15
public policy 4-5
puritan ethic 14

rehabilitation 11, 13-15, 16, 26, 28-29, 85-89, 105-106, 143-145
research (generally) 221-233
review panel process 143-144
rewards as incentives 8, 24, 45, 49-59
    critiqued 51-53
    history 50-51

role playing 145
Rothman, David 51-52
Ruiz v. Estelle 60

schizophrenia 110, 121, 125, 127-129, 151, 153, 163
Scottish Prison Service 47, 74-83, 170-171, 183, 201-207, 209-213
    survey results 209-211
scripts
    counteractive 181
    defensive 181
    feminine gender 180-182
    pseudo-reparative 181
    reparative 182-183
    repressive 182
seed and sweep 5
sentencing policy 28-29
shock incarceration 7-10, 14, 173
social learning 42, 93-95, 141, 143-144, 161-162
sociopaths 152
social therapy 71-72
sociodrama 98, 145
sour grapes syndrome 226-227
Special Alternative Incarceration 7-11
specialized offender classification 108-109
state raised youth 179-180
subcultural assumptions 170, 177-178
suicide 40, 62, 121, 139
Sykes, Gresham 90-91, 98, 180-181
syndrome (defined) 153-154
system wide planning 211-213

therapeutic community 33-34, 41-42, 87, 144, 172-173
Time 60, 87
token economies 228-229
transactional analysis 230
Transient Inmate Status 23-24
treatment (defined) 92-93

unit management 30-34, 64-65
    function 31-32
    history 32-33
    types 33-34

violence
    and hypermasculinity 176-183
    and machismo 170-171
    and social climate 185-188
    chronic 195-200
    contextual view 184-186
    discipline and treatment 197-199
    learning from 173-175
    psychology of 198-200
    romanticized 168-169
    subcultural 177-179
    visitation 72

war on drugs 46-47, 169-171